Jean Waldron

May /76

TWICE BORN

Memoirs of an Adopted Daughter

Also by Betty Jean Lifton

Children of Vietnam
(with Thomas C. Fox)
Return to Hiroshima
(photographs by Eikoh Hosoe)
Contemporary Children's Theater
(editor)

FOR CHILDREN

The Orange Monster
The Silver Crane
The Dwarf Pine Tree
Kap the Kappa
Mogo the Mynah
Joji and the Dragon
The Secret Seller

TWICE BORN

Memoirs of an Adopted Daughter

BETTY JEAN LIFTON

McGraw-Hill Book Company

NEW YORK ST. LOUIS SAN FRANCISCO TORONTO
MEXICO DÜSSELDORF

Book Design by Sallie Baldwin

123456789BPBP798765

Library of Congress Cataloging in Publication Data

Lifton, Betty Jean.
    Twice born.

    1. Adoption—United States—Personal narratives.
I. Title.
HV875.L46   362.7'34'01'9   75-9855
ISBN 0-07-037824-X

Acknowledgments

Grateful acknowledgment is made to the following for permssion to reprint material copyrighted or controlled by them:

Excerpt from *Knots*, by R. D. Laing reprinted with the permission of Pantheon Books, A Division of Random House, Inc. Copyright © 1970 by the R. D. Laing Trust.

Excerpts from *Self and Others*, 2nd Revised Edition, by R. D. Laing reprinted with the permission of Pantheon Book, A Division of Random House, Inc. Copyright © 1961, 1969 by R. D. Laing.

Portion of "The Love Song of J. Alfred Prufrock," by T. S. Eliot in *Collected Poems 1906–1962* reprinted with the permission of Harcourt Brace Jovanovich, Inc.

Portion of "The Stolen Child," by W. B. Yeats in *The Collected Poems of W. B. Yeats* reprinted with permission of Macmillan Publishing Co., Inc. Copyright 1906 by Macmillan Publishing Co., Inc., renewed in 1934 by William Butler Yeats.

© Hallmark Cards, Inc. Used by permission.

Excerpts from "Oedipus the King," Vol. II *Sophocles*, translated by David Grene in *The Complete Greek Tragedies*, edited by David Grene and Richmond Lattimore, reprinted by permission. Copyright © 1942 by The University of Chicago.

Portion of a poem by James Whitcomb Riley in *The Oxford Book of Children's Verse*, edited by Iona and Peter Opie reprinted with the permission of the publisher. Copyright © 1973 by The Clarendon Press.

Portion of "The Question," by Muriel Rukeyser in *Breaking Open* reprinted by permission of Monica McCall, ICM. Copyright © 1973 Muriel Rukeyser.

Portion of "Temper" from the book *The Fairy Flute* by Rose Fyleman. Copyright 1923 by Doubleday & Company, Inc. Reprinted by permission of the publisher.

FOR BOB
who held the thread

1 ❧ PLAYING THE GAME

Do you know who your parents are?
— Oedipus Rex

They are playing a game. They are playing at not
playing a game. If I show them I see they are, I
shall break the rules and they will punish me.
I must play their game, of not seeing I see the game.
— R. D. Laing

I said, "Who am I?"
Looking into the mirror my eyes searched for clues.
There were none.
Nor were there likely to be.
For I am adopted.
You wouldn't know it to meet me. To all outward appearances I am a writer, a married woman, a mother, a theater buff, an animal fanatic—yes, I can pass. But locked within me there is an adopted child who stirs guilty and ambivalent even as I write these words. The adopted child can never grow up. Who has ever heard of an *adopted adult*?
For most of my life my adopted state was a secret I kept from everyone, a game I played. But now I'm ready to break the rules.
Just think.
When I was born society prophesied that I would bring disgrace to my mother, kill her reputation, destroy her chances for a good bourgeois life. (It didn't raise an eyebrow for my father.) And so a kindly shepherdess who worked in a social welfare agency put me out in the marketplace where I was found by those humble folk I now call Mom and Dad.

3

When I was grown, like Oedipus, a fellow adoptee, I came across the Sphinx, that "dark singer" who waits for us all at the Crossroads of Identity.

But I am still struggling to answer the riddle.

There are some who might call this an autobiography, or a psychological journey into the past. It could even be classified as a novel because most adoptees lead fictitious lives in which real names and places are changed. Some, not all, of the names in this book are fictitious. They have to be because that's what adoption is all about: secrets.

For convenience' sake, let's call this a mythic tale. I write here of the adoptee as survivor, the twice-born, the chosen, the hero; as the illegitimate, the bastard, the changeling, the imposter, the double. I write of perilous journeys of the spirit, of labyrinths, of ghosts, of strangers with mysterious origins, of princesses and princes asleep under spells.

I say that society by sealing birth records, by cutting adoptees off from their biological past, by keeping secrets from them, has made them into a separate breed, unreal even to themselves.

However, in the myths the princess or prince can be aroused by some primal force. Some call this *satori*— sudden enlightenment or awakening. It can happen to the adopted too.

I was thirty when it happened to me. It came with the unexpected discovery that the parents I had been told were deceased at the time of my adoption had been very much alive, indeed, still might be. I was seized with a longing to know who they were—who, as the Bible puts it, begat me.

Why did it take so long, this awakening?

Like most adoptees, I had learned at an early age to numb myself in order to live in the environment into which I had been transplanted. I learned to accept that the branch must be separated from the tree, that the roots must take hold in alien soil. As a tree sleeps in winter, so did some part of me stay sleeping even while the rest of me bloomed. But now that I was awake, I was determined to learn what I could about my origins.

And so I started out on that perilous journey that Oedipus took so long ago. I did not expect to be the king's daughter, but I knew I could not refuse that call to adventure, which is the call to self.

I went into the labyrinth and emerged with what I sought—my story.

However, it is one thing to have a story, and another to tell it. I could not put it on paper. The adopted child in me felt a traitor. The child reminded me that her adoptive parents had taken her when she was helpless and raised her with the innocent hope that she would never look back. The unspoken debt was to be paid with acquiescence and silence: it is a form of emotional indenture even though it is made in the name of love. Adoptive parents demand that their stories end happily ever after, although they must know that even families with blood ties cannot be promised such a simple-minded plot, that even blood children must one day go off on their own lonely journeys of self-discovery.

It was a matter of time. I knew that someday the awakened adult must prevail over the repressed child: that she would eventually take her place on the side of truth and history.

And so I am.

Concentrating here on but one theme—striking but one chord—adoption.

It may seem at times that my pain is like the shark's fin which shows constantly as it cuts through the water, but I see it more like the whale's which submerges for long periods and surfaces only when the whole creature comes up to take the air which is its lifeline.

It is surfacing now.

Come away, O human child!
To the waters and the wild
With a faery, hand in hand,
For the world's more full of weeping than you can
understand.

—W. B. Yeats

I was seven when I was told I was adopted. It was during the Depression years in the mid-thirties and my adoptive parents, having lost a comfortable way of life in a place I shall call Corinth, Ohio, were struggling to put it all together again in a one-bedroom apartment on Chicago's South Side. They who were used to the comforts of a large house, now slept on a bed that folded into the living-room wall, while I, their only child, slept in the bedroom.

The shades of that room are drawn.
I have scarlet fever, a dread disease in those days before penicillin. There is a quarantine notice on the door of the apartment warning the public not to enter for three weeks. I lie there burning with fever, but I am a docile,

uncomplaining child. I make no demands. Although I do
not understand it then, this period is a kind of transition
from the past and a preparation for the future. I will not
rise from this bed the same person.

My mother enters the room. She is a short, amply
endowed woman with bright red hair of which she is
inordinately proud. She might be called vain but she is
not complex enough for true vanity. She is most alive
when she is socializing with friends or feeding her family;
the mundane details of existence, her matzoh balls, krep-
lach, and roast beef, are what she thrives on as fish thrive
on plankton. Yet she is not an ethnic Jewish mother like
Mrs. Portnoy or Molly Goldberg. Her own mother
migrated from England and, like her, she has a resistance
to Yiddish jokes, keeping kosher, or lighting candles on
the Sabbath. She will send me, her only child, to a
Reform Sunday school and attend temple on the high
holidays, but in the name of assimilation, she will remain
forever ignorant of the rich cultural heritage of her people.

This particular day something compels this woman,
who is my mother, to tell her child, who is me, something
she has not mentioned before. The child listens and
seems to stir from her placid state: she is to remember this
moment for the rest of her life, although she cannot recall
the exact words that were spoken. From that day the child
is defined, becomes aware of herself as something apart
from other people. I shall speak of her now as "the child"
because she is not only myself but someone about to
assume mythic proportions. She is like a creature lifted
from legend.

Camus says that from the moment one *knows*, one's
tragedy begins.

"You were not our child by birth," her mother tells
her. "Daddy and I adopted you when you were two and a
half years old."

The child stares at her. The information seems to come from nowhere.

"What does *adopted* mean?" she asks.

"We chose you."

The child looks at her vacantly. Words along with everything else have lost their meaning.

"We wanted a child and so we drove to New York and found you. You were so plump and pretty, like a Campbell's Soup baby. You put out your arms when you saw me and spoke your first words: 'Mama, Mama.'"

The child tries to picture that much younger child holding out her arms.

"Now I am telling you this as a secret," her mother continues. "You must never tell anyone, especially your father. It would break his heart. I promised him never to tell you. He wants you to think he is your real daddy."

Then perhaps relieved to have gotten this troublesome task over with, the mother leaves the room and goes on with her cooking, cleaning, and talking on the phone as if nothing has happened. She has finally done what the adoption agency probably advised long ago.

The child just lies in the room. Now she is truly in quarantine. The sign tells it as it is: she is someone different, tainted, dangerous to society. Perhaps her mother unconsciously understood this when she chose this time as the most appropriate to tell her she was chosen.

How else can the mother be forgiven?

Someone has sent the sick child a book. It is *The Little Colonel* by Annie Fellows Johnston, and although it dates back to 1895, it has been reissued now because Shirley Temple, that smiling, dimpled, curly headed moppet, has just made a movie of it. This latest edition is replete with photographs from the film.

The child stares for hours at those pictures, and waits

each day for her mother to read a new chapter. The plot of this quaint book would not ordinarily be important, but it is now because the Little Colonel's story and her story are about to become inextricably bound to each other.

Stated as briefly as possible, the Little Colonel (Shirley Temple) has just returned with her mother to the South, leaving her father, a Yankee, to try to recoup his lost fortunes in the North. The mother's father, the Colonel (Lionel Barrymore), disinherited his daughter for marrying a Yankee and does not know his granddaughter. When he meets her by chance while she is stealing strawberries on his estate, he is charmed by her flamboyant temperament, so much like his own, and allows her to visit him secretly:

"Child," he said huskily, "you will come and see me again, won't you, no matter if they do tell you not to? You shall have all the flowers and berries you want, and you can ride Maggie Boy as often as you please."

When news comes that the Yankee father has taken seriously ill, the Colonel, rather than lose the love of his granddaughter, forgives his daughter, pays the medical expenses, and takes everyone in to live with him on the old plantation.

The crisis of the book is the father's illness, with the mother crying to her faithful mammy: *"Oh, Becky, I just know Jack is going to die, and then I'll die too and what will become of the baby?"*

The child who is listening to the story suddenly asks: "Where is *my* father?"

The mother pauses. For one brief moment she is on her own, off in a void perhaps with her own dead father who so inconsiderately put a bullet through his brain when she was four. Now it looks as if the father in the book is going to die too.

"Your father is dead," she replies.

"And my mother?"

"Dead too." She is departing from the story, the book's and her own, as her emotional needs begin to take over.

"Then who took care of me?"

"You had a grandfather who loved you and you lived with him for a while. But when he got too old to keep you, he brought you to the adoption agency where we found you."

A writer could say that this adoptive mother was plagiarizing, a moralist could say she was lying, and a psychiatrist could say she was confabulating. But as her story and Annie Fellows Johnston's merged, she must have begun to believe it, for she held to it tenaciously from that time on.

And the child believed it too. She was very moved by the plight of her own grandfather, whom she pictured very much like the old Colonel in his white ducks and Panama Hat, taking her, like the Little Colonel, off to the agency. It wasn't so bad being adopted if you looked like Shirley Temple and your grandfather like Lionel Barrymore. She could understand how it would be impossible for him to keep her when he got very old. Day after day they strode off to the agency, Technicolor smiles on their faces, songs in their hearts, because they knew she would be lucky enough to find some wonderful new parents to raise her.

Of course, sometimes in that darkened room the magic of the Little Colonel did wear off, and the child asked a few more questions.

"What did my father die of?"

Since the father in the book had recovered, the mother had to think quickly. It would be too cruel to give him the fate of her own father.

"He was shell-shocked," she replied.

"What is shell-shocked?"

"A head injury you get in the war."

"And my mother?"

"She got pneumonia grieving for him and died too."

"Oh." The child could tell she did not want to discuss it anymore.

Sometimes in the night the child would shed some tears for the father who had died from the thing called "shell shock" and for the mother who was so sad. At such moments she had two sets of parents in her life and although she did not understand it then, she was in the process of becoming two people: the adopted child of this woman who had been reading to her and the unreal child of this fantasy couple who loved her and died.

Reality and unreality were already becoming mixed up—a state they would be in for many years.

There were other things happening in that room. "Remember it is a secret," her mother keeps warning her whenever she asks questions. "Your father must never know that you know."

The child swears to the secret and because children take such promises seriously, she never discusses with her adoptive father the one subject that, had it been aired, might have made them close. She and her mother are conspirators now. They are collaborating on a labyrinth, a fearsome maze worthy of the great Daedalus himself. The mother shows the child how to place the secret, her bull demon, in the center.

Over the years the child will faithfully guard this monster of whom she is both ashamed and afraid; and only in the stillness of the night will she imagine wandering down those tortuous passageways to throw some part of herself to it. Sometimes the monster lies waiting there in the center of the labyrinth, but at other times seems to be one with it.

The child understands that she is the sacrifice on which the monster feeds.

It can be argued that this mother is not to blame, that she is the victim of a traditionless society that has provided her with no communal rite of passage for anything as momentous as taking a stranger's baby into her home.

Primitive societies and old cultures devised ceremonial rituals for that moment of separation from the old group and incorporation into the new. Adoption ceremonies were as necessary as those around birth, marriage, or death.

In China, in a much earlier period, my adoptive mother and her husband would have exchanged blood and gifts with my natural parents, and she would have been encouraged to simulate birth and nursing.

As a Chamar, that caste of tanners and leatherworkers in northern India, she would have taken part in a cere-mony in which my natural parents would incant over me:

> You were ours by a deed of evil,
> Now you are the daughter of these people by
>   a virtuous act.

Then all the clan members would have sprinkled me with rice to complete my purification, and she would have cooked a ceremonial meal.

But in reality my mother had no such way of cleansing her adopted child of that evil deed that hangs over most adoptions. And so she simply recast history to her own satisfaction: marrying off the parents and then doing away with them.

And she was not alone in this myth making. Countless modern adoptive parents who found the natural parents a threat and inconvenience once they had produced the baby, have resorted to such measures, What easier way to get rid of excess characters than to kill them off from the beginning. (Novelists have been known to be just as ruth-less if it will help them get on with their action.) The number of adopted adults I've met with parents wiped out in automobile crashes is staggering.

I don't know what stories abounded in the horse-and-buggy days—"Child, your poor Mama and Papa were carried off by a runaway horse!"—but alibis weren't needed so much then. Adoption goes back to Biblical times (the Ten Commandments which guide our Western civilization were entrusted to an adoptee named Moses, who, incidently, returned to his own people), and was useful in Europe as a legal means of continuing property rights and bloodlines, but it hasn't been until the last forty years that the records have been sealed and the need to camouflage the adoptive family as a *normal* one has become so desperate.

Why?

At first secrecy was rationalized as a means of hiding the shame of the child's illegitimacy, but in recent years it seems to have had more to do with the adoptive parents' emotional need to live *as if* they had produced offspring of their own. The social-welfare agencies have encouraged this delusion with the guarantee that by matching hair- and eye-color along with religious background, they could artificially create families as durable and wholesome as natural ones. And we all know how wholesome *they* are.

Sometimes I have to remind myself that these same smug agencies that have set the policy of secrecy that so plagues adult adoptees now, were originally brought into being to save us all.

And in truth we did need saving.

The history of childhood is no cozy bedtime story: it is strewn with the corpses of unplanned babies done away with by drowning, exposure, starvation, smothering, strangulation, poisoning, you name it. Babies were once held in such low esteem that Romulus and Remus wouldn't have been able to found Rome if a wolf more maternal than their own mother hadn't been willing to suckle them.

Pliny said infanticide was the solution to overpopulation.

Except for the establishment of adoption agencies, some of those practices might still be going on. I might have been abandoned on the street, or sold by an ad in the newspaper to the first caller, no questions asked. The agencies have at least transformed unwanted bastards like me into desirable commodities worthy of good treatment. Now instead of making a profit from their charges as cheap labor, adoptive parents are expected to invest in them.

Some investment.

All of this may be to their credit—but still I say the agencies did not go far enough. They did not grow with the babies or the times. They thought their job was over once they had placed the available infant in the available crib. They did not understand that it wasn't the end: it was just the beginning.

But I am getting ahead of myself. We are still concerned with that adopted child in Chicago, and no matter what the anthropological, psychological, or social reasons for her mother's erratic behavior, she has to cope with it.

It confuses the child that this adoptive mother, once so tender and reassuring (there are golden memories of that lost home in Corinth: swinging from the apple trees in the backyard, being comforted after falling down the stairs, napping in crisp playsuits on the open porch) has become increasingly hysterical and demanding as the Depression years drag on.

Poverty has jangled her nerves, perhaps throwing her back to her own destitute childhood which was shattered by that blast from her father's gun. Much that must have been vulnerable and creative in her was blown out with her father's life. By the time I knew her the vacuum was filled in with a system of absolutes through which no wind of contradiction could blow. She had created an enclosed personal cosmology whose borders and inhabitants she controlled with fanatical intensity. No one would escape her again—especially the child.

Often when she could not have her own way, this adoptive mother would keel over into a dead faint. It was an era when women were prone to such spells of delicacy—passive-aggressive assertion as it's called now—when every well-stocked bathroom boasted smelling salts. Once, after a minor altercation, the child found her mother stretched out at her feet, her face set in a grimace so alarming and yet so false, she couldn't help giggling.

"That's not nice to laugh at your mother," admonished the young Polish girl who came in once a week to clean. She could not understand that the daughter was glimpsing beyond the façade of everyday behavior into the unfathomable depths of the psyche, and was afraid.

Even now, years later, I who was that frightened child, wonder if the intensity of that mother's hysteria was not the fruit of a barren womb. Or am I being too psychological? Is it possible that at such moments when she could not completely control the child, this mother saw her as the changeling she really was? Since changelings are fairies left in place of stolen human children, could it not be said that the adopted are changelings who replace the children who might have been?

The effort to reconcile this alien fairy child with that lost natural one might have been too much for this adoptive mother. Perhaps her swoons were a chance to enter some other realm of consciousness where she could communicate with the fairy world:

> Come at my call, oh fairy mother!
> Come and remove your offspring.

Food and drink she has received,
And kindness all from me.

Here she shall no longer stay,
But depart for your fairy realm.
Restore the Lost Child, oh fairy lady,
And food shall be left for thy people.

Ideally the wicked changeling would be gone when
the mother awoke, and in her place would be the good,
sweet, obedient child, all curly haired and dimpled like
Shirley Temple. Of course, the real child was never
returned, for adopted children are permanent changelings who are doomed to impersonate the manners and
fidelity of the natural child who might have been.

And so when that didn't work, the mother would
reverse her tactics: instead of turning the anger in on
herself, she would give the child a sharp slap across the
face. She must have known instinctively that when all
else fails, you can usually banish changelings with an act
of violence. Boiling water has been known to get rid of
them too, as well as special herbs, large fires, and the
threat of being thrown into the lake.

But only women in folk tales seem to be attracted to
the latter remedies and this woman of whom I am writing
was attracted to no myths or legends but her own. Indeed,
her methods worked in their own way. The changeling
fled, into herself, and since fairies are shape shifters, this
one assumed the guise of a docile daughter eager to
please. She did not want to use her energy in these
primitive battles. She was storing it up unknowingly for
future encounters when there would be more basic issues
at stake

Those years in Chicago from the age of five to nine are
the bleakest the child will ever know. She is shy and

withdrawn, does not seek out the more precocious children who live in her shabby yellow brick apartment building. She drifts down the back alleyways of her neighborhood on her way to public school in a trance: she is really the Little Colonel sauntering down tree-lined paths on her grandfather's estate, her mouth still dripping with strawberry juice, her nose intoxicated by the fragrance of flowers.

Sometimes her reveries are broken by the local bullies who leap out from behind garbage cans and tease the younger children. Once they tie her to a lamppost and run away. She does not tell her adoptive parents about her fear of these boys, just as she does not mention her thoughts of her real parents.

Secrets sprung from that original secret are proliferating within her, entering her bloodstream, becoming an integral part of her nervous system, though they will never show on an x-ray or in any other laboratory test.

I see a child crying as her mother throws a doll down the incinerator. The doll is one of the few friends she has ever had, and now it has been torn from her arms because it is dirty. The child thinks it came with her from wherever it was she came from. But if this was so why did the mother keep the doll all those years, and why is she throwing it away now? When the incinerator door closes, the doll joins the child's parents in that fiery void which separates the living from the dead, the past from the present.

The happy moments are Saturday afternoons. The movie house around the corner has matinees and the child goes alone each week, buys a bag of buttered popcorn and an all-day sucker, and indulges her stomach while her eyes feast on King Kong and every imaginable monster that has ever stalked the screen. But those fan-

tasy creatures are nothing to the Minotaur in her labyrinth which is beginning to shape itself in her unconscious, to excrete itself in her dreams.

On the way home she is accustomed to seeing Dick,
the half-wit man in the wheelchair who sits on the corner
by the movie house calling out to people as they go by.
Everyone knows Dick, with his drooping lower lip and
slurred way of talking. Just as every village has its idiot,
perhaps every neighborhood has its Dick. The bullies
shriek at him: "Tom's Dick is hairy!" He is used to their
taunts. He laughs imbecilically.

The rumor is that Dick has been shell-shocked in a
war, has a metal plate in his head. Now that she knows her
father was shell-shocked, a new loathing of Dick overtakes
her. She avoids the corner where she sees his chair. She
does not look at him. She begins to fear him.

One Saturday afternoon, coming home from the movies, her eyes meet Dick's as he sits in his wheelchair.
Suddenly she begins to run as if for her life. She looks
back and sees that Dick is following, his hands racing over
those wheels which propel him like a demon pursuing
her.

She flees into the circular courtyard of her building
and looks back once again as she reaches her entryway.
Dick is now at the mouth of the courtyard and turning in.
She stumbles up the dark stairway to the third floor and
into her apartment. Breathless she runs to the front window and looks down into the courtyard. There is Dick
wheeling himself around that circle, pausing at each
entry. Then he goes out slowly, and finally wheels himself
out of sight.

This is the first time the woman who was the child has
put Dick on paper. He rides that wheelchair eternally.
Then he was the ghost of my father, but now I know he is
the ghost of war, or rather what war does to the young. I
saw him, twisted and deformed, in the American military

hospitals when I was a correspondent in Korea and Vietnam, and already I could picture him in his electronically controlled chair which, though more technologically advanced than Dick's (as was his war), would look the same to a child's eye.

I also know now how the meaning of the word *shell shock* was distorted unintentionally by my adoptive mother. To her it was a head injury from the blast of a shell, serious enough to cripple a man and cause his early death. According to psychiatric dictionaries it is a term used for *psychic* disorders brought on by warfare. Soldiers on active duty were known to develop hysterical paralysis in their arms or legs which could be relieved either by hypnosis or suggestion, or removal from the front. In Korea it was called "combat fatigue" and in Vietnam "traumatic neurosis."

Still for me, "shell shock" will always have its own special meaning. Even now when I know my natural father was not shell-shocked, in fact, was too young for the First World War and too old for the Second, I associate him with the maimed, especially those veterans with metal plates in their heads. An adoptee's natural parents never completely lose the aura of fantasy, both positive and negative, which once surrounded them, even after they are found.

❧ ❧

The scene now shifts to Ohio, where the family has returned. There is more money and a comfortable house at the end of a blind street. The timid child has grown into an active teenage girl gaining confidence.

The secret is also flourishing now. Never has it been revealed to the breadwinner of the house, a quiet, short, balding man who fulfills his duties at work as doggedly as his wife pursues her domestic chores.

He is responsible, this man who was to act as my

father. Like so many of that generation of self-made, independent businessmen, he was brought over as a young child from Eastern Europe—a locale now known as Lithuania. I never knew his parents though I have a dim recollection of being introduced to someone they called Bubby, a frail figure in a hospital bed with a white cap on her head and no teeth in her mouth. She left five sons behind, but what else she or her husband did or felt in life, I never knew.

My father spoke no more of his parents' dreams than his own. I would learn of *shtetls* from fiction writers like I. B. Singer; but long before they vanished along with their inhabitants into the Holocaust, they had vanished from the imagination of Reform Jews like my father. Perhaps it was the vacuum their absence created that made him a silent man. He used the words of his only language, English, the way a carpenter uses nails: for a practical purpose.

Where did all the Yiddish go—that language of his forebears? Not one word came out—not even in a joke, But then my father didn't tell jokes; perhaps because he would have needed Yiddish.

The reason my father came back to Corinth was to start a wrecking company with his youngest brother Sid. For a short while the business partnership between the two brothers went well. Their burgeoning firm was soon bidding for some of the biggest jobs in the city. But it was only a matter of time until the flamboyant temperament of my uncle ran afoul of the conservative nature of my father, and there was a falling out.

Sid opened a rival wrecking company across the street, and the two brothers, each bidding against the other, must have turned away when they met by chance in the course of a day. I can remember flushing the picture of that perfidious uncle down the toilet when the announcement of his venture got a big spread in the newspaper.

Such was my fierce loyalty to the quiet, obstinate man who was my adoptive father.

At home my father was almost as docile as I. His social life was programed by his wife, who did all the necessary talking and arranging for him. He went routinely every Friday and Saturday night to the homes where card games had been organized, and played host on the nights scheduled at our home. But other than that there was little play in him. He didn't seem to need sports, hobbies, golf, tennis, gardening, fishing, swimming, travel, reading, music, or theater. His wife chose his clothes, ran his bath, made his food, and looked after his house and daughter.

It was only when he disappeared into his mysterious world of business that my father belonged to himself. There, like a sultan, he ruled an empire of dismantled buildings, huge cranes, mammoth trucks, and black workmen who slaved without union wages but to whom he was forever lending five or ten dollars on their salary in true plantation style. He was good at this work. He could go to a site to bid and in a few minutes figure down to the last penny what it would cost to cart away those treasures of wood and iron and steel that were hidden to the untrained eye.

Our house was built from the red bricks, the thick beams, and the fine lumber of those mansions my father tore down. It was made from the very best of other people's homes—a rose-tinted marble mantle from one estate, dark wood paneling from another, imported tile roofing from still another. Just as I came from the fragments of others' lives, so did the house I grew up in. And the street where it stood—filled with conventional, middle-class Jewish families all seemingly unaware of the war that was to tear Europe apart by a more ingenious wrecking company than anyone could imagine—was blind in more ways than one. Even today I cannot see a dead-end sign without being catapulted back to it. There is something about such a street that turns you back on yourself and gives you a sense of limitations that an open-ended road does not.

As I sat looking out the window as a child, hoping that something exciting would loom on the horizon—a circus, a caravan of gypsies, a prince on a white horse to carry me away—I already knew in my changeling heart that even clowns and gypsies would not survive the stultifying atmosphere. They had only to inhale once and they would settle right down and become proper burghers. The prince, himself, would go into business, and leave for work promptly every morning at eight in the Pontiac or Buick for which he had traded his horse, and return faithfully at sunset each night to water the grass. Something about the unquenchable thirst of the lawns merging into each other without fences, hedges or definition, was stronger than any one individual.

The last years of his life my father suffered from diabetes, taking daily insulin shots and giving up one limb after the other, which he replaced with wooden ones. I remember him making his way awkwardly on those stiff substitutes to his large Buick to drive himself to work. He kept moving in his prescribed orbit until the day he died, in his late sixties. He was a brave, stubborn man. I learned something unspoken from him about how one goes on.

My mother and I are in the kitchen doing the dishes in those days before the automatic dishwasher. She washes and I dry. These are rare moments for us to be together in one spot for she is seldom still. Only at this hour when she is at the sink, letting the boiling water exterminate the dirt which is her mortal enemy, is there a chance for discussion of this secret topic which I manage to slip in from time to time.

"Mother, tell me again about how you found me."

And then once more I hear the story that I had almost thought was a dream during those years in Chicago. The same words about the young man who died of shell shock and the young woman who succumbed Camille-like from grief.

"But how did you happen to go to New York?"

"We heard from our temple about a Jewish agency there, founded by Rabbi Wise. And so we drove to New York and stayed at a hotel. You were two and a half years old and living in a foster home. You weren't speaking yet but when you saw me you held out your arms and said, 'Mama, Mama.'"

Tears of joy always well up in her eyes as she remembers this particular moment. I continue drying the dishes.

"Everything we had was stolen that weekend from our hotel room. My mink coat, Dad's good suit. But I didn't care because we got you. We took you to a department store and bought you beautiful clothes. You were so pretty, with such a wonderful smile. You sat on my lap all the way home in the car."

I say nothing then, just keep on drying.

In fact, I am always careful not to dwell on the subject too long. Just touch it lightly like a hit-and-run driver, and come back from another direction on some other night.

To survive the tedium of these after-dinner routines, I am busy on a project I have set for myself: to memorize every stanza of "The Raven." I recite out loud as I master each phrase:

> Once upon a midnight dreary, while I
> pondered, weak and weary,
> Over many a quaint and curious volume of
> forgotten lore—

Even without knowing Poe's own story of adoption and alienation, this mournful poem connects with some darkness within me:

> But the silence was unbroken, and the
> darkness gave no token. . . .

One night when I opened the subject again tentatively, my mother said something that should have jolted me. I had inadvertently struck a vein that had not been mined before.

"Did you have a lot of children to pick from?" (The term *chosen* never grabbed me the way adoption agencies say it's supposed to.)

"No, you were the only one the agency had at the time. You see I said that the baby had to be *legitimate*. The social worker said I looked like an intelligent woman but didn't talk like one—that all children are legitimate once they are adopted. But I said I didn't care, the child I took into my home had to be of married people. She said we were in luck because she did have one child whose parents had just died and whose grandfather couldn't care for her."

My mother's point seemed to be that a virtuous woman like herself could not compromise on the virtue of others. By holding firm she had gotten what she wanted— good old legitimate me. I did not understand the significance of her protestations then because I still believed her story about my parents. Instead of fastening on the subject of legitimacy, which doesn't mean too much to children, I mourned for those young married lovers who, like Romeo and Juliet, died each time their tale was told. However, I knew it would hurt her feelings if I tried to talk about them, so I went on with my memorizing:

> Nothing further then he uttered—not a
> feather then he fluttered—

Till I scarcely more than muttered, "Other
friends have flown before"—

Another night.

"Did the woman at the agency know anything more
about me?"

"No, just what I told you. She did say you came from a
good family. Your grandfather was a rabbi, I think. She
thought you might grow up to be a prodigy."

"Did you want any other children?" I asked later that
week.

"We did think of getting a boy. And there was one
offered us by an agency in Cleveland. But when we went
to see him, his skin was covered with sores from some
kind of allergy. I didn't want anyone around like that. I
decided not to take him."

Now I had another character in the drama to think
about: the boy who might have been my brother. I saw
him lying with his open sores—which must have been
eczema—in a bare room furnished only with the disap-
proving glances of my mother and father. I felt sorry for
him. What happened to him? Did he grow up in an
orphanage or did someone take him, sores and all? What
was he like? Would he have liked poetry as much as I did?
Would it have been fun to have a brother?

I was beginning to understand that there is some
arbitrary fate that rules our destiny. Why did the boy who
might have been my brother go somewhere else? And why
did I come here?

"Do you know if my grandfather is still alive?" I hadn't
asked this before.

"I've told you all I know." This is said impatiently.
"And be careful not to drip over everything."

The past slammed shut again like the lid of a tomb that has been raided by vandals.

Quoth the Raven, "Nevermore."

My aunt who is visiting from Chicago follows us into the kitchen one night. This energetic woman, married to the older of my mother's two brothers, was always a figure of glamor to me. With her wealth, her philanthropy—her shepherd was one of the first dogs to join the Canine Corps in World War II—she whirled about busily in a larger world than the one we inhabited, although much of her leisure was as trivial. My mother adored her, deferred to her. Now with bracelets jangling, rings glistening, my aunt regally picks up a dishcloth and is helping me dry. Like Scheherazade, she enobles the occasion by telling us a story.

It is about her best friend's adopted daughter. What makes her bring up this forbidden subject in front of me? Surely she must know I'm adopted.

My aunt is telling how this ten-year-old girl had insisted on being told exactly where she came from, and then demanded to go back and see the place for herself. And so her mother packed her bag, took her to a nearby orphanage and left her there for the night.

"Believe me," says my aunt, "that child really cried to come home. And she has never mentioned the subject to her mother again."

How triumphant my aunt is as she describes the downfall of that ungrateful girl, as much as to say, it served her right, the traitor. I listen and say nothing, but I nod in such a way that there is no mistaking that I share the outrage of these two women. I want to be loyal and play the game their way. Their boundaries give me a sense of belonging, demarcate the only turf I know. And any-

way, what have I to do with that girl's quest? My parents
are dead and I already know with the knowledge of those
who have brushed it, that death is irrevocable. I know that
I will never see anyone related to me on this earth,
anyone who looks like me, shares my eyes, my nose, my
mouth, my hair.

One does not pursue ghosts. Or does one?

One evening, in a dispute with my mother over something trivial, I got one of those sudden slaps across the
face. I ran to my room, slammed the door and fell against
it sobbing. "I hate her! I hate her!" in impotent rage. And
that night as I lay in bed I had the uncanny feeling that
my real parents were in the shadows watching me, sympa-
thizing. They were sending me strength to bear all the
indignities of this existence. Just one signal from me and
they would step forward and reveal themselves. All my
love for then welled up, and then another emotion—fear.
I was afraid to confront these ghosts: death had taken
their humanity just as it had taken their lives. At the sight
of those phantom parents my secure world might crum-
ble; I had to get them to leave. I had to ignore them,
behave as if they weren't there.

I pulled the covers up over my head and began deliberately thinking of things at school, quiet, ordinary things,
and gradually the intensity of their presence diminished.
They were sensitive to my fears.

They were also persistent but although they returned
often on other more felicitous occasions, I never had the
courage to embrace them. As much as I longed for them,
I turned away.

Fortunately, the dead are resourceful—at least these
parents of mine were. Sometimes they turned themselves
into bugs, the better not to frighten me. Once, walking
down our street, I distinctly recognized that the caterpillar

crossing my path was my mother. I was very careful not to step on her. What an irony that would be—to be squashed by your own daughter. My very deference was my acknowledgment that she was there.

My father usually chose the form of winged spirits—flies, butterflies, even moths.

"Fly," I would say, as he buzzed over my head. "I know you are my father given one more chance to return to earth in living form to look at your daughter's face."

Luckily, as far as I knew, they never fell victim to the vacuums and swatters and detergents of the many maids who came and went under my adoptive mother's scrutiny. So immaculate was that house kept that a burglar coming across it would have thought the inhabitants were away on an extended trip.

Even I was subject to extinction—at least any proof of my physical presence. In my own room I was like an invisible guest: I could not flop down on the bedspread for fear of wrinkling it; put posters on the walls for fear of damaging them; touch the curtains for fear of soiling them. Not only that, but the guest's every movement was monitored: I could not stay up beyond the allotted hour, could not take phonecalls, could not keep the light on.

Sometimes I read under the covers with a flashlight so that my mother could not see the light through the crack under the door.

> "Blow out the light," they said, they said
> (She'd got to the very last page):

Or I would bunch up the throw rug along the door so that it would block the evidence. Adoptive people are especially good at such tricks.

> "Blow out the light," they said, they said,
> "It's dreadfully wicked to read in bed";

The light under the cover was like the light that burned within me with an intensity that at times was unbearable.

> Her eyes grew black and her face grew red
> And she blew in a terrible rage.

The pain and burning of Winesburg was in me, and like the young boy who narrates the tales of those suppressed lives, I knew I would not stay long in Ohio. Outwardly I was still the sweet submissive daughter, but within a strong will was developing, a sense of purpose that would propel me forward when I needed the force to fly.

> She put out the moon, she did, she did,
> So frightfully hard she blew.
> She put out the moon, she did, she did;
> Over the sky the darkness slid,
> The stars all scuttled away and hid—
> (A very wise thing to do.)

People with secrets always leave clues. They leave traces unwittingly, maybe because they feel guilty and want to be caught.

There was an old secretaire with a folding top in the upstairs hall which my mother would open to pay bills, write letters, or talk on the phone. It was the nerve center of the house because the person sitting at it could command the downstairs through the open stairwell while keeping tabs on what was going on in the bedrooms fanning off from the hall.

This desk was something like me: usually it was closed innocuously into itself, but when it was open it revealed its true complexity, a row of ornate wooden panels flanking narrow cubbyholes and miniature drawers. One day my fingers accidently (does anything happen by accident?) dislodged one of those panels. I discovered it could pull out like a drawer; that it was hollow. Inside was a lone piece of paper. I unfolded it. It had my adoptive name on it, my adoptive parents' names, my birthdate and a place—Staten Island, New York.

I folded the paper quickly as if it was contraband, put it

30

back in the panel, pushed it in, closed the desk and fled to my room like a fugitive. I had stumbled over the past like a marker on an overgrown grave. Only this marker announced a birth—mine. It was the only proof I had of entry into this world.

It did not occur to me then to wonder why the certificate did not have my original name. If I had lived two years with my natural parents I must have had a name. It was not until I was an adult that I learned that when a child is adopted its birth certificate is amended with its adoptive parents' name. History is rewritten. The original certificate is sealed away in court files and only the amended one is ever issued to the person. The adoptee, no matter what age, even should he live to be over ninety like Picasso and George Bernard Shaw, cannot be old enough to know his real name.

What cunning there is in this taboo about the adoptee's original name.

In primitive societies the name was believed to be a vital part of the individual, and therefore kept secret. He who possessed someone's true name possessed the soul as well, and could force that person to obey as a slave obeys a master. Ra, the Egyptian god of the sun, said: "My father and my mother gave me my name and it has remained hidden in my body since my birth, that no magician might have power over me."

Did the social workers and adoptive-parent organizations hope that by seizing the child's original name they could possess that child forever? Such things did not occur to me then. I had not yet come upon Frazer's *The Golden Bough*.

I wondered why this certificate was sitting alone in the secret drawer of that inscrutable desk.

Did my adoptive mother recognize it as counterfeit, something to be hidden away?

Did she ever plan to show it to me? Was it hers, or mine?

Something else.

The certificate with my adoptive parents' name on it made it sound as if I were their real daughter, born to them. Shouldn't it have said on the bottom in small print that I was the dark twin of that other child who should have been?

My mother had once told me that she couldn't have children because of my father. She was much too inhibited to discuss it in detail, but the implication was clearly that it was all his fault. I tried to picture the girl who might have been born to them were it not for that defect in my father: she floated before me with flaming red hair to match her mother's. I gave her a temper to match, too, so that she could stand up to her in a way that I, given my special status, could not. But then, since these were really her people, she would probably be less rebellious than I, more accepting of her lot.

I was aware that I was secretly impersonating this double. I was acting. I took drama lessons to improve my technique. I appeared on local radio programs. The secret gave depth to my talent. It made me unique. It assured me a way out: it was an escape hatch when the time came to go.

I didn't even tell my best friend, Marjorie, my secret, although we shared everything else: the high-school plays we acted in, the poetry we wrote, the aspirations of an adventurous life of the spirit. When we filled out school forms together, I always put Corinth as my place of birth so that she would not recognize me as the alien I was. How could I ever explain New York? The birth certificate had jolted me with its reminder of my lie. I fully expected that government agents would appear at the door some day to confront me with all the fraudulent papers I had signed. I wondered how serious a felony forging one's birthplace was.

There we were—Marjorie and I—sitting one of those wilting Midwestern afternoons in an ice cream parlor where we were accustomed to meet midway between our two houses. Suddenly she said to me: "Are you the *adopted* Hersch girl I heard about?"

Her question came so unexpectedly I must have flinched, but I only remember replying in an unconvincing monosyllable: "No."

"Oh," she said, just as falsely. "I just wondered."

"It wasn't me." I had to deny what I really was while knowing what I was not. And in the process, I was not.

Marjorie and I went on sipping sodas. She never mentioned the subject again.

I had no brothers or sisters to wage the sibling wars with. In those youthful skirmishes, I gather, one forges the mettle one will carry for life: one thrusts and parries and learns the art of advance and retreat. Within that microcosm one gets visions of one's ultimate place in the Great Pecking Order.

Marjorie came the closest to giving me a measure for my growth. And though we were antitypes in some ways, she the more analytical, I the more aesthetic, we both shared enough of the other's province to love and compete with each other. I knew I was a mystery to her, just as I was to myself, like a puzzle with some essential piece missing that keeps it from making sense. I think she saw me as more romantic and vulnerable than I really was, while I saw her as more rational and practical than she could ever hope to be.

Ironically, she was the one fated to die young like those Romantic poets I was forever quoting. There was an antagonistic tone in her letters to me during those last years of her life. She seemed unaccepting that I, the dreamer, was the bird that got away, while she, the more ambitious, was not able to escape physically from the Midwest. She was enraged by her inability to grasp what alchemy it was that made me free. I could never tell her. I thought of that when news came of her death just as I was searching for my natural mother. There was a line she'd had in *Stage Door* when we played in it together: "My it's dark in here!" that we continued using as a greeting over the years. Now we were separated by a darkness even deeper than my secret. "Marjorie," I wanted to call out to her, "I can tell you now. It *was* me!"

I kept my secret from the boys I dated also. As a member of the high-school pony chorus, a dancing troupe modeled after the Rockettes of Radio City Music Hall, and choreographed by one of its former directors, I was popular. I kept my poetry books at home when I was out with my dates, none of whom were incipient Thomas Wolfes or Scott Fitzgeralds. They were not tortured enough. They would marry eventually, go into their fathers' businesses and move into the suburbs just beyond their fathers' homes. That's the farthest they would ever get—the next suburb. It was known as progress. They never recognized me for the changeling I was, nor realized that I was just passing through.

Our phone rang all the time with invitations to the school dances, the proms, the movies, the night clubs across the river in Kentucky, and to Coney Island, an amusement park which one reached by taking an hour ride on the Island Queen show boat. But while I chatted about this or that I was always aware that my mother was on the other extension. What was she listening for?

At night she waited for me to come in from dates. The car could not pull up to the house without the lights going on and her appearing in some window in her nightgown. I hoped my friends wouldn't notice her there. She was like the woman in a Thurber drawing who envelopes the house in her arms. She occupied the night. She seemed afraid of what might happen to me, that there might be something in me she could not control. Bad blood, could it be? She never said so. I wondered if she would have behaved like this with her natural daughter. Sometimes I thought she would, that there was a yearning in her to be outside with young people, out of the dreary unromantic routine of her own antiseptic life.

Sometimes after my date had walked me to the door and left, she would come downstairs to me with outstretched arms. "Hold me," she would say. "I am your mother, hold me."

I would wrap her in a hug for a decent interval until I could escape upstairs. Sometimes she would follow me and crawl into my bed. She should have had a son, I would think at such times. She should have taken that boy in Cleveland, sores and all. He could have held her in his big male arms. Or maybe a natural daughter's arms would have been long enough, strong enough—mine were not.

At such moments she was asking from me something she could not articulate, and which I could not give.

Could a natural daughter have given it? Is there a blood feeling between mothers and daughters that the changeling cannot experience?

My mother was close to her own mother, a gentle, compulsively immaculate woman who was always supportive of me, although I was to learn that she had opposed the adoption, even moved out of my parents' house at the time. But now she and my mother were always together: shopping, going to movies, planning family dinners. They seemed to share the same nervous energy, as if the severed umbilical cord was still discharging electric current. And yet—my mother had to leave high school to help support her two younger brothers when her stepfather suddenly took off. She must have resented having to take over this adult responsibility. Circumstances had never permitted her to be coddled.

Was that what she was asking of me?

The insights I have now into my mother's psyche and my own struggles to free myself from her were not obvious to me then, nor was I preoccupied with these undercurrents of everyday existence. Life for the young, adopted or not, moves with its own energy, taking joy in its vitality, its omnipotence. A smothering mother gives something on the positive side of the ledger too—a feeling of being loved and wanted, which is perhaps as good a counterbalance as any for the adoptee's existential feeling of estrangement.

One night when I was getting ready to go out on a date, I hurried to the guest-room closet where the good coats were kept. Just below in the garden my mother had set out eight card tables for a dinner party that was now in progress. I could hear the guests joking and laughing. The door to the closet was stuck. I pulled on it impatiently and the full-length mirror which was attached by prongs on the outside broke in half, the top part breaking loose and crashing down on my hand. Blood splattered everywhere. I screamed: "Mother! Mother!"

I was dimly aware of the confusion of voices down below, chairs being pushed away from tables, shouts that help was coming. My favorite uncle, Saul, who was not really a relative but my parents' close friend, got there first. Unlike the others, he seemed to know just what to do. He tied a towel around my arm like a tourniquet, wrapped my hand in another towel and started toward the stairway with me to speed to the hospital. Halfway down the steps I saw my mother hysterically trying to climb up, so frightened that she was stumbling, half lying across them.

"Are you all right?" she cried out to me.

I was able to reassure her I was as I was hurried past by my uncle and father. My hand got a few stitches in the emergency room where it was discovered that the glass had landed well enough below the thumb and high enough above the wrist to make it a minor injury. I even went out on the date that night and my mother's party continued its course. I have only a thin scar to show for it now.

But I have never forgotten the way my voice instinctively cried out: "Mother!" when the glass fell, and how she struggled to get up those stairs, ineffectual, but full of concern, her whole being absorbed in my disaster. This kind of love is surely no less than one feels for a natural child. Fate in its perversity had paired us together. She was my mother and I was her daughter.

My date that night is the only one that matters to me in my high-school years. He is named the most handsome in the class by the yearbook, whose divine pronouncements are never wrong. We dance well together. We win prizes. We have midnight snacks in drive-ins. We sit in parked cars in dark places. It is the forties, before the Age of the Pill: it is the age of the Madonna and the Whore. We Madonnas do everything but the ultimate. As John Barth put is so well in another context: "We verged on much and didn't touch the verge."

Surrounded by the timelessness of youth, the future stretching like a great plain beyond us, we hold each other while the band plays "There Will Never Be Another You" on the radio. It would be so easy to stop the journey now, remain landlocked in this car with him forever after. But there is something churning in me that knows this moment will be over when the station signs off. He is not

yet awakened to the ambiguities of life while I have the
need to escape now.

And so we come at each other from different direc-
tions and pause in mid-flight those starry midwestern
nights of our youth, and move on.

🙢 🙢

I am in college now, a freshman at the University of
Illinois. I go there because my Chicago cousins have all
gone there, married girls from the same Jewish sorority
and settled down. Fortunately my family and their friends
coveted the invisible mantle of learning for their children
even if they did not pursue it for themselves.

I am courted by the Jewish sorority which has been
alerted I am coming and is unaware that their prize
rushee is a changeling. I accept because I have never had
a sister, and the prospect of sixty of them under one roof
is a marvel that an adoptee can easily have illusions about.

That freshman year is an initiation into many levels of
being. It is the first time I have lived away from home,
except for brief forays into local summer camps. The waif
in me is euphoric at belonging to a group at last. I do not
know yet that this sorority world is just a mirror image of
the insulated, bourgeois community I have left behind:
that in our silk hose and high heels, our expensive dresses
and extravagant fur coats, we are but mimics, parodying
the only values we have ever known and the people we are
being groomed to become.

We are still virgins.

We soon learn the necessity of belonging, that not to
belong is not to exist. We come to pity those shabby souls
who were not tapped for sorority or fraternity: they form a
group outside of communal life, languishing on the
periphery, while we sit securely around the fires of sister-
hood. We come to understand that their voices are too
strident, their clothes too loud, their manners too vulgar,

their families (especially the New Yorkers) too remote.

Inside the sorority house, of course, we freshmen are pariahs. We do all the menial chores and submit to set study hours for which we are lined up each night in the dining room from eight to ten. We are expected to bring good grades and glory to the sisters.

However, it was soon clear that *true* glory came not from academic standards but from those set by the boys in the Jewish fraternities. The Second World War was raging outside our windows, but the fraternities were filled with 4-F's and wounded veterans. One had a crippled hand, another had shrapnel in his back, another walked with a limp, but no one talked about this war which was going into its last year. Millions of people were being incinerated while we danced each night for an hour after dinner and until one in the morning on weekends. Unlike us, the incinerators had no curfews. Sunday afternoons we read the papers with our dates, but the screams of the headlines did not penetrate our consciousness.

We were sleepwalking, jitterbugging, partying through history, this collective of sororal and fraternal elites.

I was the pledge president that first semester, a position I used like a smoke screen to hide behind. But it became impossible to fool my fellow pledges collectively. With instincts like beasts of prey they came to understand that although they had chosen me in the beginning for surface qualities they could recognize, there was something fraudulent here that was not in a true leader. My loyalties were not with the pack. I might be an active reporter with the college paper, which was good, but I was not around when the social events of the house were being planned, which was bad; I might be popular with the fraternity boys, which was good, but I was not getting involved or pinned, which was bad.

Where was I when decisions had to be made about the next hayride? On the shore with Trelawny tearing Shelley's heart from the fire.

Where was I when the costume party was being planned? In Bloomsbury having tea with Virginia Woolf and Katherine Mansfield (whom I always felt closer to as a fellow outsider—New Zealand somehow always being equated with Ohio in my mind).

Where was I when the strategies for the midyear rushing season were being plotted? Off on my own cloud with Shakespeare, Keats, E. E. Cummings, Gide, Tolstoy, Dostoevsky, unaware of the storm clouds gathering nearby.

A pack of sorority sisters wants to be led by someone with its pack interests at heart.

A subclique was forming around the well-adjusted members of the freshman class. One of its ringleaders, Sandy, a tall, gangly girl from a small Iowa town, was considered a howling success at socials because she would don a misshapen porkpie hat and corncob pipe and bring down the house with her own version of "One Meatball."

But the thing that interested me about Sandy was that every day at mail call she received a post card from her father with a different proverb in the top left-hand corner: "If at first you don't succeed, try, try again," "Rome was not built in a day," "It matters not how long you live, but how well," "Every day should be lived as if it were our last."

Each card was like a secret message on how to get through life. I envied Sandy a father who verbalized the struggle and sent these lifesavers while the rest of us had to do with cookies and candy from home.

Sandy—"smile and the world smiles with you"—made an ideal social chairman. She and her cohorts organized fun and games and took notice of the concerns of the house while I was becoming increasingly involved with the "independents" I met in classes and on the paper where I was a junior editor. Some of them wanted to be writers as I did. I was coming to recognize that their *not* belonging was through strength, not weakness; that many of them had *chosen* not to belong.

However, not only the pledges were seeing me for what I was. Big Sisters were watching too. They were beginning to suspect that something indefinable—which they would attempt to define—was amiss with the pledge president.

On the night of our initiation we were told to go to bed as usual. Some elder would be up for us later. The whole third floor was one large bunk room: we lay nervously on our narrow cots waiting for we knew not what.

One by one a sister came for us, blindfolded us and led us downstairs to the living room. When it came my turn, I was told to kneel down with both elbows on the ground in front of me. Then the blindfold was taken off. I found myself blinking into a mirror encircled with candles, the only light in the otherwise dark room.

A voice told me to look into the mirror while it spoke— to look into myself. It said that I was a good student and successful with the boys and my outside activities, but somehow I had been a disappointment to those assembled here. The problem had been discussed seriously and everyone was worried about me. My head was too much in the clouds. I would have to try coming down to earth if I was to exist happily in this world.

I saw my naked face without make-up staring back at me as they spoke. Without the dark pencil I used over my blond eyebrows, it seemed my features were missing; I was looking into an unmarked map.

Then the blindfold was reapplied and I was led back to the dormitory. No one spoke, in fact, none of us ever discussed what had been told to us in secret that night. Perhaps everyone had received some critical appraisal, perhaps that was the purpose of those sessions. My cheeks were burning with humiliation, but I was also relieved. They had discovered me to be an imposter, but they had not guessed the depth of my deception: that far from not twinkling in unison with the others, I was like some star positioned in the wrong place in the sky.

The next day our energies were taken up with Hell Week. Dressed crazily, we had to stand on street corners calling out to people, raid the boys' fraternity houses, walk down dark corridors where creatures jumped out at us or buckets of water were dumped on us.

None of this touched me: I was no longer floating in the clouds—I had landed with a thud on earth. I knew that I could not stay here, that this was just a side station and a local track. I had to transfer to some main line. I had to go where the things that were considered unreal in me were real.

One pledge sister who had transferred from a college in Minnesota and knew the procedure, helped me draft letters to Barnard and Radcliffe. Barnard admitted me immediately, Radcliffe put me on a waiting list. I had waited all my life. No more. I accepted Barnard without hesitation.

My parents were proud that I had gotten into an Eastern college, but they did not understand the consequences: it was the beginning of my journey away from them.

And so on the last day of my stay in the sorority house, I said goodbye to all my sisters. Lunch was as usual filled with the excitement of letter reading. But the regular post card from Sandy's father had not arrived. Instead there was a telegram telling her to come home. Her father had committed suicide.

In New York at Barnard I found the real sisters who spoke my language. But though we read poetry together—"I grow old . . . I grow old . . . / I shall wear the bottoms of my trousers rolled"—and swore to burn with a hard gemlike flame, and listened to Raymond Duncan in

his toga and sandals, and talked of World Federalism in
the Lion's Den at Columbia, and wrote melodramatic
plays in Minor Latham's workshop and acted in the Columbia Players, although we did all these things together,
we did not share our secrets.

Years later we met at a luncheon—married, divorced,
widowed, single—and revealed our liberated selves.

One of us had been raised by an unwed mother who
had a brief affair with a famous Russian poet; another
sired out of wedlock by a prominent American critic, had
been brought up by a grandmother after her mother had
committed suicide. I was the only one given up in adoption. We were discovering each other anew: it was not
how we had progressed as writers that mattered to us
then, but how we had survived as women dragging our
lumpen secrets behind us.

However, in those student days I did not associate
New York consciously with the place of my birth and
adoption. It did not occur to me to look up the agency my
mother had spoken of in the phonebook—I knew it must
have Rabbi Wise's name in it—to walk past it or even go in
to seek answers, for the secret was slumbering deep inside
me as the beast slept in the labyrinth. I was concerned
with a different kind of rebirth, concentrated only on my
freedom and future, not the past.

During holidays I rode the train back and forth
between my new life in the East and the old life in the
Middle West. Always I felt like Sherwood Anderson when
the endless flat plains of Ohio came into view, and always
I felt the driven joy of Thomas Wolfe when the train
returned to Grand Central. And when I chose to stay on
and work in New York in television after graduation, the
message of E. B. White's essay on this beloved city was
always with me: the commuter gives New York its restlessness, the residents its stability, but the ones who come
from the Middle West seeking something, give it its soul.

I would have gone on to graduate school in literature or drama if my parents had been willing, which they were not. Either I was to come home and settle down or get a job in New York to support myself. I was offered a car to choose the former; although I don't think anyone took the possibility very seriously. Dean Millicent McIntosh had indoctrinated her girls too well.

"Get a profession," she had told us. "Don't marry until later, after you have found your vocation." And she gave her own life as an example: she had become a scientist, married in her thirties, had her first child at thirty-five and five children by the age of forty. Twins helped.

Yet she had not warned us that someone graduating with a B.A. in literature and fine sensibilities does not have much practical ability. About all I had was courage. I studied typing and speedwriting and over the next few years took a series of odd jobs seemingly unrelated to each other but all within the media world—secretarial assistant to a blind TV writer, copy writer at the *Journal American*, scriptwriter for the quiz show "Beat the Clock," and finally one that I hoped would give me background to produce shows of my own, production assistant on a weekly TV drama, "The Big Story."

It was all very challenging, but there was a price.

My double was tugging at me. The model daughter, the red-headed one my adoptive parents should have had, the one I should have been, would give me no peace.

"Go home," she said.

For although I was in regular communication with my parents—visits, phonecalls, letters—I felt enormous guilt toward them. I was not keeping my side of the adoption bargain. They had taken a daughter to comfort them in their old age and here I was living half a continent away.

They were not martyrs, they let me know they were lonely. The docile child they had raised was no longer under their control. Not only was she too far away from them, she was turning down "the chance of a lifetime" in the form of Larry, a multimillionaire from Indiana, who had been dating her through college and whose family they knew. They asked only that she marry him, settle down in the Midwest and live happily ever after. It was the way it was done in the movies. Was that asking too much?

I understood how they felt. Here I was giving up a diamond-studded life in the real world for some dingy garret in New York. Cinderella was choosing the pumpkin. I loved Larry, but as a brother; I wanted another dimension of life that his money could not buy for me—that of the mind and spirit. I was wise enough to know I could not make him happy. But at the time, saying no to my parents and to him, I felt I was an ingrate who would never make anyone happy, least of all myself.

I became unable to eat. I had bouts of nausea and dizziness. Though I had never heard of the word, I was developing the classic sysmptoms of neurasthenia. My mind felt like a Rube Goldberg contraption. I could not sort it out, nor could I tell the two college friends I was living with what was bothering me. I was guilty. I needed sanction, but I didn't know where to find it.

That Christmas I went to Florida to join my parents at the home Uncle Saul and his wife had retired to. But all the while I was with them I kept fighting back the anxiety that threatened to overwhelm me. I was the dutiful daughter played by a robot. If my parents noticed how bad I looked, how artificial I was acting, they said nothing. Denial had become so much a part of our relationship that it extended mercifully to this moment. We kept the illusion of a close family.

However, Uncle Saul's dark, compassionate eyes missed nothing. He was a clothier from Kentucky, but in his youth for one brief period he had been an opera singer, and within him there was still a poetic vision of life. We always recognized something special in each other—something yearning and thwarted that made us close. Still we had never discussed my adoption.

One night after dinner I was lying on the back lawn while they were playing cards inside. The sturdy blades of grass loomed like green giants over me in my weakened condition. I was like Gulliver, tied down by my own doubts and fears. The stars mocked me with their certainty. I wept, and my sobs relieved some of my tension. But I knew that the tears would not wipe out my problems.

Uncle Saul came out and sat down beside me. "You look terrible," he said. "Too thin. Haggard." He told me that my whole problem might be that I was adopted and felt insecure about my true background; that this was making me incapable of loving or giving myself to anyone.

"Until you solve your doubts about yourself," he said, "you will probably never be able to marry or be happy. Why don't you see a psychiatrist who could help you sort things out?"

I listened mutely to his words, emitting only occasional sobs. He told me that he was speaking like that because he loved me, and that I should stay in New York away from the domination of my mother. He urged me to find out what it was I really wanted to do, and do it. He did not say he was giving me the advice he had not been able to follow in his own life. Then he held me for a moment the way a man holds a woman—he put his lips on mine—but I did not feel like a woman then. I was still a waif, an adopted child.

Sherwood Anderson wrote somewhere that we all need love, but the world has made no plan for our lovers.

The screen door opened and my mother came out. "We're waiting for you to play," she told him. He disappeared inside.

I left the next day for New York. He died shortly after that of a heart attack. I never saw him again.

> *Once upon a time, long ago,*
> *There lived an orphan boy,*
> *Created of God,*
> *Created of Pajana.*
> *Without food to eat,*
> *Without clothes to wear:*
> *So he lived.*
> *No woman came to marry him.*
> *A fox came.*
> *The fox said to the youth:*
> *"How will you get to be a man?" he said.*
> *And the boy said:*
> *"I don't know myself*
> *How I shall get to be a man."*
>
> —Tartar Folk Tale

When I got back to New York I called Columbia University for a referral to a psychiatrist. It was the time before all student clinics were staffed with specialists to handle what we've come to know as "identity" problems. I was referred to a young psychologist on the East Side. I went to him the very next day and poured out my dilemma: I had very little money to pay for treatment because I could not ask my adoptive parents to help me— indeed, I was afraid to tell them I was seeking therapy for fear they would order me back home. I told him I felt adrift in the course I was taking against their wishes, and asked him if he thought I should make them happy by marrying my wealthy friend and settling down in the Middle West.

He was a very sensible and straightforward person, this psychologist, who would become well known for his newspaper columns and radio programs advising confused people like me what to do. In retrospect, I am grateful to him for giving me what I needed most: plain old common sense.

"What do *you* want to do?" he asked.

I told him I wanted to stay in New York and become a writer. That I did not want to think of marriage just then.

He made it sound so simple.

"When a person is starving," he said, "food is the most important thing. When a person is poor, money is important. But once one gets food and money, those needs are met and the real needs deep inside a person will still be there. You must only think of what those real needs are, and be true to them."

He was affirming everything I believed but didn't think I had a right to act on. I saw him just a few times and was able to stop feeling guilty about staying in New York. The pain of my failure as a daughter was still there, but it was not destroying me. I could cope with it. I would try to do the essentials: keep up the rituals that would satisfy my parents. But I would not sacrifice myself and my own needs for a life I did not believe in.

Of course, I was a little afraid of being on my own in New York, of maybe not making it as a writer, of maybe never finding anyone I loved enough to marry, but that was the challenge. New York always gave the promise of some new person, some new opportunity, some new adventure just around the corner.

It was a throughway, not a blind street.

Unconsciously I must have trusted New York from the beginning because this was the place I had come from. Here I was, adopted child metamorphosed into adopted adult, retaining some touch of the ingenuousness that the Midwest gives its young, while seeking the worldliness that each generation asks of the East.

What to hold on to—faith in people, trust in self, creative goals.

What to let go—dependence, conventional thinking, virginity.

This last was no longer of value to me now that I had severed my romantic ties with the past. I wanted to be free on all levels—but are the adopted ever free from some nagging fear inside them?

What if they get pregnant? What if there really is such a thing as bad blood?

I tried to submerge that fear—after all, I had been born in wedlock.

Late one Sunday afternoon I came in early from a date instead of going on to dinner. I wanted to finish the play I was writing for a course at the American Theater Wing. I used a headache as an excuse. It seemed a chance decision.

My former roommates had both married and I was sharing a drab two-room, furnished apartment on the Upper West Side with Anne, a fellow midwesterner. Now that I think of it, there was nothing of either of us visible anywhere, not a picture that we hung, not a bedspread, not a touch that identified us as the occupants. We were like transients camping out, serious about our careers, but not settling into any one place, as if not daring to play house until someone came along and tapped us for that role. No matter how liberated we thought we were, no matter how long or how often we held or changed jobs, something in us knew that our future lives did not depend on our ability to establish ourselves permanently in a profession. There was an unstated assumption that eventually we would marry, and the locale of our husband's profession would determine where we hung our own small shingles.

The phone rang. It was Doris, who worked in advertising. "Is that you, B. J.? I didn't expect to find you home."

"I came back early."

"I was calling Anne to find out if she wanted a date tonight since I thought you were out. But now that you're there, how about it?"

"I don't think so." Still I wasn't definite.

"I've got this blind date my aunt fixed me up with, a psychiatrist, and he's got a roommate who wants to come along. We're going to an Italian restaurant. Please help me out."

"Maybe another time."

"I need you now."

And so I met Bob on the other end of a double blind date, but Doris' end, not mine.

I tried to act interested in the roommate, but I knew immediately when I saw Bob that someone special had come into my life. He was tall, with that dark, intense quality that so many New York Jewish intellectuals seem born with, horn-rimmed glasses and all, as if region, not chromosomes, determines physiognomy. But he was something more than that. It was the eyes—warm and receptive, and connecting when they met mine. There was a compelling energy there too, a suggestion of hard-driving power not yet unleashed.

I see us at the end of the evening filling that colorless living room with our animated conversation. Bob and I spoke as if to everyone, but we were really sending out signals to each other that we were on a similar journey for self-expression and fulfillment. We had come from such different places, but our destination was the same.

When we said goodnight, I knew Bob would call soon.

And he did, shortly after I got in from the studio the

next evening. We went for a ride along the Hudson River in his steel-gray Oldsmobile convertible which was like a flash of fantasy in such a serious nature.

I was amazed to hear myself telling him about my adoption. It just spilled out. And it didn't faze him. He didn't think I was a gorgon or a freak. He received it compassionately, as he received everything, recorded it, and then put it away as if it had no significance to us other than its revelation bringing us even closer together.

Bob had been raised in a middle-class home in Brooklyn. He had been exposed to the world of politics and theater by a devoted father who had managed to work his way through City College and enjoyed nothing more than playing angel to the Broadway musicals of his former classmate, E. Y. Harburg. Because he had received part of his medical training during World War II, Bob owed the military two years service. That was the way it worked then. If he volunteered, he would go in as an officer; if he didn't, he would be drafted as a private. He had just volunteered and requested France. Now he was waiting to hear when and where to report.

"Will you visit me in Paris?" he asked one night when we were speculating what it would be like to be stationed overseas.

"I might."

I was studying French then for a trip I was scheduled to take to Europe the following month when my show was off the air. I had been planning it for years, especially a tour of the Greek Islands where I intended to trace some of the myths I was trying to shape into television scripts for children. No one had commissioned them, it was just something I wanted to do. Looking up the Greek gods was for me what looking up blood relatives would be for others.

Still I was reluctant to leave when it came time to sail.

Bob had not yet heard from the air force. We had been seeing each other a few times a week, but not long enough to be sure this was anything more than an intense spring encounter. He saw me off on the ship with a corsage and champagne. I waved to him from deck when we pulled anchor; he looked so small and vulnerable from my Olympian height.

Goodbye, America. Goodbye, Statue of Liberty. Goodbye, Staten Island. Goodbye, Love.

What was I doing on this ship moving away from the one person I cared about, the only one real to me?

On my second day in Paris I received a cable at my small pension: "Arriving 6 P.M. Orly." I ran through the airport when I saw Bob coming toward me. We held each other as if we had been separated for years.

"I got my orders," he said. "I have a few weeks before reporting to California for a transport plane. I've been assigned to Japan."

"Japan! I thought you asked for France."

"I did. I guess that's the way the military works."

That was just the half of it. But we didn't think about it then.

We danced in the streets of Paris on Bastille Day, July 14. We liberated ourselves from the past and the future. We visited the Greek Islands together, lingering at Delos to catch a glimpse of Apollo. We wandered for hours through the precipitous silence of Delphi. We stood breathless at the navel of the world. But the Oracle did not speak to us—she was too busy posing for tourist pictures. And besides we didn't speak Greek.

I knew that if I didn't marry Bob when we got back to the States, he would be gone for a long time. But I wasn't sure I was ready for marriage. I think adopted people seldom are. There is this frenzied turbulence that's always nipping at us—like the gadfly after Io—to keep us moving. The need to escape being trapped again pulls against the need to belong.

Bob represented the world I had unconsciously been moving toward. In some ways he was the solid, reliable Taurean bull, but there must have been a Gemini moon in ascendance at his birth for him to be attracted to anything as impractical as a mercurial Gemini—and an *adopted* one at that. That moon was still rising, exerting its pull. There was a poetic restlessness in him, that quality that he himself would one day term *protean*, that allows one to take spontaneous leaps from one level of being to another in the process of adding yet another dimension to the self.

I was leaning toward marriage but I kept having a recurring dream that had plagued me for years—breaking away from the altar just as the ceremony is about to begin. Something in me still wanted to be free.

But did I want to be *that* free?

Something stronger in me was saying: "Go with him. Make new dreams."

We were married in Ohio on our way to the West Coast where Bob had to report for his flight. My parents gave a big wedding at a large hotel with all their friends attending, a few of mine, and Bob's parents and close relatives from New York.

Bob's father, for whom anything beyond the borders of Broadway was a remote Siberia, sent us playful messages with his eyes as he dutifully went through his paces. He had loved his son fiercely, and now he was offering me a love just as generous and loyal. My mother-in-law was less vital, but also warm, and adopted or not I was part of the family.

My mother, entrenched in lace, wept tears of joy, but maybe the tears were mingled with regret that I had not found someone closer to home, less foreign than a New

Yorker, (although he did get credit for being a doctor), and who wouldn't be taking me so far away.

My father was silent, but beaming.

"Be happy, Cookie," was all he said. Still practical, even in marrying off his only daughter, he asked one of his construction photographers to take the wedding pictures. The bride came out looking like the side of a wall.

And she flew to Japan alone after seeing her husband off on his military transport.

2 ❧ MYTHIC LEAPING

A fairy world which seized my soul as gently as a child the wings of a butterfly.

—Lafcadio Hearn

It could be said that my own unreality made me available to the unreality of Japan: adopted people come from one unknown and move with little baggage into another. Japan, where everything was the opposite of anything I had ever experienced—reading from right to left, sleeping on the floor, smiling when one is sad, giving one's last name first—was strangely familiar to me. I felt at home immediately. Had I been here in another life? It was a question that a Japanese might ask.

It was 1952. After seven years of occupation, America was in the process of turning the country back over to its own people. The solar winds of a new war were now blowing thousands of American G.I.'s into Korea. These were the salad days before Vietnam. Like the Barbarian hordes of Mongolia who swept into China only to be absorbed over the centuries by its great culture, so now was America taking its first fateful steps toward absorbing and being absorbed by Asia. We were witnessing what some have called the stirring of the Asian dragon and others the decline of the Western world. Flung so unexpectedly into this exotic stage of history, Bob and I had to improvise our own lines in a drama we had not been following.

Who knew anything about Japan or Korea—then?

Not long after I arrived in Tokyo, Bob was assigned to Korea. If Japan was associated in the American imagination with paper fans and flowered kimonos, Korea was made up of the hills on which our American boys died— Pork Chop Hill, Hamburger Hill, and so on down the menu. For years there had been the dry, repetitious. accounts of such and such a battle on such and such a hill: one week it was ours, the next week it was theirs. The warriors had become so many chessmen, hopelessly stalemated until no one cared any longer who would make the next move.

"Can't you get your orders changed?" I asked. "Surely they won't send you over when we've just been married."

We were sitting on the floor of our straw-matted room in a tiny Japanese hotel in Shinjuku—the Greenwich Village of Tokyo. I hadn't wanted to stay at a big tourist hotel like the old Imperial, and having come over on my own rather than waiting for the military to send for me, we were not eligible for base housing.

"Let's experience Japan immediately," I had said. "Let's live like the Japanese."

But now after one day alone in the hotel, I knew it wasn't authentic after all. It was little more than a small-scale bordello where our G.I.'s on Rest and Recreation (R & R, as it's known), chased scantily clad Japanese girls in and out of the rooms, and up and down the corridors. I had been waiting to tell Bob this discovery when he came back from the base with the news of his sudden transfer.

"I was the logical choice," he said. "The only one in the unit without a wife."

"Without a wife!"

"You're not officially here, remember."

It was true. Bob's commanding officer owed me nothing. An air force psychiatrist was needed in Korea to visit the various bases and determine who should be kept on active duty and who sent back to hospitals in Japan or the States: in other words, to evaluate the shell shocked. It was a six-month tour. And Bob *was* the logical choice.

We had a week together in another small hotel near the Ginza before his flight, but a feeling of foreboding lay over everything we did. It didn't seem possible for things like this to happen to people like us. Until the last moment I kept expecting a reprieve: a new set of orders. It didn't come. That was the thing about Asia—it was making Americans realize that life did not necessarily have a Hollywood ending. The G.I.'s standing with us that chilly dawn in the dimly lit waiting room of Tachikawa Air Base seemed to be grasping this too. They picked up their things quietly when the transport plane was announced on the intercom: "Flight 243 leaving for Taegu."

"Take care of yourself," Bob said, trying to smile. Trying to keep *my* spirits up. He was only worrying about me.

There was a momentary shuffling of bags and as the men moved down the field I watched him become indistinguishable from the rest.

Then I turned back to the second-hand Chevrolet convertible he had bought for us on base—that cavalier symbol of another life. One part of me, the part that had always been alone, was once again the abandoned baby adrift in an alien world. But another part was exhilarated at the adventure that lay ahead, at the freedom from familial restraints and obligations that had followed me even to New York. Although I would miss Bob, I had not been married long enough to have established an emotional dependence: I was more used to the single life. I knew I could manage . . . I always had.

The car moved off the base, out through the shanty towns of "one-night cheap hotels" which had mushroomed up around it, and on past misty villages of thatched roofs clustered cozily together. It started to rain and the windshield wipers clacked like a metronome back and forth, giving a melancholy rhythm to my thoughts. It seemed preposterous that anything could happen to Bob in Korea, but then everything seemed preposterous. Ours was the generation of Pearl Harbor, of war posters with buck-toothed dwarfs leering out with the promise of death in their eyes, but now it was the Chinese, those once noble peasants of *The Good Earth*, along with the North Koreans, who were the sinister, murderous hordes.

As I reeled off the countries of Asia, separating enemies from friends, it seemed they were little more than colored fragments in a historical kaleidoscope, changing patterns with each turn of events. The identities of nations were proving just as quixotic as those of individuals.

The outskirts of Tokyo came into view. Intrepid, ignorant of even the full depth of my ignorance, armed with nothing more than an amended birth certificate, a Barnard degree, a marriage license, and a hotel key, I was about to confront a civilization that had been evolving for thousands of years and in those last, lingering moments of the American occupation was blinking at me like a stunned tortoise who has had its shell ripped away and is in the painful process of growing a new one.

It is hard to say whether I adopted Japan or it adopted me. But though I was the eager one, encouraging this new relationship, Japan remained a mysterious foster parent, alternately stern and sentimental, aloof and shy. She did not casually offer strangers a home.

I would have settled for any kind of home at the beginning. I had decided to live with a Japanese family as a way of learning the customs of the country, but after weeks of looking at rooms in the homes of unemployed generals (of whom there seemed to be a staggering number) and being turned away for reasons that were never stated (was it because I was a foreigner, and an American at that?), I was becoming discouraged.

My English-speaking rental agent, Hoshino, a part-time college student who considered his job beneath his dignity and only tolerated it for the five percent commission involved, would keep up my flagging spirits with his endless supply of aphorisms such as "Don't look for trouble till trouble looks for you," or "If you don't go into the lion's den, you do not catch his cubs."

Hoshino was shamelessly fascinated with my convertible and loved to push the button that sent the top flapping down. Immediately, no matter where we were, a crowd of children would materialize and we would become the center of attention. As we zoomed off, he would beam like a high lord accepting the admiration of the people. "General MacArthur used to ride in an open car too," he told me.

He had a lot of time to enjoy the car since I soon realized he knew no better than I where we were going. Part of the problem of looking for an address in Tokyo is that the houses are not listed in numerical order, but rather by the date they were erected. Many streets and alleys have no names at all, just tapering off into dirt paths.

When, after hours of searching, we finally reached our destination, the general's wife who invariably received us (while her husband kept his dignity intact behind closed paper sliding doors), would listen unimpressed as Hoshino told her over endless cups of tea about his own aspirations as a scholar (this so she would not look down on him and address him in language used for inferiors or servants) and about my Barnard degree (which was my best, and possibly only selling point). We would then be shown a dark Western-style room facing north, although I had requested a straw-matted one to the south, and subsequently reunited with our shoes with the vague promise that Hoshino would hear from her after she had consulted the general. I came to understand what that meant —we've changed our minds about renting, or it's no longer available.

"Maybe I should just find myself an inexpensive hotel," I told Hoshino petulantly one morning when I didn't think I could swallow another cup of tea, let alone another rejection.

"Do not be discouraged," he replied cheerily. "Even Buddha's face does not wear a benign smile the third time."

It was long past the third time when we found Fumiko's house. Obāsan, who showed us the small tatami room opening onto a section of the garden, was more vivacious than those other austere general's wives as she introduced her daughter Fumiko, who was working as a typist on an American base and hoped to practice her English with the boarder, and Fumiko's two little girls who peeked at me shyly from behind their mother's skirt.

Hoshino told me that both women were widows, and since I assumed that the men had fallen on some Pacific island, I did not probe for details.

The room was exactly what I wanted, and perhaps appreciating my enthusiasm, Obāsan concluded the arrangements right away. I was to move in that night. I felt as though I'd found a castle, although in truth, there was no hot water, no flush toilet, no heating other than a small gas burner and a charcoal hibachi, and no bed other than the two folded mats in the cupboard which I would put down each night on the floor.

Obāsan told Hoshino that I would be like a daughter in the family.

I was to learn that Japanese women have an innate sympathy with those of their own sex, probably from years of being exploited in a male-dominated society; a sympathy like the one American women are just beginning to develop in their liberation movement. My new friends were very solicitous toward this foreign sister who had just been separated from her husband and was so far from home. Although our arrangement began as a financial one, they shared the routine of their lives with me, from shopping at the small food market down the road to attending the Nō. From them I would learn the depth of Asian feeling for family and the continuity of the generations.

We are sitting that first night on the floor at the low round table in their sitting room which opened into the same section of the garden as mine. Fumiko pulls a few albums out of a lacquered chest.

"You must see our family, Betty-san," she says. It was as if she were saying:: "Behold our ancestors who have gone before if you want to understand us. We are nothing more than an unworthy extension of those enshrined on these pages."

I meet them all, from Fumiko's father, the General, short and obese, and her husband, tall and formal in the wedding pictures, to the most remote of the aunts and uncles. Their life cycle laid out before me, I see them through childhood, adolescence, marriage, parenthood, and death. Never in any of these pictures do they relax: they stand or sit together, shoulder to shoulder, chins out, eyes straight ahead, as if already they feel the gaze of their descendants—and the American—upon them. They defy the beholder to find the secrets that must have been packed away like their treasures of porcelain and jade, box within box, in dark, hidden recesses of their storehouses.

Later that night Fumiko helps me lay my *futon* (bed mat) on the floor and closes the wooden shutters to the garden.

"But Fumiko, I need air."

"We do not keep the windows open," she says firmly. And then she mumbles something incomprehensible about robbers or evil spirits or germs, I am not sure which, lurking out there in the dangerous night air.

Maybe it is the power of suggestion, but after she has gone I am glad of this custom of shutting the houses up tight. I begin to imagine that the ghosts of the General and Fumiko's husband are hovering out there in the garden, resentful of the American living under their roof. Would they try to seek revenge?

I pull the quilts up over my head much as I did as a child, and seek a coward's escape into sleep. I do not know that the spirits of the glorious dead who die in battle go instantly to Yasukuni Shrine where they become deities to guard the Emperor. No self-respecting spirit would be concerned with an insignificant American woman.

But I, who am still ignorant of my own ghosts, could hardly be expected to understand those of the Far East.

At night Fumiko's ancestors, bound each to the other by invincible ties, reeled about in my brain. I was like a link from a chain that had been allowed to break, something that could not happen here. I did not understand then that the knowledge I was slowly gleaning from how this old society functioned, would give me insights I would need later in my search for who I was in my own.

I had just discovered Lafcadio Hearn, who, coming to Japan in 1890 as a journalist, had settled here for the rest of his life, taking a Japanese name and wife and opening the country to the West with his interpretations of its culture and literature as effectively as Perry had opened it forty-four years before with his fleet. Hearn had also been separated from his natural parents at an early age, and though the circumstances were different from mine, I recognized him as a kindred spirit looking for a spiritual home. His two-volume *Glimpses of Unfamiliar Japan* was making my new world familiar.

"What country is your family from?" Fumiko asks me one night. "You look French. Do you have French blood?"

"I don't know, Fumiko."

"You don't know!" she gasps in disbelief. Then deciding it must be a language problem, she tries again. "I mean, were your parents from France?"

"I don't know," I repeat dumbly. For a moment I consider telling this foreign sister everything, but old habits are hard to break and besides, adoption, as we know it, was not in her vocabulary. Children here were adopted from known bloodlines, and then only for the expediency of continuing the family name and ensuring that someone was fulfilling the numerous obligations the dead make on the living to care for the ancestral graves and perform the ritual ceremonies. Sons-in-law might be adopted if there were no other sons, and often adults were adopted by elderly couples with no heirs. But how could I explain to Fumiko that I had been raised by people who did not know my natural parents—and that I did not know them either.

"You don't know," Fumiko repeats after me. She looks as if I have announced I had fallen from the sky. In fact, she might have accepted that more readily than my ignorance, for the legends of her country which I had begun to dip into were filled with miraculous births: Momotarō, the Peach Boy, bursting full-blown from a peach; the Bamboo Princess, found as a radiantly beautiful young girl by a woodcutter inside a bamboo tree; the Mud Snail Son, born as a mud snail to a human couple who had prayed to the Water God for a child in any form.

I was intrigued by these mythic characters who did not come into the world through ordinary channels and had already begun writing their stories down for children much as Lafcadio Hearn had done before me. I noticed that although they allowed themselves to be raised by simple mortals, they seemed driven by a sense of destiny they had to fulfill. Momotarō, with nothing more than a bag of rice dumplings and the help of a dog, a pheasant, and a monkey, went off to defeat an island of ogres, bringing their stolen treasures back to his adoptive parents. The Bamboo Princess renounced the Emperor's earthly love when her time of exile from the moon was over, leaving behind her the elixir of immortality for which Mount Fuji, the never-dying mountain, is named. The Mud Snail Son insisted on accompanying the bags of rice to the landlord's house for his poor father until, as in "Beauty and the Beast," he was metamorphosed into human form by the pure love of a faithful maiden.

As I read these tales I knew they were telling me something I had yearned to know as a child: something about the mystery of origins, about journeys and destinations, battles to be fought and won, and knowledge that was intuitive from the moment of birth.

However, it was through the *kappa*, that mischievous water elf whose roots are as deep in the folklore of Japan as his home is deep in the river, that I tried to express myself in what was to become a series of children's books.

About the size of a ten-year-old boy, *kappas* have greenish yellow skin, a shell on the back like a turtle's, a face like a monkey's, and most important of all, a bowl full of watery fluid in the top of the head which is the source of their magical strength. Should they lose the water, they become weak, and may even die.

Like all folk creatures, including the popular leprechaun, *kappas* are both loved and feared. They dance gaily by the light of the full moon but they have been known to pull people and horses into the river where they can, and usually do, drown. They also steal into the fields for cucumbers and eggplants, much to the chagrin of the farmers.

But in spite of these questionable habits, or maybe

because of them, Japanese artists have always identified with the saké-drinking *kappa*. Ryūnosuke Akutagawa (of *Rashōmon* fame) wrote a classic satire on Japanese life in his novel, *Kappa*; Usen Ogawa painted them in meditative poses contemplating the fleeting beauty of life; Ashihei Hino wrote tales that revealed the *kappa*'s innate goodness in contrast to man's more coarse and ungenerous nature; and Kon Shimizu drew *kappa* cartoons that lampooned modern society.

I was attracted to the *kappa* as a shape-shifter, and all unconsciously began telling *my* story through him. In my *Kap the Kappa*, Kap, who is prince of the river, spills the water from his head when he is caught by a fisherman. In a state of amnesia he allows himself to be dressed as a human child by the fisherman's wife: "Little *kappa*, prince of joy / You will be my little boy. / No longer will you roam the river wild. / Tomorrow you will wake a human child." He is passed off as an *adopted* son from another village.

But at the time of the full moon, Kap's true *kappa* nature forces him to dance secretly on the rooftops and steal cucumbers from the fields. Eventually, when his real identity is discovered by the villagers and by himself—"he knew he was not like any of them / he was the *kappa*, / not a real little boy." —he realizes that he must return to the river from which he came and discover his *kappa* origins.

It was perhaps my first step toward the labyrinth.

One morning, Constitution Day, Fumiko and Obāsan invited me to accompany them to hear Emperor Hirohito speak to his people. It was the fifth anniversary of the Japanese constitution drafted by the Allied Forces, and the first one since the end of the Occupation.

We went in my open convertible, Obāsan raising her parasol as she sat in the back like a daimyo's wife going off in a palanquin. Mother and daughter were wearing their best kimonos—"Material the Emperor gave us when my father died," Fumiko said—and I could hear them chattering like schoolgirls as I chauffeured them past the crowds of downtown Tokyo. Through the rearview mirror I could see them—Obāsan, whose dainty oval face might have been drawn by the deft hand of a master painter, and Fumiko, whose irregular features suggested a coarser brush and more careless strokes. They were not unlike our Southern families after the Civil War: stripped of their lands and wealth, they still wore the mantle of tradition with unflagging pride. And even though they had taken me, a foreigner, into their home, I knew that their inner reality remained unshaken. It was not that they did not know that things outside had changed, it was that emotionally they must behave as if they had not.

The Imperial Palace grounds, all three hundred acres of them, are situated in the heart of the city; but unlike the White House or Buckingham Palace, on display for all to see, the Emperor's palace, like his court life, lies hidden behind high stone walls and deep moats.

"Before the war we were not allowed to look at the Emperor," Fumiko was telling me as we walked through the gates and took our place in the sea of kimonos around us. "When he passed, we had to bow our heads. But things have changed, *ne?*"

Yes, things had changed because occupations are something like adoptions: no matter how benign or well-meaning, they obscure the subject's origins, alter the identity. Even the Emperor of Japan, whose royal family dates back to the mythical Emperor Jimmu in 660 B.C. was not immune from having his own personal mythology tampered with. In return for not being tried for war crimes, the Emperor had agreed to renounce his divinity and accept mortality as his bitter cup. To prove his good faith, he had to strip his family tree of the dazzling Sun Goddess, Amaterasu Omikami, and other less luminous deities, much as one might divest a Christmas tree of its bright lights and tinsel to prove there is no God.

"The ties between us and our people do not depend upon mere legends and myths," he had told his people then. "They are not predicated on the false conceptions that the Emperor is divine and the Japanese people are superior to other races and fated to rule the world."

Yes, the Emperor, like the adopted, had been forced to accept the rewriting of his own history. But even though the West dismissed his past as "mythology," he had come naturally to those legends he lived by, unlike the adopted who must live by false myths under the rubric of reality.

Now on Constitution Day, the Emperor appeared before us on the high platform erected for this purpose. He was wearing a Western suit which made him look more like a conventional businessman than an ex-god, but the very old bowed their heads as if the radiance of his presence was still too much for mortal eyes. He was by reputation a gentle man, a dedicated marine biologist, who until the Occupation had lived in an atmosphere as rarified as that of his exotic fish in their enormous tanks. But now the filter was shut off: he moved in the same element as the rest of us.

Almost.

Still there was no question that the Emperor held what was left of his country together. His tree may have been stripped, but it was not chopped down. The Japanese believe that pruning a tree and then artificially reshaping it, will force it into possibilities of even more spectacular beauty, releasing energies unaccessible to an ordinary tree. The Emperor had that aura of nobility about him that emanates from those bonsai which have sacrificed naturalness for form.

Fumiko was whispering that when Hiroshima and part

of Nagasaki lay in ashes, the Emperor had raised his curtain and spoken directly to his people for the first time in history to help them accept defeat: "You must endure the unendurable and suffer the insufferable," he had said, speaking the old Court language in a high voice that must have made him sound like a god calling to them from ancient times.

Now here he was seven years later, having endured and suffered the Occupation with them, his words reaching out in benediction over his loyal followers in a language they could understand: "Let us thoroughly embrace the tenets of democracy and keep faith with other nations."

I looked at the rapt expressions on the faces about me, most of them old and as deeply furrowed as their fields, and knew that although democracy was as foreign to them as defeat, the Emperor's will was still their will.

"Let us march hand in hand toward the consumation of national reconstruction and share the blessings and happiness it will bring our land," the Emperor concluded.

And then Fumiko and Obāsan and everyone shouted: "Banzai! Banzai! Banzai!"—Long live the Emperor! And for that moment all of Japan seemed to resound with "Banzai!"

But things never were as they appeared at any given time. Always the Yin-Yang dialectic was at play. Just when I felt I had grasped an insight, formulated a truth, something would happen to make me realize I hadn't understood at all.

Outside the Palace grounds college students, in the somber black uniforms which mark their tribe, looked at the dispersing crowd with disdain. They reminded me of the young men in the East-West discussion group I had started at Fumiko's house as informal English lessons, but which had turned into a course in political history for me. High-strung, proud, critical, uncompromising, those students were helplessly aware that their heritage had been destroyed by Japan's defeat in the war. As children they had been taken to the national Shinto shrines, they had recited the Imperial Rescript in school, visited the palace grounds with awe, but everything they had been taught to believe had been proven false: Japan had not been saved by the kamikaze—the divine wind—which had blown back Kublai Khan, even when her young men took that name on their suicide missions.

As survivors the students had had to reexamine everything. Their identity problems made mine seem simple.

Even Fumiko's life was not what it seemed to my unacclimated Western eyes. Like me, Fumiko harbored a secret anchored perilously close to her heart. Why had I not guessed that she who had been blessed with a mother, father, grandmother, grandfather, great-grandmother, great-grandfather, indeed, a whole cosmos of known ancestors to ward off the abyss, should not have had her bull demon too?

The revelation came when we were having tea after returning home from the Constitution Day ceremonies.

"Japanese women must be very happy with the new Constitution," I was saying. "Now they have equal rights with men, can vote, get divorced, inherit property." I was repeating what I had read in the English-language *Japan Times*.

"Japanese women are not happy," she replied flatly. It was the first time she had spoken to me in such an unguarded way. Her voice had a weariness I had not heard before.

"Do you mean war widows like yourself who are alone?"

"Betty-san, I am not a widow."

"What do you mean?"

"My husband is not dead."

"But I thought . . ."

"I know. . . . I tell everyone at work. It is easier that way."

"But where is he?" I hadn't wanted to put it so directly.

"He lives down the road a few miles—with a former geisha." She giggled nervously. "He even bought her her own bar. He is a bad man, *ne?*"

And then Fumiko told me how her arranged marriage with an eligible young man from a prominent business family had dissolved into a mere front for the continuation of his line and the life of debauchery which he led every night away from home. The proud officer whose picture I had seen in the album had served in the war all right, but had come home very much alive—to the geisha, not to Fumiko and her daughters. Indeed, he had even berated her for not having sons.

"Why don't you get a divorce?" I asked.

"You don't understand," she said, waving her hand back and forth in front of her face in that familiar gesture she used whenever she disagreed with something I said. "People look down on a divorced woman. She is . . . how shall I say . . . damaged goods."

"But you're still young," I protested. "You still have your life before you. You should marry again."

"I will never marry again," she declared. "The only happy women in Japan are the widowed and the unmarried."

For a moment her features fell into total disarray: the lines under her eyes were dark and exaggerated; her face was drained, even old. Then she must have remembered the discipline of the ancestors, for she sat up straight as if posing for a picture in one of the albums.

"Please don't worry—I'm better off this way," she tried to reassure me.

"I'm not worried. It's just that I thought your husband was killed in combat like your father in the last war."

Now Fumiko let out a piercing laugh, covering her

mouth with her hand so that it exploded into her palm. "No, Betty-san, my father did not die in the last war."

"But you said he was a general." I was totally confused.

"He *was* a general, but he died in 1937—in China— from high blood pressure. Drinking too much saké!" Again she went into peals of laughter. "If he had been killed in the last war, our family would not have received silk from the Emperor," she explained after she had composed herself again. "Too many generals died then. We were lucky, *ne?*"

"Yes, Fumiko, you were very lucky."

That night I sat for a long time looking into the garden. The ghosts out there had been exorcised, but now my own had been unleashed.

Something within me made me identify with the ex-geisha turned bar madam whom Fumiko's husband had gone off with. She belonged to that floating society known as the "Water World" which flows through the nights of men's desires, and evaporates at dawn. For Japan did not destroy its marriages over illicit relationships; instead it set up a demimonde quarter where men could act out their romantic fantasies without disturbing the stability of the family system upon which the nation is based.

Japanese literature and theater were filled with maudlin tales from this Water World: stories of renunciation and longing, restrained passion, and double suicide pacts that seemed to nourish the Japanese spirit. Proper housewives and mothers who could never hope for the sexual license given those indentured geisha and prostitutes, wept through long afternoons at Kabuki over their star-crossed lives.

And I wept with them.

For although I still believed that my natural parents were properly married and properly dead, there was a lingering mystery over why my other family members had let me be cast adrift.

Where were my aunts and uncle and cousins when my

old grandfather had to give me up? There must have been some reason why they had not claimed me. Something about my past seemed to belong to the shadows and sorrows of the Water World.

I think I knew that someday my own story would unravel before me like one of those Kabuki tales, but now I was to learn stories of other children much less fortunate than myself.

It was while I was working for the *Japan Times*.

"Sure you can do some features for us," Kempei Sheba, the wiry editor told me in his colloquial English when I stopped by his office looking for a job.

At first he sent me over to the old Imperial Hotel to interview visiting dignitaries like Henry Luce and Eleanor Roosevelt (and later he would send me to Korea to cover the end of the war and the repatriation of prisoners), but now he had the idea to get an American slant on Madam Sawada's mixed-blood orphanage in Oiso, a seaside resort south of Tokyo.

This story had begun long before I arrived in Japan, in fact, from the moment the first Occupation troops landed. Japan, never having been defeated in war, had never been occupied. She had the custom of servicing her own troops with women from the Water World, but there was no precedent for how to satisfy foreign ones.

At first everyone hid their daughters, but gradually when it became obvious the Western "barbarians" were not butchering people on the streets, the girls slipped out—especially the ones from poor families, which have always known how to look the other way. These girls, whom we call camp followers, became known as *pan pan* girls to the Japanese. They were rumored to be making more money than salaried men.

The Americans may have been nervous when they landed, but they soon caught the spirit of this male-oriented society. They had never met such compliant, self-sacrificing women before, never enjoyed such sexual and emotional freedom. (No shotgun weddings here. In fact, the Occupation discouraged marriages.)

It was fun, this playing house in tiny straw-matted rooms with miniature teacups, being served and catered to, being daddy while someone was mama. It was a game these men had played in an expurgated version in childhood with their sisters and their friends when they weren't playing war with the boys. It was a game even more enticing when you were grown up—and certainly more amusing than war.

But like all diversions, it was not part of the reality of their lives. This was an interlude, a brief affair until it was time to settle down back home with the girl next door in a real house with a mortgage.

The number of women and children abandoned when the American soldiers rotated home would have been staggering even for a Puccini: the sensibilities of Madam Butterfly were a luxury in an era when a few months or even a year of temporary liason was the norm. The women they cohabited with so briefly, the children they spawned so casually, were put out of mind after they left those shores, just as colored lanterns are snuffed out after the dance.

However, until their fathers returned to their homeland, the mixed-blood babies got the best that good old Uncle Sam could supply: condensed milk from the P.X., jars of strained, sterilized food, teething rings, wind-up toys. But not for them Mom's apple pie. These children were the remnants of a consumer society that discarded what it had consumed; they were the dark, disposable side of the American dream.

Japan was stuck with the problem, but what could she do with those blond, blue-eyed devils, or the ones with black, frizzy hair, all of whom were a mockery of her visage and a reminder of her shame?

Some *pan pan* girls solved the problem efficiently by

dumping the babies in garbage cans and dance-hall latrines. Others more squeamishly abandoned them at shrines along the road, or under the seats in movie theaters. Infanticide, while never openly acknowledged in any culture, East or West, had been prevalent in the Tokugawa period a few hundred years before when there were too many mouths to feed. Children are always expendable if they threaten a society's survival, especially children who look like freaks to the neighbors and hinder the mother's chances of getting a husband in the future.

Now enter Miki Sawada—the daughter of one of Japan's most illustrious families, married to an eminent diplomat, converted to Christianity, looking for a higher purpose. She, like so many of her affluent contemporaries in that rarified stratum, had been influenced by idealistic foreign governesses who had taught them about "social services," something alien to Japan where each family unit took care of its own.

Madame Sawada saw this moment in her country's ill-fated history to start an orphanage modeled on those of Dr. Bernardo which she had seen in England on her trips abroad. Using a bequest left by one of those governesses, Elizabeth Sanders, for some unspecified good deed, she persuaded the Episcopal Church to buy her family's confiscated estate in Oiso to start an orphanage for the abandoned mixed-blood babies.

By the time I came along, the orphanage had been struggling for about six years. Churches in America were actively helping to support it, and so was Pearl Buck, who was encouraging intercountry adoption here much as she would do later in Korea.

It was a breath-taking piece of property, this summer villa where Miki Sawada had played as a pampered child. High walls protected its manicured grounds which swept down to the sea. Madame Sawada, herself, showed me around. She was living here full-time now, having left her husband to his international affairs and her own children to their governesses.

With the boldness of spirit and independence that only women of high social status or outstanding artistic talent could get away with in that time, Madame Sawada had set up her wonderland of unwanted children.

She pointed them out to me: there was Shizuko, found under a seat at the Nichigeki Music Hall, who was proving docile, although not very bright; George, found crying to the jazz music in a Tachikawa dance hall, who was still a crybaby; Sammy, found in a purple muslin kimono in the palace grounds, who was finally beginning to walk at the age of three; Helen, fathered by a Military Policeman in Yokohama, who was very bright but a problem child; and Ikuo, found with the end of his umbilical cord uncut under the eaves of a farmer's house near an American base, who was nicknamed "Tōjō" because he was forever sticking his tummy out and saluting to get attention.

He got a lot from Madame Sawada. Tōjō was one of her favorites.

There were about a hundred children altogether. I remember being startled by their beauty, their features a combination of racial characteristics that only a painter would have the imagination or the courage to juxtapose. They were like fairy people created to show us our best possibilities, but they were already marked, doomed, reflecting our worst degradation.

When I came upon some of them at play, they were in a fairy ring holding hands and circling around as they sang the Japanese equivalent of "Ring Around the Rosy": "*Kagome, Kagome,* bird in a cage / When will you come out?"

"That one is the Colonel's daughter," said Madame Sawada, pointing to a three-year-old girl with short, blond hair, pug nose, and blue eyes. I felt a surge of longing to take the hand of the Colonel's daughter and join the fairy circle, for I knew I was one of them, circling about in the cage fate had created for me.

We had the same designer, these children and I. I wanted to take them all home and be their mother.

But I was still the adopted child then. I had no home except my room at Fumiko's; and I knew she would eye these children as dispassionately as she did the black and white mongrel puppy I had rescued from extinction only the week before. Standing there with Madame Sawada, disguised as an objective journalist, I could only feel pain for the special destiny I knew lay ahead for these orphans as outcasts in Japan when they eventually had to leave these protected grounds.

Round and round I watched them go that day, near the gate where Miki Sawada, tied to her nurse's back, once watched her soldiers going off to war with Russia; round and round near the spot where her grandmother had taught her how to raise silkworms and to spin the silk threads; round and round by the gnarled pine tree she and her brothers and sisters had climbed; round and round near the azalea bush by the zig-zag, hilly path where her mother often lingered lost in thought; round and round under the window where her father stood reading his Chinese classics.

"I often wonder what my parents would think if they knew what I am doing now," she once remarked. "Perhaps they would say as they so often did when they were with me: 'Miki again up to her tricks.'"

Surely even her parents could not have imagined such tricks as these: no one else had stepped forward to pull the mixed-blood children out of the garbage cans. Miki Sawada had proved herself a revolutionary in her determination that these outcasts should have a place to grow up physically. She would see that they were baptized, fed, clothed, educated, and if need be, buried. There was a place for their cremated bones and ashes in the crypt under the chapel, since even in death they would not be claimed by their mother's clans.

Some of the urns were already full. She told me of one mother who had arrived with a dead black baby in her arms: she had been so embarrassed by his cries on the train, afraid others would notice he was black, she kept the blanket over his face, not realizing she was smothering him. Madame Sawada had her take the body to her Buddhist shrine for cremation and then bring the remains back to the orphanage for burial.

"The box was so small, and the bones rattled about so pathetically," she recalled.

When it was time to leave the orphanage, I passed a young Japanese woman in kimono standing in front of the gate. She was bringing her son, fathered by an American, whom she had kept for six years. But the strain was becoming too great: she had to go out to earn a living, her mother could no longer care for him. The neighborhood children were taunting him. Madame Sawada had said she would take him.

The boy, dressed in a clean white shirt, short pants, knee socks, stood at her side listening to his mother express her gratitude. His sandy hair which was wavy, his flat nose which was freckled, his blue eyes which were fearful gave him away as an imposter in this land so intolerant of any deviance from the norm of sleek black hair and dark eyes.

Now the mother turned to say farewell to her son. Japanese of whatever class do not show their emotions publicly. She must have already said goodbye, this mother, but now she just nodded at the boy, bowed to Madame Sawada, and walked down the narrow lane that led to the main road.

The boy was crying hysterically: it was probably his unfettered Western blood expressing itself. Madame Sawada asked me to wait while she took him inside. I sat in the car for about ten minutes and was just about to leave and come back later, when she came running out to me. Her face was flushed with excitement, as if she had just won a victory.

"That child," she said. "He was so disobedient. He would not take off his clothes to nap with the rest of the children. So I gave him a good slap and then he obeyed. He must learn who is the authority here or else we will not be able to discipline him."

I blinked, almost as if I had received the slap myself. A Zen slap—that knocks you into reality. As I drove away I felt as helpless as that boy.

The plight of the mixed-blood orphans, Amerasians, as they've come to be known, haunted me. Japanese journalists were curious about them too, even a little guilty, especially about the black ones who were going to have the hardest time. Most of them were street children who were not even registered at birth by their mothers— therefore, did not officially exist. They were called *kuronbō* (blackies) or *hitokui jinshu* (cannibals) by other children. One was not supposed to have dark skin in this country where the elite used hats and parasols to protect themselves from the sun that darkened the skin of the laboring classes. And, of course, the Japanese were not unaware of the prejudice America felt toward her black people. With so many prejudices of their own (the *burak-umin* are an outcast group as segregated as the untouchables in India), it was nothing for the Japanese to assimilate the biases of others as facilely as they had styles of painting, dressing, or living.

The black children also fascinated the Japanese as a form of exotica.

There was an article in a magazine in which the writer mentioned hearing two black sailors in a bar commenting on a half-black boy who was singing "Black Cherry" as he begged for yen.

"That boy is not Japanese," said one sailor.

"He is not a brother either," said the other.

Whose boy was he? No one seemed to know.

When Bob came back from Korea we set up a little house in the rice paddies between Tachikawa and Tokyo. On a clear day we could see the snow-capped cone of Mount Fuji. The farmers who were our neighbors accepted our presence much as they must have accepted the Occupation: stoically. Some of them even brought us gifts of seaweed in keeping with the custom of welcoming newcomers to a neighborhood. They nodded in greeting when we passed them working their small patches of land, and the only hint we had of disapproval was the night our jeep's tires were slashed after our dog had been running loose. It was their way of saying to keep the dog in his place—tied in the yard.

Bob was somewhat confused when his bride of six months greeted him with a request to adopt a child, and a mixed-blood one at that. "We're not ready to have children yet," he protested. "And when we do it should be one of our own first."

Adoption is biologically alien to the unadopted.

Of course, I knew I wasn't ready for children either, my own or others. There was too much traveling I wanted to do in the Far East, covering political events and gathering legends. But the Colonel's daughter and that weeping boy seemed to beckon me from another realm that had nothing to do with the mundane routine of the very family life I had spent so much energy escaping from. I was a changeling ready to take another changeling by the hand.

Still I was relieved when Bob stood firm on the issue. I

was not yet ready to settle down responsibly to the demands of child care. It was an impractical impulse—but the children were real.

One day a Japanese reporter we knew asked if we would appear in a film a friend of his was directing. It was about a half-black child in an orphanage. We were to be in the sequence where the boy dreams about the people who might adopt him.

We arrived at the studio to find the director had asked a few others to participate that night: an Indian couple, a black soldier with a Japanese wife, and an all-Japanese couple. We each took turns walking in pairs down the long barren room toward the camera. The light was blinding. The child was not there.

It did not strike me as ironic that I was portraying a potential adoptive parent—what intrigued me was that I was a fantasy in someone else's fantasy.

3 ❀ INTO THE MAZE

There was a dinner and at it a man, a drunken man, accused me in his drink of being bastard. I was furious but held my temper under for that day.

Next day I went and taxed my parents with it; they took the insult very ill from him, the drunken fellow who had uttered it. So I was comforted for their part, but still this thing rankled always, for the story crept about widely. And I went at last to Pytho, though my parents did not know. But Phoebus sent me home again unhonoured in what I came to learn, but he foretold other and more desperate horrors to befall me . . .

—Oedipus Rex

There is first of all the question of origin, which often looms in individuals who are driven to be original.

—Erik Erikson

We came back from the Far East not at all the same light-hearted couple who had left three and a half years before.

We hadn't even followed our original schedule. A week in Hong Kong had developed into Bob's two-year research project on the subject of "brainwashing." During that time I had traveled in Vietnam and Southeast Asia as a journalist filing for the *Tokyo Evening News* and American magazines.

What did it all mean—to the world? to us?

We had to sit quietly at our desks to absorb everything. We settled into our first American home—a hundred-year-old colonial house in Cambridge, Massachusetts, which we filled with our acquisitions of old chests, porcelains, scrolls, folk toys, and wood blocks, much as the Yankee sea captains had done before us—and began writing our first books.

Bob's was on the brainwashing project, a formulation of how the Chinese had changed men's minds. He was hoping to unravel the mystery of this process that had intrigued him ever since captured American G.I.'s had spouted confessions in North Korean camps run by the Chinese.

"There's a store of guilt in all of us," he would say. "If you keep wearing a man down long enough in a completely controlled environment, you can stimulate all the guilt he's built up over the course of his lifetime. You can convince him that he's really done something wrong. And in this case, Westerners did feel guilty for the way China had been exploited by the larger powers."

They'd have an easy time with me, I thought. Criticism and self-criticism, that's something I know a lot about.

I was having trouble with my book from the beginning. It was to encompass my experiences in Asia—the end of the American occupation of Japan, the end of the Korean war in stalemate, the beginning of our country's active role in Vietnam, and, of course, all my material on the Chinese in Hong Kong. China had been closed to Americans then, but one felt the vastness of it, the pull and the force. In fact, China crowded everything else out, just as she must have centuries before when she was the Great Middle Kingdom, center of the universe, around which all neighboring countries revolved and paid tribute.

I had files filled with notes, but although I labored for the next few years to express these various experiences and impressions, my book never had the right tone. I could find no voice to speak through, no style that seemed natural.

I became hung up on style—as if it were an ornate curtain behind which I could hide, rather than a diaphanous one through which to reveal myself. Robert Frost said that style is that which indicates how a writer takes himself and what he is saying: "It is the mind skating circles around itself as it moves forward."

But the first-person *I* in my book was a shadowy, unsubstantial person, floating, not skating, through each experience. I might have been the Chinese philosopher who woke each morning asking: "Am I a man dreaming I am a butterfly, or a butterfly dreaming I am a man?"

I did not understand that I who had so carefully documented the histories of the people I was writing about, had no history of my own to set theirs against. Like a true creature of the nether world, I had no shadow.

My book struggled valiantly to be born, but it lacked some vital chemical to give it life. It was made up of exquisitely polished fragments, but like me it could not coalesce into a whole. I mourned over that manuscript as one might a stillborn baby. The children's books which I continued writing and publishing during this period could not comfort me, just as the living can never successfully replace the dead. For although the *kappa*, the *amano-jaku*, the *tengu*, and other folklore creatures were saying in metaphor and parable the things that mattered most to me, I was hidden within them, just as the demon-secret was hidden in the labyrinth. I yearned for a form that could confront life directly, that could throw off the mask.

When I was overwhelmed with the book, I would take off for the Cambridge Records Office and research my old house's genealogy as if it were my own. I felt related to the names on that long list of deeds, proud that I was part of a continuum going back to the mid-eighteenth century— one of us had been on the Lewis and Clark expedition.

Even the poltergeist on the back stairway whom I traced to Benjamin, the brother given that half of the house in 1810, seemed kindly and well-intentioned. I accepted his noisy antics as one might the sleep-walking habits of a dotty old uncle who cannot help himself. His existence was corroborated by the former owner, psychoanalyst Lucy Jessner, who remarked when I mentioned him tentatively: "Oh, don't worry, he always stays on the stairway and never comes into the bedroom."

My ghost, my house, then, gave me a spurious sense of family heritage and relationship to the flow of history. I did not yet have the insight that I would have to come to terms with my *own* origins before I could deepen myself further as an artist or a woman. Before I could have a style.

Still all unknowingly I was listening for the call: I was ready.

Do things happen by chance, or are they predestined? Joseph Campbell says that a blunder, apparently the merest chance, can reveal an unsuspected world that draws the individual into a relationship with forces that are not rightly understood. It may sound the call to some historical undertaking, or mark the dawn of a religious illumination. He refers to it as the awakening of the self, or the call to adventure: "The familiar pattern has been outgrown; the old concepts, ideals and emotional patterns no longer fit; the time of the passing of a threshold is at hand."

And so it happened, as if by chance, that I received a phonecall from my favorite cousin, Carol, some years older than I, who was married to my father's nephew. She had picked up a bit of family gossip from her sister-in-law who had stopped by on her way home to California. Did I know that my father had gone to Harvard and been killed in an automobile crash with my mother?

Carol, the only person other than Bob to whom I had confided my secret, had been startled to hear that casual remark. Although we had never dwelled on the subject, Carol realized that this was not the version she had heard from me. As we spoke, I felt the ground shifting under me.

"What do you think?" she said.

"I can't think. I'll call you back."

That moment of news about a car crash was much like the moment Oedipus must have experienced when a drunken man at the banquet accused him of being a bastard. For Oedipus had grown up much as I had, believing a myth. Oedipus could have ignored the drunken man's remarks instead of going to Pytho to check them out, and I could have ignored that distant cousin's gossip and gone on about my life. But Oedipus first went to his parents, Polybus and Merope, and asked them the truth of the man's words. They had their moment and they flubbed it: they denied any knowledge of what the man could mean.

By chance my adoptive mother was coming to visit us the following week, and although it had been years since I had mentioned this subject, I decided to confront her with what I had heard. She was alone now, my father having died the year before. And so one afternoon when we were sitting in the living room of my old colonial house, I brought up the subject which had lain dormant between us for so many years.

She didn't flinch when I told her what I had heard. "I don't remember," she said as calmly as if I had asked her that cousin's phone number. "You should have asked your father."

"It is too late for that," I reminded her.

"Listen," she said, covering her tracks, "when your father and I went to New York to adopt a child, we wanted a boy. But your father said to take a girl when we saw you. He said a girl would be with me in later years, while a boy would move away."

Her eyes filled with tears, their source not yet defined.

"But you are not with me. I see other mothers being taken care of by their daughters. Not that I want to be taken care of. God knows I don't. But you live so far away. And you seldom come to visit. Everyone is talking about it, how you are letting me live alone."

The tears were for my father, for herself, for what the public thought. We both knew she would never leave the apartment she loved and the community she depended on to come East with me. But she had no private self: she was a literal reflection of the values and prejudices of her friends: somehow mothers should be living near their children. The tears now came streaming down her face as they always did at some point in our reunions.

I tried to steer the conversation which was careening wildly around my guilt back to the story that Carol had heard.

"Is it possible my father didn't die from shell shock?" I asked, hoping by rephrasing it I could get a response.

But she had recovered herself again. Once more she repeated the story I had heard so often in my childhood.

"Then how did the rumor of a car accident get circulated?" I persisted.

"I don't know. Maybe she's right. I don't remember details like that anymore. Dad would know."

Now a few tears specifically for Dad.

"All I can remember is that we wanted a legitimate baby and we found you. And you came running to us with your first words: "Daddy! Daddy!""

I dropped the subject, as Oedipus must have done. I could not point out to her than in an earlier version she had me saying "Mama! Mama!" If this could be changed, what other details might not be based on her own fantasy life. But what was the use of prolonging the agony—these scenes between us were too painful. I resolved never to bring up the subject again. We each had our roles now and we had to continue to play them. I resented this woman who was my mother by a fluke of fate and a legal decree, but a primitive love still held me to her. Or was it guilt? Or gratitude? The Japanese speak of the debt that can never be paid: that's what held me to this mother—a child's helplessness and this debt. Or are they one and the same? Does it hold all adults to the parents they have grown away from—or only the adopted? "Oh the pity of it, Iago, the pity of it;" kept running through my mind like a mantra as I sat there looking into her large, empty, teary eyes.

I so wanted to say something kind to her, something she craved that would reassure her. I wanted to tell her that although I appreciated what she had done for me, there was a world out there beyond us and the experiences we had shared together. I wanted her to know what I had seen in my travels: the revolutions and wars and lives caught up in them; I wanted her to hear the insights I had gained (Hadn't she read those voluminous letters I had sent?); I wanted to explain to her who I had become and that I was still in the process of becoming, thanks to the mothering she gave me in those earlier years.

But she was frozen in the past, hers and mine, clinging to my childhood as one might to an heirloom that was the last link to some loved one.

"Mother," I wanted to say, "I've tried to be a good daughter. All through college I came home on Thanksgiving, at Christmas, on your birthday, on my birthday, on Mother's Day. I wrote, I called (I still do), but nothing has ever been enough. You are the keeper of the archives of my past and even though you have distorted the records, I shall let you go free. But just look at me now, recognize me as the grown married woman that I am."

I looked into her eyes, but I saw only myself as a little girl.

Now her voice became soft and pathetic; she, too, wanted everything to go right with us during this visit. I could sense her loneliness, her fear of old age, and I became frightened, as if her fear had entered me. For there is a symbiotic relationship between a mother and child, adopted or not. A bind between you and the one who raises you, who shares your history. I could not bear the pain of it, but still I was incapable of comforting her, just as I was incapable of satisfying her insatiable emotional needs.

Would her own daughter have known how to protect her from mortality?

"Her own daughter would have fled long ago," Bob once said when I was brooding morbidly like this.

Now in spite of all those years away from her, here I was seized by the same old panic when we were together again. But I was determined to keep my resentments secret from this mother who had taught me so well the fine art of secrecy. Even though such polite distancing is more appropriate with strangers, it was kinder at times such as this. I had to protect her from those truths which could hurt her, just as I had to protect myself from those falsehoods which could destroy me.

Still I knew that deep in that unarticulated, repressed part of her, the part that had gone underground at the sound of her father's gun, she knew the truth—that the secret we once shared so tacitly had grown into a monster between us. If unchecked, it could devour us both. We faced each other like enemies whenever the monster stirred: I became once again the ugly changeling who would never grow into the enlarged dimpled version of Shirley Temple who sang and danced in all mothers' dreams.

If only I could have said those things to her then. Instead I suggested lightly, "How about a movie this afternoon?"

I can't remember what we saw.

Carol and I talked again shortly after my mother's visit. She had written her sister-in-law who had confirmed by mail the same story about the car accident. "I think we should call the agency that arranged your adoption and find out what did happen," she said.

I hesitated. The idea of making such a call, so elementary to others, seemed earthshaking to me: like asking the boatman Charon for the passenger list on that fateful day's crossing of the Styx. All unknowingly I had reached the borders between life and death at which the taboos stand guard. One does not tamper with these sentries: one observes their *Off Limits* signs. Society has put all that is attractive but dangerous to its functioning under their jurisdiction.

Now for the first time I was consciously aware of those invisible taboos that ruled my life and kept my emotions in check.

Bob, however, was not intimidated by them: he refused to acknowledge their existence. I watched him pick up the phone and put through the call to that adoption agency with the nonchalance of one about to place an order with the grocer.

The call was switched to the executive director, Mrs. White. Bob explained briefly that he was a psychiatrist seeking more information about his wife's past. Mrs. White suggested he make the request in a letter so that she could know if what he sought was in her files. At the time neither Bob nor I realized that most adoption agencies under the rubric of "confidentiality" give only select material, if any, to an adoptee who comes inquiring, and never the names of the original parents. If he had known, he might not have been able to carry off the call as a natural request which he expected to be filled.

The letter Bob wrote was two pages long and covered just about everything we knew to date. In explaining why we wanted to know what was in the agency files, he said:

> Without this knowledge my wife feels confused about her identity, a person without roots. I am certain that learning more about her parents—their racial backgrounds, their

interests and professions, or anything at all pertaining to them—would be a very great emotional benefit to her. As a psychiatrist I want to emphasize how very important this knowledge is to my wife's emotional life, and particularly to her ability to feel some kind of heritage, whatever it may be. I cannot tell you how deeply grateful we both feel for the part your agency has played in giving her the opportunities she has had in her life. And I need not tell you how much we would appreciate your contribution to her well-being.

Bob, who was to become a pioneer in the field of psychohistory—the coming together of a person's psyche with the age he or she lives in—understood instinctively how important it was that I exhume this information about my past, which until now had lain dormant in the grave my adoptive mother had assigned it. I addressed the envelope and dropped it into the corner mailbox. It was like posting a letter to God.

For the rest of that day I felt calm. I knew I was betraying my adoptive mother by this act, just as I felt she had betrayed me by telling a story that might not be true, but I no longer wanted to live in her hysterical fantasy world. I wanted myth and reality to merge: to know who I came from, what blood was in my veins. I wanted to live consciously, to get rid of the confusion and chaos cluttering my mind. To be real.

However, that night, awakened by the thunder-and-lightning storm that rattled the frail structure of our house, I felt the winds of panic and remorse blowing right through me. It was wrong to have sent the letter, wrong to pry into the past. It was only in the sunlight of the next morning when the world seemed calm again that I was calm again, and believed I had a right to know.

All during the next week I fluctuated between certainty and doubt. Bob was immersed in his own psyche, having started his personal analysis as part of his analytic training. But I felt no temptation to go into therapy myself.

"I wouldn't want to relive my past in the Midwest over again," I said. "I don't consider it a part of me anymore."

"Whether you're analyzed or not, it is part of you," he reminded me. "You can't amputate those years of your life like you can a limb."

"I wish I could."

"You'd be slamming the door on yourself," he warned me. "You are what has evolved over all these years. Even if you learn about your real family, there would still be the life you have lived until now. You would still be you."

But dwelling on my adopted past didn't interest me. I wanted to explore the myth, to luxuriate in my new knowledge, to brood over the car crash and the possible new characters who might emerge from the wreckage. I began looking into the mirror as I had as a child for the eyes of my father, the nose of my mother, the ears of my grandparents. I began trying to imagine what my parents might have been like as people, something I had not done before. At thirty, I was probably already older than they when they died: they would be like children to me.

The letter from Mrs. White arrived two weeks later. It began:

> Unfortunately there is very little information that I can give you since our old records have so little in them. I can share with you what there is, but I am afraid that the information will not add very much to what you already know. . . .

And then I learned the "official" facts, phrased in such a way that they managed to corroborate my adoptive mother's version while avoiding the real issues:

> I note that your wife was placed for adoption when she was almost two and a half years old. During this early period she lived with her family, and later was placed at the Home for Hebrew Infants. Our record indicates that her great-grandfather was an Orthodox rabbi and the relatives were intelligent and successful people. However, there are not specific facts given regarding your wife's mother and father, other than the fact that they were both born in this country and were of good intelligence.

The letter ended with Mrs. White's willingness to talk to both of us personally if we would like to make an appointment.

I read that letter over and over, but each time my parents slipped through the netting of her words as if nothing would encompass them. They were suggested in that letter, but they were not there. They were still dead.

Bob made the appointment for the following week. Our plan was to go into New York together but for him to go to the agency alone. I rationalized that she would tell him more if I were not there. But, in truth, I could not have gone with him: I, who had traveled alone through war zones in both Korea and Vietnam, did not yet have the courage to enter the front door of that adoption agency.

I was to wait for Bob under the clock at the Biltmore Hotel, a popular trysting place for New Yorkers. Sitting there I felt the minutes of my past were being checked off by the sturdy hands of that stalwart timepiece which has served so many generations of lovers and strangers on their various assignations.

Hickory dickory dock, the mouse ran up the clock.

That last night of the Korean War I had sat in a bunker at the front with a few G.I.'s and their officers watching the pudgy hands of an alarm clock edge their way toward 10 P.M., the designated hour of the ceasefire. We knew that if the Chinese and North Koreans failed to observe it, and lobbed mortars in instead, we would probably all be killed. Now I realized that it was not bravery that made me stay there with those men that night rather than accepting a ride back to the rear lines: it was the same lack of rootedness within me that made dying seem as unreal as living. The hands of that clock held our collective fate, and I belonged at that moment to a group of people with an intensity I had never experienced before. Perhaps this is the emotion that holds men to war—that feeling of camaraderie that makes each feel he is not alone.

The clock struck ten, the mouse ran down. All was quiet. Someone said: "This is the Great End."

Hickory dickory dock.

Now I was about to enter the Great Beginning. I jumped up when I saw Bob's head in the distance bobbing above the others in the lobby just as it had in Japan where he loomed a giant among the Lilliputians. He was striding briskly, smiling in anticipation of seeing me.

"Sit down," he said. "I have real news."

We settled on the bench directly under that impassive clock while he prepared to read to me from the white index cards on which he had his notes.

"Did she tell you *everything?*" I couldn't wait.

"A lot. I couldn't look at the files, but she pulled some things out for me."

I didn't let him start. "How did they die?"

"They're not dead—at least as far as the records show."

I felt as if a mortar had just landed.

"Not dead? What do you mean?"

"Just that. There's no record of shell shock or a car accident."

Then he read from the cards: "Your name was Blanche Silverstein. Your mother's was Beatrice Silverstein. She and her family came from Freeport, Rhode Island, but they moved to New York before you were born. Your great-grandfather was an Orthodox rabbi in the Bronx. Your mother was nineteen when she gave you up."

He looked up to see how I was taking it. "Ready for more?"

I nodded dumbly.

"All the information is about your mother. She gave birth at seventeen, breast fed you for five months, and then put you in the Hebrew Home for Infants, which was not an adoption agency." He paused. "Sounds like she wanted to keep you. She used to visit you there."

Back to the card: "You weighed seven pounds at birth. Later had light hair and blue eyes. You were chubby, a good eater, and listen to this, you had a winning smile."

We both laughed at that.

"Mrs. White said the records imply there was a conflict in the family about whether or not to keep you. The family in the mother's line had some prominent people in it—professionals and college graduates, but her father was a glazier."

"What's a glazier?"

"I don't know." Again we laughed.

"Your mother took a job with a dress firm to support you, and then decided to give you up when you were two. You had been very ill with mastoiditis. You were put into a foster home for four months until your adoptive parents came and took you to the Midwest. The adoption came through two years later."

He put the cards down. "That's all I have, but it's a lot, isn't it?"

"My name is Blanche Silverstein."

"Hello Blanche."

"I hate Blanche."

"You don't have to use it."

Again we laughed. We were giddy. Then he had an appointment to see his editor and I had to see mine about a new children's book in production. We were to meet on the train back to Cambridge.

The euphoria was still with us on the ride home. We went over the material carefully. Was Beatrice married? Mrs. White made a point of saying there was no record either way in the file, but was she telling the truth? If Beatrice had been married, wouldn't there have been a record? Would she be giving her child away? If I were legitimate, why did I have my mother's maiden name?

But the most important piece of information that kept tugging at me was that there was no record of either parent's death. They seemed to have been very much alive at the time of my adoption. And if they were, who were those ghostly presences standing in the wings of my childhood, sending me messages of strength from the other world?

Everything was collapsing within me.

I moved through the next few weeks in a kind of stupor. I had my story, and although it was far from complete, at least it was the closest I had ever come to any reality about myself. I found myself weeping uncontrollably for I knew not what. Sometimes it seemed to be for Beatrice, my real mother, so young to face such a decision as giving up her child, so brave to hang on for so long. I knew the wound must be something old to her by now, grown over with scar tissue, but it was fresh for me, as if I were now bearing the pain for her.

Yet I knew I was also weeping for myself—the self I might have been.

"Carol, my name was Blanche," I reported as soon as I got back to Cambridge.

"Sounds French. Maybe your father was French." Carol had a French grandmother.

"My Japanese family said I looked French."

"They ought to know."

We both laughed. There were so many laughs in those days, along with the tears.

"Carol, it seems certain now that the child was given up because it was not legitimate."

We had taken to calling the child "it."

"Maybe your mother fell in love with a Frenchman but couldn't marry him because he wasn't Jewish." Carol was a non-Jew who converted to marry my cousin.

"Is it possible he died just before or after I was born?"

"It's possible he was still alive—but married to someone else."

We played this scenario. My mother is a young girl from Freeport rebelling against her parents. She becomes involved with a married man and is impregnated. Her family sends her to New York to relatives so that the community will not learn of her disgrace. She has the baby but cannot decide whether to give it up. She puts it into a home, hoping the father will divorce his wife and marry her. He does not. The relatives persuade her to think of the baby's future and let it be adopted. She gives up the baby.

Such is the fiction the adopted invent.

"Let's think about what Beatrice might be like," Carol says one day over tea.

"Beatrice . . . Beatrice," I repeat her name, trying to make it something familiar.

"She must have married in all this time," says Carol. "She may have a family of her own, children she could keep."

"Then I would have brothers and sisters. I always wanted a brother." I think of that boy in the Cleveland home.

"But has she told this family about you?" Carol asks.

A good question, but we do not understand its significance at the time. We have not yet thought into the psychology of anyone in the adoption drama except the adoptee—me.

"Anyway, they'd be half-brothers and half-sisters," she continues. "How would they feel if you came on the scene? Would they want to know about you?"

The terrain is so unexplored, so limitless, it stretches to infinity from all vantage points.

"You know, I don't think your real mother could have been married," Carol says another time. "A married woman does not give up her child."

Carol has no children. Years ago she and my cousin tried to adopt but they couldn't get a baby from either the Protestant or Jewish agencies because of their mixed marriage.

"But why did my mother insist that I was legitimate?"

"Because it sounded better," replies Carol knowingly. "As long as she was revising the story, she put in things she wanted."

Now it was my turn to revise the script. I made it into a James Barrie play where one has the options to see what might have happened had the plot gone a different way.

Beatrice decides to keep the child—me. She grows up in New York. I see her sitting with a group of little girls in

Rumplemayers on Central Park South. They are celebrating a birthday party such as the one I had observed from my table not too long before on a visit to the city. These girls were more mature, less innocent than the ones in the Middle West. Their faces had already congealed into firmer, more determined lines, already they were miniature replicas of their smartly dressed, heavily made-up mothers who sat gossiping at an adjoining table. I had felt like a spy watching them.

Now I am watching myself.

But is that *me* sitting there with those privileged upper-middle-class girls? I remind myself that Blanche would have lived with a poor, working mother who was straining to support her. Maybe it would have become too much for this young mother and she would have put Blanche into a series of foster homes like the ones Norma Jean ended up in. She would live with the identity of a bastard if that mother were not married. Her sense of not belonging might be a more basic alienation from society than growing up in an adopted family.

But was she a bastard? Who was her father? Why was there no mention of him in the agency files? Until now he had had a concrete, shell-shocked reality, more vivid than that Camille-like mother. Now he was nonexistent. A cipher.

And what about this rabbi-grandfather, this Southern colonel, the most real of all the phantoms to me? What void did he suddenly disappear into? No mention of him as a loving, nourishing figure strolling hand in hand with me into that agency. Surely such a touching detail would have been noted in the files.

I am feeling sorry for myself.

"The adopted are just accidents thrown on the wheel at the wrong time by a drunken Potter," I announce to Bob.

"Everyone is an accident whether born in wedlock or not," he replies.

I love him for that.

"But at least everyone else knows who their real parents are," I argue, refusing to be fully consoled.

"Most people would be happy *not* to know," he quips.

As a psychiatrist Bob knows how often people are temperamentally alienated from their blood parents and relatives, and I know this too. But it does not help.

"What if your real mother turned out to be insensitive, gross, overbearing?" Bob asks me one evening while I am brooding. "What if she's not the poetic fantasy you've created in your mind?"

"I wouldn't care," I reply. "At least I'd know who she was."

"What if she's bourgeois and pedestrian?" Bob persists.

"She couldn't be."

"But what if she was?" He is relentless. "Would it destroy your fantasy world? How would you feel?"

It is like one of those long, shaggy conundrums children pose to each other.

"I'd feel better knowing, no matter what she was."

"Think about it," he warns. "Perhaps it is better to live with a dream than to seek reality and be plunged to earth."

He doesn't mean it, but he is testing me. I picture myself hurtling like Icarus down through the sky, my wings melted by the searing brilliance of the sun. Could I survive being plunged to earth? What would it do to me as a writer—deepen me or make me commonplace, unimaginative, bitter, cynical? My head is whirling.

Ring around the rosy.

We go round and round on this. Round and round like those mixed-blood fairy children in their magic circle.

Neither Bob nor I realize that I am beginning to circle

the labyrinth. Slowly at first, drifting with a discussion of searching out Beatrice to learn the part of the story not in the agency files, and then faster and faster as the speculation becomes a possibility. I break away.

No more! I never intended to search for my natural parents.

The very idea is as overwhelming as the idea of calling the agency once was. I have incorporated my taboos too well, digested them so thoroughly that they form part of every fiber of my body.

Who, me, do such a thing as look for my natural mother? Never! I am innocent!

This is precarious territory we are trespassing on. It threatens to open up and swallow the one identity I have; as manufactured and shaky as that is, at least it is *me*.

I'm circling again—if I met my real mother would it destroy the reality of my adoptive family unit—the only family I had ever known? In other words, if I found Blanche, who belonged to that natural mother, would there still be an adopted me to belong to my adoptive parents?

I remembered reading about a schizophrenic woman who had twelve selves, or was it sixteen, inhabiting her body at different times, each one surprising the other at the most inopportune times. At least I had only two to contend with—but which was the real one?

Ashes, ashes, we all fall down.

Bob is not religious. He prides himself on his Jewish heritage in a secular way. I am more mystical, entertaining vague ideas of reincarnation in a pantheist universe. I still do not trust this Jehovah, this Jewish god. Look what he did to me—separated me from my natural parents, farmed me out to the Midwest. Still these turbulent days I find myself often in a state of hysteria that verges on prayer: "Oh, God," I mumble—not caring if Buddha or Jesus or Jehovah tunes in—"give me strength to develop what is the reality of this me, whose existence was never tabulated in the original plan. Give me the perseverance and wisdom to put it all together, and survive."

When I am not discoursing with the powers that be, I tell myself that what is important is to keep writing, keep creating. A recorded existence is a real one. A legitimate one. Maybe even think of creating a child: for the first time now I can psychologically consider carrying a baby in my womb. This new knowledge about Beatrice, as sparse as it is, is something concrete that connects me to the physical world. And if it does that, then it is *right* to have this information about her—and to seek more.

Every day we ride our ambivalences like waves in the sea, and sometimes the breakers keep carrying us closer to that shore we are not sure we want to reach.

I knew that I could not go backward. To go forward meant going alone into Mrs. White's office at the adoption agency. I had to hear it all for myself. Then I would know what I had to do. After all, I told myself, the agency had been the Great Go-Between. The agency was in the labyrinth business, and like plumbers who hide sewer pipes in the bowels of the earth, it buries its pipelines deep in the underbelly of society.

I managed to convince myself that only the agency could give me the threaded sanction to enter the maze that stretched ahead, and return whole. Only the agency had the map, the original drawings of the labyrinth.

I walk through the front door of the agency to Mrs. White's office.

The agency is the Big Mother, taking from one woman, giving to another. The agency is the Procurer, the Dispenser, the Recording Angel, the Pimp, the Shepherd. The agency is the Executive Director.

Mrs. White shakes my wet hand and motions me to a chair.

The agency is the ancient Chinese sage who has seen

millions of babies come and go, some of them to palaces, some of them to shanties, some of them to the bottom of the river. Perhaps it has even seen some coming back like me, transmogrified into adult versions of themselves.

I feel calm as I sit on the other side of the desk facing her, the woman at the top.

The agency is the All-Seeing, All-Knowing, All-Forgiving Mother.

She speaks: "I've told your husband everything I can from our file."

I see her now. She is matronly, matter-of-fact, businesslike. A pro.

"Your need to come here seems most unusual."

"Many people must have come back asking for information about themselves," I venture respectfully. I have come in with the courage of a lion, now I am meek like a lamb.

"Very few," she says. "And you seem more intense than the others."

She is confirming my worst fears: I am really a freak.

The agency is the Nonapproving, Avenging Mother.

"I think my search is a normal one," I continue casually. "How could anyone not want to know her background?"

She concedes a little. "I suppose it is normal to have feelings of curiosity."

What does she mean by "curiosity"? Is she using it in a pejorative sense? Is she implying that adoptees are motivated by *idle* curiosity?

"If a questionnaire were sent out to adoptees," she says, "perhaps we would find that everyone has felt as you do at one time or another. And that if they were not too guilty, they might have come in."

The agency is the Manipulator of Guilt.

I know about guilt too. But still I want to shout: "Why should they feel guilty? They did not give themselves away. They were the unknowing objects in the transaction. No one asked them. The guilt is on you. The blood is on your hands too!"

"I cannot tell you anything more than I have already told your husband," she is repeating. "And in retrospect I realize I should not have given him your mother's name. You might go out and try to find her."

She smiles a cunning smile. We understand each other, the two of us, this agency and its former baby. We know the baby wouldn't do a thing like that. Naughty, naughty to even entertain the thought.

The agency is the Stern Nanny.

"If you don't mind my giving you advice, I think you should seek therapy to try to understand *why* you want more material," Mrs. White says, standing up.

Our interview is over. The agency has given its time, nothing more. It has given all it intends to give. It does not dispense sanction. Even should the baby throw a tantrum, the agency will not relent. The baby nods demurely as she leaves, throwing that winning smile that so charmed Mrs. White's predecessor thirty years before.

We shake hands. The door closes behind me.

I feel flushed with a warm glow. Just making the pilgrimage to this Temple of Forbidden Secrets has helped me leap over some invisible hurdle into selfhood. I have touched some inner conviction within myself, laid a new cornerstone in my development. I have achieved one of the small satori's on the way to the Big One.

I walk confidently into the warm noon sun. I am on my way to making the fate that was imposed upon me my own.

However, back in Cambridge my courage failed. I found I still could not act without some kind of sanction. Bob could not give it to me, nor could Carol. They were too close. I needed the impartial wisdom of a seer.

In another age I would have consulted the Oracle of

Delphi. I would have sought out priests who analyzed the cawing of birds and inhaled the dark fumes of caves. But in Cambridge the only analysts were psychiatrists who spoke in the deep, gutteral tones of Freud, the Viennese medicine man, whose cures they had carried over the seas to us. Like their guru, they knew how to equate taboos with neurosis; how to evaporate the vapors of ambivalence; how to cleanse the mind's pollution and cut the silver cords. Or so they claimed.

The analyst I chose for an hour's consultation was an authority on the psychology of women. I wanted a woman. Perhaps she would have Ariadne's thread in her sewing box.

It was the next stage of the journey.

She listened gravely to my story about my adopted childhood, my secret, my dilemma, and then she spoke: "Your need to look for your mother is neurotic. You are rationalizing why you must know who your 'real' parents, as you call them, are."

So, too, had Jocasta tried to discourage Oedipus from seeking the truth.

"You should have therapy first before considering a move like this," said the analyst. "You should understand yourself before seeking out your parents."

"My search for my parents is to help me understand myself," I replied.

"You will find out who you are in the years you lived with your adoptive parents," she pointed out kindly, but firmly.

"But I was living in a myth about my past," I protested. "And now I've learned that even that myth was based on lies."

"The myth becomes integrated into one's life and psychology and is as good as the real history. Do not seek anything else. You do not know what things you may overturn."

"What could I learn that it would be better for me not to know?"

"It is best to let things stay as they are," she cautioned, avoiding a direct answer to my question. "The biological mother is unimportant in a case like this. The only reason you want to find her is that you did not have a good relationship with your adoptive one."

"There's more to it than that," I objected. "I would want to know, no matter who had adopted me."

"Your mother may not even want to see you."

"I have to take that chance," I replied.

The analyst and Jocasta were keepers of the status quo. They had to ensure the uninterrupted continuity of the generations.

"This could be very unpleasant for your mother," the analyst was saying.

"It might make her happy," I countered. I didn't know from what wellsprings I was drawing my nerve.

She continued: "Is it fair of you? I think not. And if you find your mother, you will still be unsatisfied. You will have the need to find your father."

"Is that so terrible?"

"You must understand what it is you really want to know," she said, trying a new tack. "Will the fact of your father being a lawyer or a doctor or a businessman help your identity? I think not."

Her tone clearly implied he would be none of these. Madman, murderer, rapist—why didn't she say what she saw in my past?

We had reached an impasse. Now the analyst invited Bob, who was waiting in the outer room, to join us. Because he was a colleague, albeit a much younger one, and I his wife, she spoke more directly than she might have otherwise in such a consultation.

"Your wife is on a neurotic search, masked under the rationalization that she is seeking reality," she told him in front of me. "She seems to feel that what her life has been until now is not reality."

Bob rose loyally to my support. "She hoped you might understand the importance of the search."

"No one has has asked me if they should look up their natural parents before," she informed him. "I do not think that most adopted people have this need. Your wife may not be hurt by it, but no matter what she discovers, she will still be unsatisfied. If a child thinks there is a burglar in the room, you cannot allay his fears by switching on the light. He will find a burglar elsewhere. You must find out *why* he is afraid of the burglar in the first place."

Then she turned to me: "You have already made your decision about what you are going to do."

For the first time that hour I agreed with her.

"But," she continued, "this is a compulsion you have to follow through. You will not be satisfied." And then as if to soften her sharp prediction, she added, "I'll be happy to help you if you want to return to me after you have looked up your mother."

I thanked her kindly, but I knew I would never return there. If she could not comprehend my need now, how could she help me later?

And so I came to know that I would search for my mother, that no one can give you sanction but yourself. It is the authorities' role to guard the taboos against each generation that defies them.

I had to go into the labyrinth armed only with the faith I had in my heart. I would spin the thread as I went along.

There are hundreds of manuals for adoptive parents like *How to Adopt a Baby, How to Tell Your Child He/She is Adopted, How to Believe it is Okay Not to Tell Your Child He/She is Adopted,* and so on.

But there are no manuals for the adopted like *How to Grow Up Adopted, How to Have Healthy Fantasies About Natural Parents, How to Survive as an Adopted Adult, How to Get Sanction to Look Up Your Origins, How to Maneuver With Mother's Maiden Name.* For in truth, by the time adoptees have managed to grow up emotionally as well as physically, that is, mustered the courage to search and acquired a name to search with, their mothers may have been married once or twice, and moved as many times in the process.

What does one do? Does one spend the rest of one's life playing Sherlock Holmes, following clues, looking in old phonebooks, rummaging through old records and graveyard listings, knocking on doors of old addresses—hoping that some action will magically spring the lock which holds the door to the labyrinth?

One does—there is no choice.

The following Sunday Bob and I put our gangly Wei-maraner pup in the back seat of the convertible, and took off for the scene of the crime—Freeport, Rhode Island. I was going there like a pilgrim seeking the truth, and was not surprised to see the golden dome of the city hall beckoning me like the spires of Mecca.

I looked into the good book and found two Silversteins listed—Samuel and Isadore—and then our car cruised slowly through their silent, suburban landscape and past their unsuspecting homes.

I was Princess Blanche making the Grand Tour of my Origins.

Our huge pup, in the spirit of the occasion, stood up on his seat like a mighty potentate surveying the scene. His lineage was almost as mysterious as mine. Surely as complicated. The Weimaraner is an invented breed, and though his family line traces back to the time of Grand Duke Charles Augustus in the duchy of Saxe-Weimar, and there are dark rumors about the mixing of German and Russian blood, no one knows where he got his yellow eyes and his gray ghostlike coat.

Because of his improbable heritage, I bestowed upon him the nonsensical name, Runcible, coined by that master of nonsense and whimsy, Edward Lear, for his runcible cat. It was Lear who sent the Owl and the Pussycat out to sea in a beautiful pea-green boat, and the Jumblies out in a sieve. He would have known how to smoke Samuel and Isadore out of their haunted houses: one of them would become my age'd Uncle Arley perched on a heap of Barley, on whose nose there was a cricket and in whose pocket a railway ticket; and the other would turn out to be that old man of Whitehaven, who danced a quadrille with a Raven, till they said "it's absurd to encourage this bird" and smashed that old man of White-haven.

Would *they* smash me? I had the need to believe that someday all the *theys* would condone my lonely journey.

> And everyone said, "if we only live,
> We *too* will go to sea in a Sieve—
>> To the hills of the Chankly Bore!
>> Far and few, far and few,
>>> Are the lands where the Jumblies
>>> live
>>> Their heads are green, and their
>>> hands are blue
>>> And they went to sea in a Sieve.

Then we put our runcible dog in our runcible car and journeyed back over the great Groomboolian Plain to our runcible house in Cambridge.

"Carol, we found two Silversteins in the phonebook. I have the addresses and the numbers. What do we do now?"

Carol was as new to this kind of enterprise as I was, but she was game. "Let's not call them yet," she said. "Let's go to the Record's office there during the week and look up Beatrice's birth certificate. That way we can learn some of the family names."

Being descended from Nathan Hale on her mother's side, Carol had a natural bent toward genealogy.

A few days later we drove to Freeport and had stiff martinis with lunch at one of the hotels to fortify ourselves. The old police building where the vital statistics were kept was musty and nearly empty. I gave a clerk my mother's maiden name and he pulled out some books of birth records under S. I couldn't believe it. In just a few minutes I, who had no legal right to look at my own, was actually looking at my mother's birth certificate. She was real, even if I was not.

This is what I learned from the records.

My natural mother was born the third daughter of Samuel and Sophie Silverstein in the same year as Carol. That made her forty-seven.

My grandfather had been married before, but was divorced from his first wife, by whom he had a son.

My mother had a younger brother, Oran. His birth certificate was there too.

My grandmother's wedding certificate told me she had been a widow when she married my grandfather. He had been listed as a picture framer and cabinetmaker on his first wedding certificate, but he was down as a glazier on this one.

In brief, a widow born in Russia and a divorced man born in Austria had joined in America to beget my mother who had joined with someone somewhere to beget me.

There was no wedding certificate for my mother in that office. No death certificate for my grandmother or grandfather.

"Those records must be in New York," said Carol. "The whole family must have moved there."

We spoke in whispers but our excitement attracted the attention of one of the senior men at the desk. He walked over to us.

"Do you need any help?" he asked suspiciously.

Suddenly I felt guilty again, furtive. I did not want him to know I was looking at my family records.

"No," I said, trying to sound natural.

"Well, use a pencil, not a pen when you make notes." He didn't know what else to say. "We don't want to get the records marked."

And to Carol: "No smoking in here."

He walked away, but then turned back, unable to resist asserting his authority further. "What's your name?" he snapped at me.

"She doesn't have to give that," said Carol quickly.

"I need it for my files since you are using my material."

"They're public records," I said. "I have a right to use them and besides—I'm with the press."

"Let's see your press card," he demanded.

I looked into my wallet thinking to give him an old accreditation card from Vietnam when I realized it would have my name on it. He might know my mother's relatives and tell them I had been here. I didn't want anyone to know—yet. I told him to give me a few minutes to find my card.

He stalked back to his desk and reached for a phone. Carol and I ducked out the side door.

We ran like fugitives.

We were fugitives.

We were guilty.

We were breaking the taboo.

We were criminals.

We were trying to find my mother.

We were looking up mother's maiden name.

We were not playing by the rules of the game.

We were shaking as we fled back to the hotel and ordered another round of stiff drinks. I understood the elated tension of bank robbers who make a successful getaway. But soon we were absorbed in analyzing the notes we had taken there.

"Your father probably was *not* Jewish or he would have been forced to marry your mother," Carol mused. "There would have been a wedding certificate."

There seemed to have been no marriage.

"The next step is the Records office in the Bronx," she went on. "That's where she put you in the home. Maybe she got married there too."

The possibility of actually finding this woman who was my mother came flooding through me again.

"What would I feel if I saw her?" I asked Carol. "Would I recognize her? Would we be strangers? Would she want to see me?"

"She'd want to see her daughter," said Carol, who had no daughter.

I looked at her gratefully—her delicate face with its finely chiseled features and luminous eyes—and knew at that moment I could never love any mother as much as I loved her.

Carol and I are getting into the spirit of things: we are beginning to enjoy our detective work.

During the Christmas holidays we drive to the Bronx and look up wedding records. This time there are no problems. The clerk gives us the right book and moves away.

I turn to my mother's wedding certificate, see her handwriting where she has signed her name.

The letters are large, open and innocent, like a child's. What could be more wondrous than my mother's signature? There is no guile in those letters, not even pain. She has signed herself Bea. It is less formal, more modern. She is married by her grandfather, the Rabbi. Her age is listed as twenty. The groom, listed as a manufacturer, is a few years older.

But his name, this husband of my mother, is a common one—Goodman. There are twenty of him with the same first initial in the Manhattan phonebook.

"We'll go to the New York registry and look up business firms in *Polk* and *Dunn and Bradstreet*," says Carol. She had once been her husband's executive secretary. This is a world she feels comfortable in.

But there were no firms listed with my mother's husband's initials. I did not want to call the others with the same surnames because I didn't want to alert anyone that

I was trying to find Bea. It was still a secret: hers and mine. If that's what the agency meant by "confidentiality," then I was willing to respect it. No one but my mother should know I was looking for her.

We had come to a dead end here. The search had to be for my mother's husband in order to find her. But how could that be done without arousing his suspicions? He might not know about me.

I would advise anyone now, if they could afford it, to go to a tracer's bureau. But at the time it seemed sordid to have a private detective prowling about my secret world, and I feared the expense would be prohibitive. And so we appealed to a lawyer, a friend of my father-in-law, to help us find this manufacturer in a field where he had many clients. We did not tell him why, just that we wanted to contact his wife. The lawyer, sensing our need to keep this confidential, respected our request for privacy.

I felt guilty for not confiding in my father-in-law. He would not only have understood but would probably have tried to help. But I was still made up of conflicting selves and antiselves. So much of me was still submerged because of the secrets of the past. I never asked myself to whom I was being loyal in keeping the fact of my search from close friends and relatives.

We waited to hear from the lawyer.

On Bea's birthday, the date I had seen on the birth certificate, Bob and I bought a bottle of champagne and toasted her. I drank to the mother I did not know. It was like a novel: the plot was in the making even as I drained the glass.

The letter from the lawyer came the following week. He had learned that Bea was divorced from Goodman and remarried, but his informant did not know her new name or where she lived. However, he did know that Howard, her son by the first marriage, was in graduate school at M.I.T.

I had a half-brother at M.I.T.

I wanted to run down the streets of Cambridge shouting: "I have a brother! I have a brother!" I might have already passed him in Harvard Square. I determined to look more closely at the students on the street to see if someone looked like me.

I went to the M.I.T. directory and looked up his last name. He was there—an engineering student living in one of the dormitories.

By now I was intrepid. I didn't need Carol or Bob. I could do this job alone. I called my brother's dorm and told the switchboard operator I was trying to find a certain student named Goodman but did not want to bother the one I saw listed until I was sure he was the right one. Was his mother's name Beatrice?

The operator said she was not allowed to give out family names, but since I was a faculty wife in the area she didn't see the harm. And then she spoke the words I was waiting to her: Yes, her name was Beatrice—Beatrice Rudolph. She also gave me her address and phone number in Great Neck, New York.

The door to the labyrinth flew open.

Inside was the woman I thought to be my mother.

❧ ❧

But here is where we need an adoptee's how-to manual again. How does one proceed when one has the name and address of the woman who may or may not be one's mother?

I had to approach Beatrice Rudolph in a way that would protect her privacy if indeed I was her daughter. Going to her door was impossible—there might be someone at home with her. If I wrote a letter, some one else might open it. Even a phonecall was dangerous, since there might be someone on another extension. But I decided to try this last course.

The plan was that Bob and Carol and I would drive into New York that next weekend. Bob had to go on to a conference in New Jersey, but Carol would stay with me and act as a go-between with Bea.

On the way into the city we drove out to Great Neck and looked for Bea's house. I wanted to see how she lived. The snow flurries which had begun sprinkling the car when we left Massachusetts had turned into a raging blizzard on the outskirts of New York, blanketing the streets and our windshield.

After many false turns, we found Bea's street, and saw her apartment house. Two pink flamingos stood in the courtyard flanking a *For Rent* sign.

"We could rent an apartment there," said Carol jocularly.

"We won't see her in this storm," I sighed. I must have expected her to be standing in the doorway as I passed.

"You'll see her soon," Bob reassured me.

And we drove into Manhattan, the elements continuing to rage about the car as if they were trying to tell us something.

We checked into the Algonquin. It is a small, intimate hotel in the center of the theater district, which prides itself on a clientele of artists, writers, and actors. Each room has a desk where one can work. I had often corrected galleys and page proofs for my children's books during short stays here. It was a home away from home, a good place to meet one's mother for the first time. And to complete one's adult story.

Soon after Bob left for the conference the next morning Carol came into my room. She gave the hotel operator the number that I had gotten from M.I.T. It rang. A woman answered. Carol asked, "Is this Mrs. Rudolph?"

"Yes."

Carol gave her name and said: "I am from Boston. I have a message for you from someone you haven't seen since she was a child. This is good news. May I make an appointment to see you?"

The woman excused herself to get a towel, saying she had just stepped out of the shower. When she returned, she said, "I will call you back. Please give me your phone number."

Carol gave the hotel number, and that was all there was to it.

After she hung up, we just looked at each other. Our faces were flushed. She had actually talked to my mother. We ordered some cold soda up to the room and waited. Nothing happened. We had lunch in the room and then I had to go out to an appointment with my editor. Carol said she would wait by the phone.

When I returned in midafternoon, I found her still there. "Did she call back?"

"No, but her sister-in-law did."

"Her sister-in-law?"

"Yes, she said Mrs. Rudolph was ill and could not speak on the phone. She asked me to tell her what I was calling about."

"Did you?"

"I thought I should wait until I spoke to you. I told her I'd call back."

That's where we were now. Both sides had a go-between.

We decided that Carol should call back and tell her the truth about what we wanted. And this time we made a careful outline of what she should say. The woman's name was Mrs. Oran Silver; Bea's younger brother had obviously shortened his last name, which was why I hadn't been able to find him in a New York phonebook.

Mrs. Silver answered when Carol returned the call.

Carol said things like, "The woman I am calling about was named Blanche as a baby. She has reason to believe that Mrs. Rudolph may know about her childhood."

Mrs. Silver asked questions like, "How did she learn this? How old is she?"

Carol told her everything, including my married name and address in Cambridge. She said it would make me happy to see Mrs. Rudolph and that I hoped it would make her happy too.

Mrs. Silver promised to convey this information to her sister-in-law. She explained that Mrs. Rudolph had had an eye operation for glaucoma recently and was too weak to go out or do anything for herself yet. But she would surely call on getting my message.

Again the receiver made a decisive click as Carol put it down.

"Carol, is it possible that this Bea Rudolph is the wrong person?"

"Impossible. They're not denying anything."

"But they're not admitting anything either."

"They're scared," Carol said, collapsing on the bed.

"What are they scared of?"

"They've been taken by surprise."

I wait alone in the room that night for the call from my mother.

I've always been partial to hotel rooms. They give one a sense of anonymity and privacy. They are not cluttered with memorabilia of the past. They create a neutral shelter. Neither are they linked to the future. One begins anew each time one enters a hotel room. One inhabits the present.

Just one ring from the phone and my mother and I would begin anew. But the phone did not ring. I could not believe it. I had imagined that she would come rushing down to the hotel as soon as she heard from me. But obviously there were forces in her life that she could not break through to come to me.

A feeling of aloneness swept over me, and again I wept. But I was not unhappy. I was grappling with something real and meaningful, something tangible. And in the process I was becoming rooted to life. There was a premonition of something momentous about to happen, such as Oedipus must have felt as he approached his native city and heard the animated whispers of his forefathers.

The next morning, Sunday, Mrs. Silver calls Carol. She explains that Bea cannot meet with me because her eyes are troubling her too much. However, she, Mrs. Silver, would be willing to speak with me on the phone if I cared to call her.

Carol says she will relay the message.

I give myself the rest of the morning before making that call. Time seems to have lost its urgency, to have taken on the slow, unhurried tension of a Nō play. The main actor, who is really a spirit disguised as a traveler, moves with deliberate insouciance from the realm of the dead into present time. Eventually, with carefully measured pacing, he arrives at his destination center stage. It is not his speed or lack of it that matters, but the grace of his style, which it has taken years of discipline to develop.

I delay calling until Carol has checked out, as she has to get back to Boston that night. I delay until I can delay no longer taking that calculated step alone toward my mother.

I give the hotel operator Mrs. Silver's number. Here is my fate, operator, take it and do with it as you will.

Mrs. Silver's voice is cold and suspicious at first. I try to explain what a hard decision it was to make this contact with Mrs. Rudolph; I want her to know this was not done lightly. I do not want to upset anyone. I just want to meet with Mrs. Rudolph once, and in no way intend to inter-fere with her life.

Mrs. Silver is becoming sympathetic.

She repeats that Mrs. Rudolph's eyes prevent her going out now, but would I like to meet with her brother, Mr. Silver.

"Only if he would like to meet with me."

"He is willing. And so am I."

"Then please come to the hotel, both of you."

"I'll have to find a babysitter for my four year old, but we'll be down in about two hours—three o'clock."

Now as in the Nō play, time begins moving with raging fury. The spirit works itself into a frenzy, tears off its mask and is revealed as the personage it is—a woman. Her quest is accomplished, her soul at peace. The play is over.

Then the next skit on the program, the Kyogen, that comic underbelly of the Nō, comes on, its characters parodying all the values and philosophy in the preceding play. It is like the comedy scene that serves as a bridge between the main actions in a Shakespearean tragedy. The Kyogen is about to begin.

The hotel has given me the use of an empty studio room for this meeting. I pace back and forth as the hands of a clock again measure my destiny. I know that my internal clock has driven me relentlessly to this moment. I am about to meet a blood relative. The melodrama is so heavy that even I have to smile. George Bernard Shaw said, "If you cannot get rid of the family skeleton, you may as well make it dance."

Still I am nervous. I won't believe it until they arrive.

The hands of the clock announce three, and move on to less auspicious moments.

They are late.

Have they changed their minds?

I pace the room.

The knock comes at three forty-five.

I open the door.

Three people stand there, a man, a woman, and a small boy. The man, of slight build with thinning blondish hair, peers at me through rimless glasses perched high on a short upturned nose. His pale eyes do not match my brown ones.

There are no bells, no shock of recognition.

I am surprised to see the child. "Is it all right to speak in front of him?" I ask, leading them into the room.

"He is too young to understand anything," says this man who is my uncle.

"We brought some coloring books and crayons," says his wife, who is the Mrs. Silver I had spoken to. Her face is open and friendly; she is smaller than I had imagined from that forceful tone on the telephone, diminished now that her role is over.

We sit down and look at each other in embarrassed silence, the boy coloring dutifully at our feet. We are improvising as we go along.

Here is my uncle, the first blood relative I have ever seen. He is fidgeting on his chair, crossing and recrossing his legs. He was not type-cast for this mythic role he has been asked to play. Nor was I.

No one is able to say the first word.

"She has Bea's forehead," says my uncle's wife, breaking the awkward silence. "And the nose too."

"The high cheekbones are there," he says, and the two of them go on to agree on the shape of the face and the mouth.

Then my uncle seems to remember his official role as investigator. He sits up stiffly. He is not going to be caught relaxing until a few things are settled.

"How can you prove who you are?" he asks, not unkindly, but perfunctorily, like a civil servant in the judge's chambers.

I want to laugh. Or is it cry? Prove who I am! If I knew that, I wouldn't be here now. Which me does he want proof of?

"You must prove who you are," he repeats. There is the clear implication that I might be trying to blackmail them.

As if by divine inspiration, I do what any red-blooded American does when her identity is challenged: I pull out my driver's license. (Much to my amazement this had worked in Korea when I was challenged by a G.I. guard at the International Commission's barracks to prove I was married to Bob, and, therefore, not a spy.) Now it might prove that I was the me my uncle wanted proof of.

He examines the little card solemnly just as that young G.I. had done. The full import of this moment seems to have overwhelmed him, making breathing difficult.

Finally he says, "Is there anything else you can show me?"

We are moving from Kyogen into Theater of the Absurd.

I go to my room and return with an advance copy of my new book, *Mogo the Mynah*, which is about an outrageous black bird who will say nothing but "Nevermore."

My uncle chuckles as he looks at the illustrations. "That's enough," he says. "Anyone who writes a book must be a good person."

I curb my impulse to tell him otherwise.

Now we settle down to business. Again I tell them the story I had related over the phone.

"But how could the agency give you such information?" Oran asks. "I thought it was supposed to be a secret so that all sides could be protected."

I tell him that sometimes an agency understands an adult's need to know her birthright.

"But wasn't the agency worried about trouble?" he persists. "Something like this could lead to lawsuits—with a *different* kind of person, of course."

I explain that the agency trusted us since my husband is a psychiatrist.

As we speak, Oran admits he can understand my wanting to know about my background.

"I'm a curious type too," he says. "I would have done the same thing. Anyone would want to know."

He admits he had wondered (not all the time, he qualifies, but often) what ever happened to Bea's baby. It was good to know that everything had come out so well.

"Bea can really turn them out," his wife says. "She ought to have had a dozen."

We all laugh. Again there is a silence.

My uncle takes this as a cue to let me know I should not think his guard is down completely. "I am here to get information," he announces. "Not to give any."

"You were born in 1917," I tell him.

"How did you know that?" He is flabbergasted.

"It was in the records in Freeport."

He is clearly pleased. "What day?"

I fail that one, but I give him Bea's birthdate.

"That's right," he says.

It is more fun than charades.

"But why didn't you call me first since you knew so much about me?"

"I tried, but you shortened your name to Silver."

"That's right," he agrees again.

"Does anyone else know you called Bea?" my aunt asks.

I assure her no one does.

"Bea was worried about that. She doesn't want her

husband or son to know. Her husband is retired and home all the time. He wanted to know who the call was from."

"What is Bea like?" I ask. I want to hear about my mother.

"So good-hearted. Like an angel," says my aunt.

"She's so generous she'd give you the shirt off her back," says my uncle.

I tell them I might not have looked her up if I hadn't learned that she kept me for two years.

"Why did she keep me so long?"

"Because she was so good," says my uncle defensively. "And she hoped to find a way to keep you."

"She's a good woman," agrees my aunt.

"Weren't you afraid you'd be hurt?" my uncle queries me. "This turned out well, but what if it had turned out badly?"

"I had faith," I said. And it was the truth.

My aunt and uncle are genuinely touched by this. Now he drops his official role and begins speaking earnestly, as if with family, about his and Bea's childhood.

"Our mother was a tyrant," he says. "A cold, selfish woman. She beat me many times. I used to hide under the bed. She was mean to Bea, too. She never bought us any toys."

As he speaks I see this strong-willed maternal grandmother who had been widowed in Russia before they were born. She had come to America with two small children and married my grandfather, the glazier. But she never accepted the cruel twist life had taken in separating her from her beloved first husband, a young rabbinical student who contracted pneumonia while traveling from one village to another—to speak? to study?—and sending her as widow with her two babies into exile. Her rage consumed her—that must be it—and turned outward against this new inferior husband and the two inferior children she bore him—my mother and this uncle.

"But Bea is very close to her now," his wife interjects. "She is very *devoted*."

"I'd like to meet Bea," I venture.

"I'll try to arrange it," my uncle says, as if reluctantly recalling the purpose of this visit. "But remember, a child must learn to crawl before it can walk."

There was a feeling of good will as they left, Now we were comrades working together.

I handed *Mogo* to their little boy, my cousin.

The weeks went by.

I had explained to my aunt and uncle that we were leaving in another month for a summer in Japan to set up a long-range research project on Japanese youth for Bob. I wondered now if my mother would let me go without our meeting.

I wondered how she liked the snapshots I had sent her.

I wondered.

One night about 10 P.M. the phone rang. It was Oran. He was in Cambridge.

"I came up to go over some important papers with Howie," he said. "And I've got some pictures of Bea for you."

We picked him up in front of his hotel and drove him back to our house. He handed me an envelope with pictures of my mother. I let it lie unopened in my lap.

"I stopped at Bea's on the way up here to get them," he said. "It was safe because her husband was at the race track. If you're going to see her at all it will have to be when the races are on."

"I hope the horses keep running until we leave for Japan," I said, more bitterly than I intended.

"Oh, Bea wants to see you," Oran reassured me. "But her eyes are bad. And our mother is ill now. She has to be with her."

"What did she say about your meeting with me in New York?"

"She was thrilled to know what had happened to you. It's a hundred-to-one chance this kind of thing could come about. It was like a salve to the wound she had inside her.

"It's really strange you and Howie are in the same town," he added. "You haven't seen Howie yet, have you?"

I couldn't tell if his question was innocent or probing.

"Of course not."

I decided it was innocent.

"If I had gotten to a phone, you could have met me at the restaurant and seen him," he went on. "From across the room, you know."

I was surprised he would suggest such a thing: from being the cautious go-between he was turning into the reckless adventurer.

"Bea says she thinks it best not to tell Howie until he's finished graduate school. He has another year to go. But it wouldn't have done any harm to have seen him from a distance."

Still Oran had not gone to the restaurant phone to summon me. I was tired of pursuing what *might* have been in my life. I changed the subject back to Bea. She was the person I was searching for. This brother was something I would worry about later.

"What did she say when she saw my picture?"

"She said, 'That's me.' She felt there was a real resemblance. Howie looks like me, not Bea. But you look like she did when she was younger. Everyone said she was the image of Virginia Bruce. She even wanted to be an actress."

When Oran left I opened the envelope to look at my mother's face.

The snapshots were the smallest size, the miniature figures in them almost indistinguishable.

There was a woman sitting in a deck chair in the sun with dark glasses and a broad-brimmed hat on. There was a woman standing next to a small boy, probably my brother, with her face in shadows.

There was a woman hiding in those pictures. But hiding from whom?

Oran had agreed to arrange a meeting with Bea before I left for Japan—if he possibly could. I felt no pain at his indefinite promise. I had already had my pain at the Algonquin waiting for a mother who did not come. I had wept that night for all the years of the past and the present. I had wept all through my childhood.

I did not have to weep any more.

I was beginning to realize that my mother's eyes, her husband, her son, her own fears, were like bramble bushes growing over the path that we had once started on together. One could not run back down that path like a child innocently gamboling down a country lane. I was no longer the Little Colonel rushing headlong through the countryside to be held in her grandfather's safe embrace. The past was not there waiting to receive me. It was buried somewhere deep within the brambles that separated us in this life.

But how could I have ever thought it would be simple—this meeting with her? It had never been simple between us.

I was even beginning to dread the moment we might meet.

A Japanese writer came to tea one day during this waiting period.

How did we get into the conversation?

He was telling me about his early childhood in Hok-kaido, that northernmost island of Japan where he was born. It is there that the Ainu still live—those white-skinned aborigines whose fate was very much like the American Indians' as they were pushed back off the land into small reservations.

My friend knew he was adopted, but one day he overheard, as children do, that there was some Ainu blood in his veins. It was all very troubling, as mysterious as the Ainu themselves, whose legends say they are descended from a polar bear, the "big white dog of Heaven."

The Ainu are a hairy people, but my friend is not hairy. Still he secretly searched for and found his Ainu relatives. His adoptive family does not know he has done this.

It was a comfort to hear his secret: to be reminded (how many times must we be reminded?) that the human condition is universal. Whether we are searching for our Russian, our Austrian, our French, Indian, or Ainu blood, we are all related, each to the other.

Not too long after that Oran called. Bea would be able to meet me at his house at one that Saturday.

The horses would be running.

She would be able to slip away.

> *Naked and alone we came into exile. In our dark*
> *womb we did not know our mother's face; from the*
> *prison of her flesh have we come into the*
> *unspeakable and incommunicable prison of this*
> *earth . . .*
> *O lost, and by the wind-grieved ghost, come back*
> *again.*

—Thomas Wolfe

The day I went to meet my mother I dressed all in black. I often wore black, but this darkness was unrelieved by color: a black suit, black hat, black hose, black shoes, black purse. Not even a bright scarf. Although I felt joyous inside, this was not a celebration. This was something dark and secretive to be acted out in shadows. Property men in Japanese theater wear black to be invisible: they dart about the stage moving props and arranging the actors' costumes, their somber attire announcing they are not really there. My guilt toward my adoptive parents covered me, making me invisible as I moved toward the execution of this nefarious deed.

My uncle's house in Queens reflected the simplicity of

his life as an accountant. It was an unpretentious ranch, the kind one sees sprawling over all the suburbs of this land. When he had called, he said "weather permitting" he and his wife would not be home. But it was pouring rain and they were at the door waiting for us. "We've pulled the shades in the living room to protect her eyes," they said. She, too, needed that darkness.

She was sitting in a chair on the far side of the room with large sunglasses covering her eyes. I could not look into them. Her face was as illusive as in those snapshots. She rose as Bob and I entered.

She was much shorter than I had imagined she would be, large hipped and bosomed, unlike myself. We approached each other tentatively. I'm sure the possibility of our rushing into each other's arms must have crossed her mind earlier too, but now the impossibility of it seemed to reach us both at the same time. I put out my arm and we shook hands indecisively. Her fingers lay cold, limp in mine. Then she returned to her chair and I perched tensely on the edge of the sofa at the opposite end of the room. Bob sat near me.

My aunt and uncle paced in the doorway like heraldic lions guarding the entrance.

According to Jung, the desire to be reunited with the mother is the desire to be reborn through her. I sat and looked at the woman across from me and knew I would not have recognized her as my mother had we passed each other on the street. Jung says the mother is a symbol of the unconscious to which an individual wishes to return in order to seek a solution for his psychic conflicts. Now here she sat in the flesh, nervously twisting a handkerchief in her lap, as ill-at-ease as I was. Yet everything in my life seemed to have led irrevocably to this moment. Her voice was gentle and caring as she spoke the first words.

"Betty, I want you to know you are from a good

family." She used my adopted name, not Blanche. Then she reeled off some of the prominent New York relatives and their various professions, placing herself and me socially so that I need not look down on her, or myself.

"I expected you to look me up some day," she added to fill the silence which followed. "But I did not think it would take this long."

She began to weep at this. It was only later, much later, that I understood the true meaning of her words. She had lived with the hope that she would one day hear her daughter had fared well and was successful—perhaps that would redeem her sin. But she had also been living in fear with this secret, fear that the phone would ring one day, or the knock would come at the door which would expose her to the world.

The phone had rung, and here I was.

She was not the big, strong, all-powerful mother ready to take the frightened child in her arms and dispel the demons. She too, was riddled with demons. She, too, was afraid: afraid of her secret, afraid of exposure, afraid of that cold, domineering, loveless mother of her own. Afraid of me. She was a disconcerting combination of self-awareness and denial, but she told me the story I had come to hear as best she could. She was brave about that.

My mother was not married to my father. She had had only a few dates with him in Freeport when her family moved, according to prior plans, to Brooklyn to be near her rabbi-grandfather. When she realized she was pregnant, her wealthy aunt in Freeport tried to persuade my father to marry her. She promised an immediate annulment: all that was wanted was his signature on a piece of paper. He was a few years older, already a man about town. He refused. By Talmudic law in the old country it could be said they were already married. But nobody consulted the Talmud.

When my mother was five months pregnant, her older

half-sister died in childbirth. This sister was the favorite of my grandmother, the child of her first husband back in Russia, and now not only was she gone, but so was the baby who would have been the first beloved grandchild. Even then I was stirring like a monster in my mother's womb. I was the dark twin of that lost golden baby.

According to psychiatric literature, it could be argued that my mother had conceived me to compete with her more-favored sister, to have an equal gift to hand over to her mother. But if this was so, my grandmother was not one for such cheap handouts.

A few months before I was born, my mother was shipped off by her family to a shelter for unmarried girls in Staten Island. She went there alone, unaccompanied by a relative or friend. She went in exile to that island, the waters of whose narrow channel would seem to her as wide as the oceans that separated exiled emperors and generals from the shores of their homeland. Her grief and loneliness would be as great as theirs. And she was only seventeen years old.

When her time came, my mother went alone in a taxi from the shelter to the hospital. She does not remember the hour I was born. She stayed alone in the hospital with me, and then returned to the shelter for five months to nurse me. She had no visitors.

My mother said she was determined not to give me up. She must have been a strong-willed person—then. She hoped to persuade her mother to see me eventually and to allow me into the home. But my grandmother would still have no gifts. She refused to recognize my existence.

My mother admitted there was some talk of sitting *shiva* for her, that ceremony of mourning that Orthodox Jews hold for those prodigal children who marry out of the religion or transgress in other equally unforgivable ways, and who must forever after be considered dead.

Her grandfather, (the colonel), was a famous Orthodox rabbi in Brooklyn. He knew Theodore Roosevelt well enough to be personally notified of his death. Didn't he know that in the old country, according to Talmudic law, I was *not* a bastard. Only a child conceived in an adulterous relationship is considered such, and neither my mother nor my father was married to anyone else at the time.

In the old country it wouldn't have been so bad. But this was the new country. Was he afraid Teddy's ghost would hear? Or was he afraid of his daughter?—everyone seemed to be. The real colonel wouldn't have been afraid.

Anyway, there was no *shiva* ceremony necessary for my mother since everyone soon began acting as if I had never been born. She was finally allowed back into the house, alone. However, she must have gathered strength in her exile, for in spite of the advice of social workers and other family members, she refused to part with her baby. Rather than place me for adoption, she put me in an infants' home in the Bronx and visited me there on weekends for the next year and a half.

Once her father (also afraid of her mother) dared to sneak out secretly to visit me with her. But no one else ever saw me.

"I took a job in a dress firm to support you," my mother said. "And every Sunday during visiting hours I came with a little toy. I called you 'Bubbaleh' and you held out your arms to me. You had such a lovely smile."

Here she began to weep again, and my aunt cautioned her from the doorway that she would hurt her eyes.

"But when you were older and standing up in your crib, I would look at you surrounded by all those other homeless children, and cry. 'My child should have something better than this,' I told myself."

During this period my mother kept hoping my father would call. Once she actually visited Freeport and phoned his house. He was not there. She left her office number in New York, but she did not hear from him.

"I suppose I was hoping he would change his mind and marry me when he saw you," she explained. "Then I would have had a home to take you to.

"When you were two, you had to have a mastoid operation. They told me you would die if you did not get a family of your own. They encouraged me to let you go for adoption if I really loved you. I was afraid you would die or I would never have done it."

Again she wept, and again my aunt poked her head in to caution her.

("You had almost died before we got you," my adopted mother had told me. "A mastoid." This was one detail she had not distorted.)

An aunt, the wife of one of my mother's successful uncles, knew about the adoption agency run by that Reform rabbi, Stephen Wise. It must have been something for an Orthodox rabbi's family to turn their disgrace over to a Reform agency—but perhaps only Reform people handled such things.

"My aunt told me you would go to a wealthy family," my mother said. "That the agency knew just the right people for you."

And so my mother, at the age of nineteen, signed the papers that released her child from her care forever. She was never told where I went, or to whom. And in keeping with adoption-agency practice, she was never given a report as to my progress. So does society unconsciously punish women who produce offspring out of wedlock.

Or is it conscious?

Never in this life are they allowed to see or hear of their children again. The agencies say they are protecting the "privacy" of these mothers.

In losing the battle to keep her child, my mother was

like the luna moth who lays her eggs and dies. One part of her died, the part that was spirited and had dreams. From that moment she must have begun to change into the conventional, frightened, submissive woman I saw before me now. The only thing she kept of me was her secret: and this secret was to grow in her until it became one of her vital organs.

My mother became docile, even dutiful toward her own mother, who continued to put her down. She must have been trying to be the replacement for the dead sister whose beauty and fine character she could never hope to equal.

Two young doctors—not one, but two—wanted to marry her, she said. But she was afraid they would find out her secret. Doctors notice things like that. When she met her first husband, a year after my adoption, she married him because he "pressured" her with kindness.

A businessman wouldn't notice.

During those years of her first marriage, my mother continued currying her mother's favor, as if only this woman could give her absolution for her crime. Then her son was born.

Her husband thought it was her first child.

When my half-brother was still in my mother's womb, my father called her at her office.

"When I heard his voice, I began crying hysterically," she said. "I told him it was too late and to leave me alone. To never call me again."

He never did. We'll never know what he wanted.

After her son was born, my mother lived like a well-to-do Jewish matron. She even had a special nurse for her baby. She kept kosher out of respect for her rabbi-grandfather, and worked actively in philanthropy.

"One night a whole congregation at the temple stood up to honor my work. But I thought, 'I am not worthy of this. If they only knew what I have done.' Yet I had another thought: 'If this could happen, couldn't something nice happen too? If only my daughter could know about this honor I am receiving tonight.'"

Now she knew.

As soon as my half-brother was bar-mitzvahed, my mother divorced his father and moved in with her mother. "Everyone says my mother broke up the marriage," she said. But she did not say what *she* thought. She did admit that her mother had not mellowed over the years. "She didn't seem to care much about her grandson. She had never given me as much as a doll when I was growing up, and now she would complain if I spent too much money on Howie's milk. 'Children don't need milk,' she would say."

My mother worked in a dress shop on Madison Avenue after her divorce. It must have been during those years I was at Barnard. Then she married a second time.

"He was a sport like your father," she admitted with a shy smile. He followed the races, but she married him in spite of her mother's strong disapproval. "He had a daughter in her twenties, just the age you would have been. I always felt distant from her. I could never forget that she might have been you, and that *you* might have been living with us instead of her."

Again she daubed her eyes.

"You asked Oran if I was happy," she went on. "I asked him if you had asked that. I knew you would. But I want you to know that I felt I could never be happy after giving you up. There was always something in me unsatisfied that nothing could feed. I would look at other women with their daughters on the street and wonder if any of them could be you."

She didn't see the contradiction as she added: "No one knows you called except Oran and his wife. And they will keep my secret. I must not let my husband know. Or Howie until he's graduated."

There was a silence as the room was washed by the waves of that secret.

Now I asked about my father. He was like a presence holding us together and yet standing between us. Who was he? What was he like?

I was unprepared for her response.

She stiffened in her chair and her voice became tense. "I have spoken to you honestly today," she said, "and told you everything I know. But you must *never* ask your father's name."

Bob interrupted here to help me out. "His name is not important," he said softly. "But maybe you could tell Betty something about him."

I added quickly that now that I had heard her story, I certainly did not feel any kindness toward my father; my sympathy was entirely with her who had been through so much those first years.

She seemed relieved to hear this, and now her nemesis having been brought down to size, she volunteered the information that had been haunting her along with the secret.

"No one must know this," she warned. "He was a. . . . a bootlegger."

"A what?" I asked. I couldn't quite understand the word she muffled in her embarrassment.

"You know. . . . a rumrunner. . . . a *bootlegger*," she repeated nervously, as if federal agents might appear at the door even as she said the word.

I wanted to laugh. A bootlegger! Just like Gatsby. How romantic. How incredible.

"I'm sorry to have to tell you this," she said mournfully.

I tried to explain to her that I did not care what my father was. I had not come to judge either of them, just to learn the truth.

I asked her nothing further about my father who being

the source of me, was the source of her pain. Out of loyalty to this woman who was my mother and had tried to keep me, I closed my heart to that nameless man. It would be many years before I could bring myself to search for this part of my story.

And now the Kyogen begins again.

For Jews there may be great tragedy, but nothing is so terrible you shouldn't eat. The table in the dining room had been laid with cold cuts and open-faced sandwiches, enough to satisfy all the grown babies in that Infants' home had they arrived with me. During our talk my mother would occasionally interrupt to urge Bob and me to eat something. I could not think of food and even though Bob can always think of it, he was circumspect enough to leave the table untouched.

Now, it being almost evening, it was time to talk of food again—in earnest. Although I was a secret from the past, she insisted on taking us to a restaurant near Oran's house. We sat there, all of us, at that small neighborhood delicatessen, gorging ourselves on marinated herring, stuffed cabbage, lox and bagels, like a normal Jewish family. She wasn't afraid of being seen with me: but then this wasn't *her* neighborhood.

She was flushed and excited, and a bit unrealistic. She spoke of having me meet a favorite aunt of hers, one of those millionaires who seemed abundant in another branch of the family, but whose abundance did not spill over into her modest circumstances.

"But how would you introduce me?"

"I could say you were a niece by my husband."

She spoke of telling Howie about me—as soon as he graduated. She began listing some other prominent aunts, uncles, cousins.

I said as delicately as I could that I did not want to meet relatives, not now, not disguised as someone else. (I wasn't sure I wanted to meet them at all—perhaps it would make my disloyalty to my adopted family even more official.) We parted promising to see each other again before Bob and I left for Japan.

This time we embraced warmly.

But we were still strangers.

I saw my mother once more, shortly before we took the plane.

We had checked into the St. Moritz on Central Park South because I wanted to look out on that wonderful expanse of nature that sits like an oasis in a concrete jungle; to have a room that opened onto green, growing things the way I felt my life had opened and grown.

"This is the hotel I lived in the first year of my marriage," my mother exclaimed as she entered the room.

She had been able to meet me because her husband was again at the races. "He thinks I am shopping today. I need so many things."

Still she seemed afraid not to have some packages to take home. "I have a lot of contacts in the wholesale houses," she said. "I could buy you something nice."

I insisted we stay there in the room and have lunch. We pulled the table up against the window and looked out over the park as we ate.

She was much more relaxed this day.

"You know I've always wished your father had returned my call sooner," she said over salad. "I could have divorced my husband and somehow gotten you back."

Little did she realize how impossible that would have been.

Her first husband had been narrow-minded and stingy, she told me. The present one, the sport, was just the opposite. "I married him because he admitted he had an illegitimate daughter by a married woman he was having an affair with during his former marriage. The daughter does not know he is her father. I realized he had the same sin as mine. If he ever found out, he could not turn on me."

"But you didn't tell him about me."

"I couldn't. He would say, 'Where is your daughter?' I could not admit I did not know where you were."

She began weeping again. Now *I* had to caution her about her eyes. I seemed to turn on wellsprings of tears in *both* my mothers.

"All these years I imagined the worst," she sobbed. "I heard of a case in Boston where a wealthy woman looked up the son she had given to her doctor at birth. She wanted to leave him her estate. But she found him in an asylum wasting away with insanity and alcoholism. She felt so guilty for the good life she had been leading while he had been suffering."

Guilt, guilt, we were all drowning in guilt.

I felt warmth and compassion for Bea that afternoon. She was weak, but she admitted her mistakes; she was undeveloped, but human.

"You are doing all the things I wanted to do," she told me. "I wanted to act, to write, to have a career. But I wasn't able to accomplish anything."

"It's not too late," I ventured. "Be strong. I expect it of you. After all, you are my *mother*."

She burst into fresh sobs. "I never heard you use that word before!"

I was startled to hear it coming from my lips too. She was my mother physically, but what is being a mother? Something physical or spiritual—or just being there?

This woman had given birth to me and so she was my mother; but she had separated from me, and so she was a stranger.

Yet her whole life had been retribution for having

borne me. I had influenced this stranger's life just as she had influenced mine. She had carried her loss within her longer than she had carried me.

It was all very confusing, but I did not feel disturbed by it—yet.

I was coming to grips with some of the complexities of the human condition. My mother was locked as I was in the intricate tangle of the past: I was the darling baby, the lost child, the ache in her heart; but I was also the dark secret, the one who had almost ruined her life and threatened to again.

And for me this woman was the beautiful lost mother; but she was also the one who had abandoned me.

I kissed her on the cheek as we parted. I promised to write while we were in Japan, but to address my letters to her brother, Oran, who would relay them to her, thus preventing her husband and son from ever seeing them.

I promised to help her keep her secret.

It was a light casual kiss I gave her, like the brush of a butterfly's wing.

4 ❧ REBIRTH

A linch-pin is removed that had been holding a whole world together. The whole meaning of reality crumbles. It "takes the ground from under his feet." Participation in the world, such terms as "contact with" and "sense of reality," are empty sounds. A desperate crisis indeed. Either one restructures one's whole "real" view of others and the world and redefines one's "real" self; or one annuls the chasm between what is the case and what one knows *to be the case, by taking one's stand on what one* knows.

—R. D. Laing

On the plane flight to Japan I was filled with anxiety. I attributed it to fear of flying, which I had never had before, but it was more than that: it was fear of living. My nervous system seemed to have collapsed completely. I felt like something broken hurtling through space, no center, just a body pulled through the universe, about to explode at any moment.

I knew that anxiety is an alarm system that disaster is impending in the inner world. But in my case it was not impending, it had arrived full-blast. My alarm was electronic—buzzers, bells, sirens screamed inside me. I could not locate the master switch to turn them off.

I devoured phenobarbital like candy and lay in a semiconscious state as the plane sped past the stars in their course. I was waiting for the plane to drop from the sky. It would serve me right if it crashed, or just exploded like a meteor there in space.

But serve me right for what?

Was I punishing myself for breaking the taboo against looking up my natural mother? Was my fear of flying an outer manifestation of my fear of reprisal for going against the sanction of society?

But artists are always flying against the laws of the

community, defying the laws of gravity, I told myself. They are the closest in spirit to the comets, those eccentric masses of frozen gas that go hurtling like dirty snowballs through the skies to their own unpredictable rendezvous with the sun. And yet I knew that even the most erratic comets obey some natural laws in outer space, gravitational pulls beyond man's knowledge, that force them to an eternal return to the sun until they disintegrate.

It was too early for me to disintegrate. I wanted to complete my course even if I couldn't understand the path it was taking. The deed was done and could not be undone: but I had become undone too. Not all the King's horses nor all the King's men—not even Bob. I was in a kind of Buddhist hell reserved for the real sinners; if I were Catholic I would have believed I was possessed by demons.

I was Jonah in the belly of the whale. Erik Erikson has written somewhere that one must grasp and not regress from the sheer sense of sin over having grasped. But he failed to tell us how not to regress. I had grasped what for most people is a birthright and the price was proving too high. The analyst in Cambridge had tried to warn me, just as the Oracle had tried to warn Oedipus, of more desperate horrors to come. But the warnings should have been given to those who merchandised us as babies: a time bomb had been set then which it was our destiny to touch off. No amount of self-analysis or restraint could deter us from our course.

Even after arriving in Tokyo I was overwhelmed with free-floating anxiety which needed anchoring as much as I did. I subsisted on tranquilizers. I didn't want to see anyone. The least activity exhausted me. I had such an excruciating sense of despair that I could hardly bear to wake in the morning to face the new day. Is this what Kierkegaard meant by *dread*?

"Do you think I'm having a nervous breakdown," I

asked Bob one morning. I had been afraid to say the word before.

"I don't think so," he said. "It's a broad term. You'll be all right. Just give yourself time."

He believed in me, and perhaps he, too, didn't dare to think it might be something really serious that was happening.

We rented rooms in the home of an elderly Japanese couple who made a profession of such transactions and gave us complete privacy. While Bob went out each day to meet students and talk with possible research assistants for his future project, I sat in the room and hand fed a baby mynah bird I had found in a pet store. Mogo had died the year before, and now this helpless fledgling who had been stolen from its nest in India and was dependent on human care from its adoptive mother, somehow was a comfort. I let it jump around the room and explore bright bits of paper, while I wandered through the ruins of my psyche looking for clues as a dazed survivor sifts through the rubble of his house after a surprise bombing attack.

But why was I so surprised? Just as the primitives had to stay away from their tabooed dead, I knew that the adopted had to stay away from their natural parents who are as if dead.

Let us now pay homage to taboos: they guard the chief acts of the community—birth, initiation rites, marriage, childrearing, burial—against interference. They guard adoptive parents from natural parents, natural parents from adoptive parents, adoptees from natural parents, natural parents from adoptees. They guard everybody from everybody. They enable us to live in armed citadels safe from each other. They protect us from our deepest impulses, from that to which we are most naturally drawn. The violated taboo is programed to avenge itself, but should it fail, benevolent society takes over the punishment of the hapless offender. In my case, I didn't need society: I was doing a fine job on myself.

As if sensing that the breaking of a taboo makes the offender taboo, I stayed indoors those first weeks in Japan. Was I, like Oedipus, being punished for a fate decided before I was born? Were the inviolable laws of the gods broken when my father and mother conceived me without a marriage contract?

Was I now the defiler, the polluter, the unholy, responsible for earthquakes, plagues, atomic bombs, floods, and draughts? Must I now be humbled and exiled far from home before being purified? Was I a lesson to all adoptees not to look up their natural parents?

No! to all of these!

I would not admit guilt. Having taken my fate into my own hands, I would now take the consequences.

But how could the wound be healed, the order restored? Campbell tells us that the passage of a threshold is a form of self-annihilation. One dies to time and returns to the world womb or the world navel. One goes forward to be born again: one undergoes a metamorphosis and is renewed.

I realized that one becomes one of the twice-born, in William James' sense of the word—one who must question, suffer, and become a divided self rather than blindly accept the body of thought around one.

One willingly takes the Night Journey because it leads to the morning light.

Gradually the warm summer air restored me. Japan, that adopted country which had received me in the past, had curative powers. I began to go out. I wandered through the narrow streets of Tokyo's residential areas, past the high walls and the disciplined hedges, letting the sights, sounds, smells, and traffic of that city pass by me as I refueled myself from within. It was a relief to be a spectator at someone else's drama: it gave me respite from the violent pulls of my own.

Japan gave me the stillness, that other time sense she

expresses in her aesthetics but has lost in her frenetic modern life. I held on to this quiet while the Japanese revolved around me on their relentless treadmill.

Slowly, as Bob and I talked far into the night, I began to articulate things that were hard to admit even to myself: I had been disappointed in my mother. I had not expected to find a queen, but at least a vibrant, creative woman. Someone less defeated; someone who had willed herself to be strong just as I had done throughout my youth. I thought she would open not only her arms to me, but her house and her life. I did not expect to find the entrance barred, myself on the outside. She had been more nurturing as the ghostly mother of my fantasy than as a reality in life.

Still I did not regret this new reality. Whatever it was, it was *real*. On a conscious level I could say I was glad I had searched for her, but on an unconscious one I was devastated and had to rearrange my psychic furnishings.

Such are the rewards and punishments of those who transgress the taboo.

"The transgressions of one era are the liberations of another," Bob told me.

I knew this was true, but I needed time to internalize it. The psyche, like the body, requires time to mend.

During that brief, tortured interlude in Japan—that fragile bridge between my two stages of being—I exchanged short notes with Bea. Her first moved me deeply: "You have opened a door for me to peace of mind and contentment that I have never known before." But shortly afterward, on Mother's Day, I received a commercial card:

> This day that's known as
> Mother's Day
> Is Daughter's Day to me—
> A Day for happy memories

In which again I see
That laughing little girl
of mine
So sweet in every way
Who grew into the lovely girl
That you are, Dear, today.

She should have known there were no Hallmark Cards
for a relationship such as ours. Imagine seeing on the rack
in the drugstore, tucked in among *Get Well*, *Valentine*,
Birthday, and *Anniversary* greetings, a section entitled:
To the Child I Gave Away or *To the Mother I Never
Knew*. My card to her would read:

This day that's known as
Mother's Day
Is Adoption Day to me,
A Day for wondering and regret
In which again I see
That laughing little babe
Of yours
Whom you sadly gave away,
Who grew into the orphan girl
Who would search you out, Dear, one day.

I did not respond to her card; nor did I write her again.
The taboo, the guilt, which I had internalized all my life,
promised me respite if I would give her up. We were
making a deal, the taboo and I: I would once again honor
its restrictions just as she was doing in not openly
acknowledging me. Mother and daughter—after all they
had been through—would remain taboo to each other.
Society had done its job well.

❧ ❧

When I returned to Cambridge in the fall, I kept to my
resolve: I did not call her. I felt like a collage of all my new
insights pasted precariously together; I did not want to

disintegrate again. I had my story; it was enough. Now I would live in the present and move into the future.

I took an abortive dip into therapy during that winter. I had developed some phobic symptoms in restaurants and theaters, and thought that seeing someone a few times a week might help me understand what defenses my body was taking. According to the psychiatric textbooks which I fearfully scanned, the early years of a child's life are crucial: the baby should have an unbroken, intimate relationship with a single, primary mothering figure. But in my first two years I had experienced the very worst that can happen to a developing child: separation, loss, grief, mourning. According to all the authorities I should have become a catatonic or raving maniac by now. I pictured Blanche, a depressed, withdrawn baby going from mother to Infant's Home to Foster Home to Adoptive Home. But then where did she get that "winning smile" noted in the file? I must have been perverse even then.

Was it too late for me? Was catatonia just around the corner?

I chose another woman therapist to see once a week. (Was I still looking for a mother?) This one was much younger than the analyst I had consulted before my search, although her hair was prematurely white. I hoped it would be a sign of heightened sensibility. It wasn't. She proved to be full of the prejudices and clichés drilled into her by her trade. Nor had nature endowed her with insight that even untrained people can have in dealing with the problems of others.

Her approach was to break down my defenses by challenging me: "You must have known your parents weren't dead." "You couldn't have believed your parents were married." "You must have known that adopted children are usually illegitimate."

No, I insisted, I had not known. I had never thought about why children were adopted. I had never had an adopted friend to discuss things with. No relative had ever revealed the facts of adoption to me. I had been left to stew in it alone.

So, too, the critics of Sophocles insisted Oedipus must have known: Didn't he overhear the drunken man at the banquet say the King and Queen weren't his parents? And why, if he had been warned by the Oracle that he would kill his father and marry his mother, did he slay the first stranger on the road to Thebes and marry a woman old enough to be his mother?

But Sophocles had Oedipus cry out that he did not know.

Perhaps Oedipus and I both knew through that middle knowledge one has when one knows and does not know at the same time. At first to survive, we do *not* know; then to survive, we know.

The therapist and I reached our final impasse over "the family romance" which all children are said to experience: the fantasy that one's parents are not one's real ones, and that one is really of noble or royal birth. How could I analyze this in terms of the Oedipus complex with my adopted parents when it was a *fact*, not a romance, that I had been born to others. I needed another dimension to explore, but this woman was much too limited in her perceptions, too literal in her use of the Freudian catechism. Bob had told me that during his own psychiatric training, the emotional problems of the adopted had never been presented, although every other kind of deviant behavior known to the human animal had been discussed.

I was beginning to feel much like those concentration-camp victims, prisoners of war, and the "brainwashed" who maintain that only those who have shared their experience can possibly understand them.

I might have fared better with a Rankian, for much of Rank's work, although not dealing with adoption, was

focused on the idea of the double, the two selves, which
the adopted person also must grapple with. In the last year
of his life he had written: "Man is born beyond psychology
and he dies beyond it but can live beyond it only through
vital experience of his own—in religious terms, through
revelation, conversion, or rebirth."

A Jungian would have been aware of the concept of
the *dual mother*, something else the adoptee must cope
with. Jung saw her as an archetype that runs through
mythology and religion, and is at home in the collective
unconscious. He would have understood that the unspoken impulse of the adoptee to find the original mother was
a natural one that could be traced back through the ages,
and that if blocked and driven underground, would surface eventually in some form of illness.

"The urge and compulsion to self-realization is a law
of nature and thus of invincible power," he has written,
"even though its effect, at the start, is insignificant and
improbable."

But the ideas of Rank and Jung were better known in
Europe than here. The disciples of Freud had ironically
found acceptance in the land he abhorred, and had
turned the imaginative analytic process he developed into
a rigid, conformist system.

I gave up therapy and decided to go it alone.

And so where was I now?

I had two mothers instead of one, but since both had
disappointed me, I had none. And where before I'd had
only one secret, I now had two.

I saw my phobias as representing my conflict over
telling the secrets. I both wanted to and couldn't. I still felt
I could never let my adoptive mother know what I had
done: by destroying her myth I would destroy what was
most meaningful in her life. And that guilt would be a
worse burden than the one I carried now.

As disillusioned as I was with "experts," I began seeing another kind about this time: fertility specialists. Now that I had decided I was ready to have a baby, the baby was not ready to have me. The doctors could find no specific reason other than the irregularity of my menstrual cycles which made it difficult to gauge the time of ovulation. I tried keeping temperature charts and taking hormone pills but nothing helped. I had heard that adopted people often have problems conceiving because of anxieties over their origins; I even recalled an adopted woman in my hometown who had produced a mongoloid baby. But far from fearing I could produce such a child, I had never believed I would even have one. How could I, who was not compounded of flesh and blood as others were, do anything as natural as having a baby?

However, now that I had seen my mother's face, albeit a frightened one, I was assured that nothing in my background should produce an abnormal baby. Then why was I having trouble? Was I still unconsciously afraid? Symptoms often remain trailing behind long after insight should have removed them, just as smoke lingers long after the fire is out.

The few fertility specialists I consulted conceded that there are certain mysterious forces at play in the matter of conception. One suggested an operation as a possible solution, but he was so vague as to its need, let alone its success, that I rejected the idea.

Bob and I began considering adoption seriously now. Unlike those earlier romantic ruminations about the Colonel's daughter at Madame Sawada's orphanage, these discussions were for real. When you are adopted, perhaps becoming a parent through adoption is just as attractive as the other way. Like something you owe to the next generation of foundlings.

We had little time to explore this before the moment arrived to return to Japan for Bob's two-year research

project on Japanese youth. We rented the Cambridge house, little knowing we would not return to it, got a sturdy cage for Mogo II, who was to be smuggled under a blanket into the cabin, and a crate made for Runcible who, because of his size, was headed for cargo.
Once again Japan would influence our destiny.

Far underlying all the surface crop of quaint superstitions and artless myths and fantastic magic there thrills a mighty spiritual force, the whole soul of a race with its impulses and powers and intuitions.   —Lafcadio Hearn

In Japan one consults experts too, but of a different kind—astrologers, phrenologists, palm readers, psychics. Since my Western gurus had failed me, I knew it was time to see Seki, the phrenologist, again. He would tell me whether we should adopt a child now or wait.

I had met Seki through my old friend Seihei Okuyama, the publisher of the English-language *Shipping News*. Okuyama, a jolly, heavy-set man, had always been ready to help me during my first stay in Japan, whether it was letting me use a room in his office at night for the East-West discussion group I had started at Fumiko's home or publishing my first children's book.

It was following Seki's advice to go into publishing that had made Okuyama a wealthy man. And now he escorted all of his friends and relatives to Seki's house whether they needed counseling on a particular problem or not. That first time he took me I had gone out of curiosity to see this famous seer who had not only made Okuyama's fortune, but had also successfully predicted previous

American presidential elections: that F. D. R. would run a third and fourth time, and that Eisenhower and Kennedy would be elected. (If he had lived, perhaps he would have predicted Watergate.) But during that earlier visit all he could tell me was to become a teacher or writer and to eat lots of food with iodine in it.

Now that I had a definite problem, Okuyama was exuberant. "Seki will know what you should do about adopting," he guaranteed me. And then in his impetuously generous way he immediately ordered his chauffeured car, and the next thing I knew we were speeding through Tokyo traffic on our way to Seki's place.

Seki himself greeted us at the door. Now eighty years old, he had been ailing since I last saw him, and was greatly altered. His round Kewpie-doll face was unshaven, although his bald head still shone like a glass ball. The brown kimono which covered his shrunken body and the woolen scarf protecting his throat gave him the appearance of an ascetic monk. Even his long Buddha-like earlobes suggested a sense of sanctity. Yet something about the way the silver-rimmed glasses kept sliding down his nose, or the way his eyes twinkled behind them, gave you the feeling that here was a monk who could laugh at the moon and enjoy the illusions of a worldly life.

The tatami room where Seki received us was empty except for the shelves of books on phrenology and the occult which lined the walls and a low table on which his daughter served tea. He sat on the cushion opposite me at the table.

When Okuyama had told him what brought us there, Seki asked me to write my name and date of birth on a piece of paper. Then he lifted a huge magnifying glass between us and peered closely into my face as he had that previous time. Again I was startled to see his distorted features swimming in the glass before me, but revealing none of their secrets. Then remembering that Okuyama had warned me that Japanese women lowered their eyes when looked at, I lowered mine. I didn't want the fortune of that other American woman he had brought who had defiantly stared back throughout the whole examination, only to be told that she was aggressive, hen-pecked her husband, and that her nose was too long.

While I sat there demurely waiting for Seki to finish scrutinizing my face, Okuyama was repeating my dilemma to him: should we adopt an Amerasian or a Western child first? And if the latter, should we fly to Germany where we had heard that babies fathered by American G.I.'s were in need of homes.

Finally Seki put down his magnifying glass and spoke: "You don't have to *adopt*," he said in Japanese. "You are with child."

Okuyama repeated his words in English, without comment, like a conscientious interpreter.

I had understood him too, but still I exclaimed "What?" My limited grasp of Japanese had never been able to cope with the lack of tense for future time, and surely that is what Seki must have meant.

Okuyama asked Seki to repeat his answer and there was a short, rapid exchange between them.

"Seki says you don't have to adopt because you are already pregnant."

"That's impossible," I protested. I had been prepared for anything, even to taking the baby of a Tibetan lama, if Seki saw one in my destiny, but not for this.

"Nothing is impossible if Seki says it is so," Okuyama reprimanded me. "Seki can look at a husband's face and tell him his wife is pregnant before she knows it herself."

"Tell him that if I am pregnant it would be too early to know," I said lamely. I couldn't possibly say such a personal thing in Japanese myself, and besides, the language had left me completely.

"He says you should have a test at a clinic and you'll find out for sure if your don't believe him," Okuyama interpreted. And he added on his own: "I think that's what you should do too."

I was beginning to get used to the idea now. "If it's true, what sex will the child be?" I asked.

Seki picked up his huge magnifying glass again and looked carefully for my child. "It is hard to say just yet."

"Could you guess?" I urged him, like the greedy fisherman's wife in the Russian tale who never has enough.

He looked again. "A girl."

I could not wait to get home to tell Bob. I burst into his study in the large Japanese-style house we were renting in one of Tokyo's suburbs: "I'm pregnant and it's a girl!"

But he was not too impressed with me. "We've suffered enough over this subject without having to complicate things with false hopes," he snapped.

Nevertheless, he agreed that I might as well go to a clinic. There was nothing to lose.

It was the era when frogs were still used in pregnancy tests. I had to wait two days for the results. A frog held my fate as surely as the frog in the fairy tale held the golden ball of the princess deep within the well. Would it come up with my golden child?

Early the appointed day, I called the clinic asking for the result of the test.

"*Tashika*," replied a cheery voice on the other end of the line.

I went scurrying into Bob's study, sliding open the door without even knocking. "She said '*tashika*'!" I cried. "That means positive."

"I don't trust your Japanese any more than Seki's predictions," he replied.

Now he made the call, and his voice actually wavered as he repeated the word: "*Tashika*."

The frog had delivered. I was pregnant. I was about to

create a blood relative who would live in my house, eat at my table, share my life, just as the frog in the tale wanted to do with the princess.

When I phoned Okuyama to tell him the good news, having previously reported Bob's reservations, he exclaimed gleefully: "Our side won!"

I wrote back to the States for a girl's layette, pink booties and all. When I was six months along, I went with Bob and a large bottle of saké in Okuyama's car to thank Seki for his prediction.

He had been napping, but he was quite pleased to accept the saké along with our gratitude.

This time I spoke to him directly in Japanese. "Thank you for our little girl."

He picked up his magnifying glass and gave my features a rapid going-over.

"It's a *boy*," he corrected me.

I was confused again. "But you said it would be a girl!"

"I said it was hard to tell then. But I see now it is clearly going to be a boy."

"Seki has been right on all three of my children," Okuyama interjected here. "I couldn't sleep the night our last one was born, not because I was worried about my wife, but that Seki's prediction might be wrong. It was very foolish of me. Seki never makes mistakes on these matters."

"What will I do with the pink layette?" I asked Bob when we got home. I could already feel the baby moving restlessly inside me, sometimes I could even hold the impression of a foot that stretched itself into my side. I had imagined it in pink booties, but now I had to change my vision to football cleats.

My father-in-law cabled us on hearing the revised news: "Seki will be only fifty percent wrong either way."

During a few months of my pregnancy we lived in Kyoto, the former capital of Japan, whose treasures of temples and pagodas were spared bombing in World War II.

The dream of old Japan was still there, the elegance, the restrained grace, the formality of ancient times, even the fragrance of Lady Murasaki who wrote what is regarded as the world's first novel, *The Tale of Genji*, that romantic chronicle of court life with its secret intrigues, its doomed love affairs, its poetic awareness of the sad impermanence of things. One brushed against samurai ghosts on the streets, heard the swishing of their swords when the wind rustled the trees.

I walked through the moss gardens and cavernous temples hoping my unborn baby would imbibe some of the wisdom and aesthetics of the Far East. What better heritage could I give him. He was, after all, a gift of the Buddha.

Bob and I are visiting a Zen master, Shinichi Hisamatsu, who had once come to our home in Cambridge with Daisetsu Suzuki. We sit on the straw-matted floor looking out into a moss garden, talking of existence and nonexistence: If there was a beginning, then there was a time before that beginning. And if there is existence, there must be nonexistence. And who is to say the difference between existence and nonexistence?

I ask the Master suddenly: "Does my baby exist now?"

He points outside: "Is that inside?"

He points inside: "Is that outside?"

In the foothills of Mount Arashi, just outside Kyoto, I stop in at Giō-ji, a small Buddhist nunnery, to see my friend Anshu-san, once the most famous geisha in Japan.

For some reason I am drawn to this frail figure with shaven head, long black gown, and piercing dark eyes. My Japanese is not elegant enough for the things we have to confide in each other, and we speak through an interpreter, Tsuneko Sadao, a close friend who has been helping me with my research. Perhaps it is Tsuneko's genius to be like the bamboo letting our words bend her invisibly, for it is as if this nun and I speak directly to each other's hearts.

Anshu-san tells me that she was adopted at three months by her father's poor relatives in Nara, and sold to a geisha house when she was eleven. By eighteen she already had her first wealthy patron who took her on a trip to America; by thirty-nine she had been an actress and journalist, and owned three bars in Osaka. She was known as Teruha.

Newspapers and magazines carried stories of Teruha's love affairs in serial episodes which the whole nation followed avidly. Plays were written about her, portraits were painted by famous artists. But then weary of the turbulence of her tempestuous life, she cut off the tip of her little finger to show her devotion to her last lover, shaved off her hair to show her spiritual sincerity, and retired to this deserted hut as a recluse.

The maple and pine trees which shelter her humble abode whisper of that other geisha, Giō, who fled here with her mother and sister over seven hundred years before, after being rejected by the powerful daimyo, Kiyomori. Each day Anshu-san burns candles to the wooden statues of those three women on the altar, as well as to Hotoke, Giō's successor, who eventually joined her here. Lined up with them is the statue of Kiyomori, himself, in the seat of honor next to the Buddha.

Anshu-san says she feels related to Giō, perhaps even an incarnation. It was Giō's spirit who guided her here, and like that former dancing girl, she has found peace.

"To be released from everything is to be released from yourself," she tells me. "Maybe I am just a piece of charcoal not burning, just eating necessary food and sleeping—what other people call being old. But I like it. I am close to that state of mind of *mu*—nothingness."

She pours another cup of tea for us: it is bitter, lest one forget the true essence of life. "But not so close to *mu* that I do not feel sad watching flower petals fall quietly on a spring night. It is impossible to stop them, but I feel lonely, left behind. I *envy* them."

Something in me would like to stop all my frantic activity, to linger here with Anshu-san, but I am far from that state of *mu*—I have a child to deliver to the world and a journey to complete before I can find release with her and Giō. I drink a last cup of tea and bid her goodbye, my bows matching hers in depth and feeling. Our eyes meet with messages that need no language.

Bob and I walk on the old Tokaido highway, that ancient pass that led out from Tokyo in the period when the shoguns ruled Japan. Once Hiroshige walked this road, immortalizing it with his woodblocks of the fifty-three stations through which the traveler was checked by the barrier guards.

We rest under an old tree and wonder if it once sheltered Hiroshige. Bob pulls out a white card and writes a haiku:

> The hills of Hakone.
> Two lovers pause
> To rest their unborn child.

Perhaps he too has been here before.

Had I been in New York during my last months, I would probably have been doing natural childbirth exercises and memorizing Spock, but here there are other preparations to make.

I visit the two-hundred-year-old Kappa Temple in the Nihonbashi area with Tsuneko and for a few yen receive a small clay figure of that water elf to help me in childbirth. It happens to be one of the *kappa*'s less publicized talents.

"Have you ever seen a *kappa?*" I ask the young priest there.

"Only in my dreams," he replies.

A student brings me an *inu-hariko*—a paper dog—which is also said to be an accomplished midwife. It is believed that dogs have an easy delivery—on the fifth day, the dog day, of the fifth month, Japanese women tie a white band around their stomachs to hold their babies in place. I do not do this but I believe in the dog as much as I do the *kappa* and my small stone Jizo, who is the patron saint of children and travelers.

>   ❦ ❦

My blood relative is born in a Japanese hospital on June 19, 1961, with a bald head and crumpled face that make him look more like Dwight Eisenhower than the Buddha. But he has my fair coloring and features. As I lie in that room with my baby I cannot help but think that I who had been born on Staten Island, have now given birth on another island on the other side of the world. Other deities than the ones who were with me then are now keeping watch.

Because of Bob's presence I am not alone, as my natural mother was, yet I still feel like one of the creatures of the forest who go deep into hiding to deliver their litters. For the adopted perhaps giving birth is a deed to be done in seclusion, so disconnected is the process from the rest of their lives.

It did not occur to me to think my adopted mother should be there. I had not invited her nor had she suggested coming. This was not an experience we could share together. Our life started with the toddler whose pictures adorn her dresser—the two-and-a-half-year-old cherub looking down wistfully at the tiny locket around her neck.

The Japanese nurse comes to return my blood relative

to the nursery—my cub, my pup, my *kappa*, my baby—I
do not want to let him go. How can a mother give up the
baby that comes from the flesh of her flesh? I tighten my
grip as if she is threatening to tear him away forever.
Nothing will separate me from my son. I who had been
indifferent to giving birth become the fiercely possessive
mother who hopes she can curb her wild hunger for
closeness to her own to let go when the time comes. The
Zen priest Nange Genko said, "Deeper than a crane's cry
is the maternal instinct."

It is the Year of the Bull: a baby born in this year can
be as driving and forceful in spirit as the bull or as gentle
as the cow. I hope my son will combine both of these
qualities. It is a difficult world he will grow into.

Every night a few miles from the hospital the Japanese
students have been snake-dancing through the streets in
demonstrations against their government. They want to
be heard in the conservative citadels where the power lies.
They are lighting the fires for a generation of students
who will spend the sixties manning barricades, and
marching through the streets of Asia, Europe, and America protesting against the Vietnam War, against their
universities' narrow policies, against their governments'
oppression of the poor. Against the sins of the fathers.

Someday my son will be a student too.

We name him Kenneth, but he becomes known as
Ken-chan, for the Japanese add that diminutive to the
first syllable of a child's name. The Japanese government
does not recognize him as a citizen (even with the "chan")
although my country gives automatic citizenship to any
baby born in its territory. My son emerges as an American
who, as the statutes stand now, may never be president
because he was born on foreign soil.

However, Ken-chan is unaware of all these rules and
regulations as he gurgles and coos in his Japanese *chan
chan ko* jacket with its virile boy's samurai design and his

pink booties. But I know that some part of him will always belong to this country of his birth which recognized his coming even before I did, just as some part of my gratitude for him will always be there.

Whatever the mysteries of conception, my adopted country had somehow unlocked them for me.

❧ ❧

We hadn't planned to stay in Hiroshima for more than one day, but we ended up living there for six months while Bob studied the psychological effects of the atomic bomb on the survivors. He could not believe that with all the physical research being done, no one had thought to do this. And so my son, who was exposed in utero to Kyoto gardens and temples, was to be exposed to Hiroshima the first year of his life.

At first it seemed wrong to take him there. "No child, whatever age, should have to know about this," I told myself. "He will absorb their suffering with the very air, and some part of man's inhumanity to man will be seared into his very being." Instinctively I wanted to shield him as the father of Siddhartha had tried to spare his son the sight of poverty, illness, old age, and death.

But then I remembered that the nuclear age was my son's heritage, one that his generation would have to deal with. I could no more hide it from him than I could the sun, and that first bomb that demolished Hiroshima was said to be brighter than a thousand suns.

I needn't have worried too much. We lived in a little house on the Inland Sea looking out on the sacred island of Miyajima where the gods once dwelt. And when we drove into town I could hardly believe that this was the legendary Hiroshima: the city had been rebuilt with wide boulevards; its castle had risen again; factories were turning out automobiles and sewing machines; it had a baseball stadium with a successful team, the Hiroshima Carps;

there was an entertainment center where you could eat the famous oysters and drink the best saké; and there was a population of five hundred thousand, mostly outsiders who had swarmed in from other places after the war to take advantage of the frontier conditions.

Sometimes you thought you could forget what had happened here.

However, after meeting some of the survivors (*hibakusha*, as they're called—literally, explosion-affected people), you recognized the true face of Hiroshima contorted with pain, and you knew that they never forgot. It was already seventeen years since that first atomic bomb had fallen, August 6, 1945, at 8:15 in the morning, but for the *hibakusha*, it was always 8:15. The atomic mushroom, that multicolored cloud that rose from the ruins, still hangs in their sky.

Sometimes I took Ken-chan with me to visit the children of the Folded Crane Club in their shanty built along the banks of the Ohta river, whose seven fingers, once so bloody, now twine peacefully through the city. We would sit on the straw-matted floor and watch as those young boys and girls folded pieces of colored paper to make the paper birds for which they are known. They would fold a thousand cranes, string them into leis, and take them to the hospitals to cheer the sick and aged. The Japanese believe that a crane can live for a thousand years, and such a lei will ensure long life. These young people, survivors or children of survivors, also hoped that their cranes would warn the world about nuclear weapons.

"We shall write 'peace' on their wings, and they shall fly all over the world," they would tell us.

"Here's a story, Ken-chan," they said one day. It was different from the ones I told him, and it went like this:

Once upon a time, there was a healthy young girl named Sadako Sasaki. She was two when the bomb fell a mile from her house, and though she was thrown from a chest by the force of the blast, she was uninjured. Sadako was such a pretty girl, so active and so gay. She was the fastest runner in her sixth-grade class. Then one day she fainted in the schoolyard, and a few weeks later she was in the A-bomb hospital with the dread diagnosis: acute leukemia.

Sadako was brave in the hospital. She sang songs with her friends and folded paper cranes. She wanted to make 1,000, but one day in 1955, when she had folded only 984, she died. Her friends made the missing cranes for her, and placed them all together in her coffin.

That was the end of the story, but not the end of what Sadako's friends had done. As if realizing that the death of Sadako symbolized all their deaths, they decided to do something about it. They raised money from young people all over the country to build a monument for Sadako that would sit in the Peace Park in their city.

Ken-chan and I went with the club members to visit the monument. On top of an oval granite pedestal, which symbolizes Mount Horai, the fabled mountain of paradise, a young girl stands holding in her outstretched arms a golden folded crane. Just below her, on the mountain, a young boy and girl reach out their arms to the sky. Within the arched pedestal hang colorful leis of a thousand paper cranes each, and inscribed on the base are the words: "This is our cry, this is our prayer: peace in the world."

"Look, Ken-chan, here are some cranes!" the children call delightedly as they place a lei around his neck. Like them, he is the child of a survivor.

I look from one young guarded face to another and hope that things will be better from now on. I know that the fear is there in them that this year, or the next, the dark thing that was unleashed into the world as radiation, and is perhaps even now lurking in their bodies, as it was in Sadako's, may suddenly erupt as "A-bomb disease." Cancers may be developing, blood deficiencies, blindness. Like their birthplace, these young people are different. Hiroshima is a *chosen* city, and its survivors are *chosen*.

It is this difference I recognize in them.

"I know it may seem far-fetched," I tell Bob later, "but adoptees have a lot in common with *hibakusha*. We walk around seemingly normal like everyone else, but we've got taboos, guilts, and repressions lodging like radiation inside us."

"Anyone who has experienced a holocaust—whether internal or external—has something in common," he replies.

"But why hasn't anyone recognized the adoptee's condition before?" It's something I keep coming back to. "Why aren't we taken seriously in the psychiatric literature so that we can be helped before it's too late?"

"I suppose because the state of adoption has never been considered a disease," he says thoughtfully.

"'A-doption disease,' that's what it is," I say. And I think for the first time how I would write it up: *Something that can lie dormant most of one's life. If it erupts in childhood, adolescence, or early adulthood and is dismissed as neurotic behavior or normal rebellion, it can subside into numbness. But it can stir malignantly in some adoptees all their lives, making them detached, floating, unable to love or to trust: loners.*

"'A-doption disease,'" I repeat, "It's got to be understood."

Every August 6 the *hibakusha* die a little and are reborn.

Bob and I stood at 8:15 in the morning with them at the Cenotaph, that official monument wherein are buried the names of those who perished, and bowed our heads with the others to commemorate the exact moment of their loss.

And that night I held Ken-chan in my arms and walked with the children of the Folded Crane Club through the city to the Ohta river to float paper lanterns to console the spirits of the dead. Each lantern had a deceased child's name on it. We were singing the song of the poet, Sankichi Toge, who had himself fallen victim to delayed radiation effects the previous year. His widow, who was to commit suicide soon after this night, was with us.

The children's high voices hung so sweetly on the air:

> Give back my father, give back my mother,
> Give grandpa back, grandma back,
> Give our sons and daughters back.
> Give me back myself, give mankind back,
> Give each back to each other.

5 ❦ THE HEART OF THE MAZE

Who was it bore you, child? One of
the long-lived nymphs who lay with Pan—
the father who treads the hills?
Or was she a bride of Loxias, your mother? The
grassy slopes
are all of them dear to him. Or perhaps Cyllene's
king
or the Bacchants' God that lives on the tops
of the hills received you a gift from some
one of the Helicon Nymphs, with whom he
mostly plays.

—Oedipus Rex

When one has no knowledge of one's real parents, or if one grows up to discover that the people one thought were one's "real" parents are not, one's problem is whether to feel deprived of this identity, or lucky to have escaped it. Frequently such people feel it to be a compelling issue to discover their parents, especially their mother. There are many motives, revenge and hate among them, but there always seems to be the assumption that through establishing one's biological origin one will really know who one really is. Or at least the negative: if one does not know one's parents, one cannot know oneself. One man said, "I am a book with no beginning . . ." Yet the quest to discover who one's parents were, however understandable, cannot in itself lead one to oneself.

—R. D. Laing

Ten years have passed. We are living in another old colonial house, this one a former inn, with a large pond on which I am raising ducks while writing allegories about them and commuting to New York to produce multimedia plays for the young at such diverse places as The Electric Circus and City Center. But although my plays are experimenting technologically with film, light, and music, they are still haunted by the folk creatures and spirit of the Far East.

Bob is teaching at Yale. We have a daughter now, Karen, four years younger than Ken. Though born in New Haven, she had managed to confound Western science too: "Mrs. Lifton, we don't know if you'll ever conceive again." Even the pregnancy tests kept coming back *uncertain*. Only Seki would have known. But he had died a few years before—and that was in another country.

I have not contacted Bea in all this time. I had closed the door after that Mother's Day card, and I thought it was locked, just as the secret of my search and finding her was still locked within me.

My adoptive mother visits twice a year—she comes as regularly as the seasons—spring and fall. And on the tenth day each time she is gone. New England is foreign to her midwestern soul: old things are not as good as new. She scoffs at our old-fashioned kitchen and bathrooms, but she will go back and tell her friends the marvelous size of them.

Through the study window I watch her outside with my daughter. How patiently she sits there by the pond with Karen, who looks like Bob, not me. But she doesn't seem to mind that this child is dark, not blond as hers was. Dolls, cards, tea party, she plays them all with more enthusiasm than I have. Childhood is her thing.

It's easier for us both with the children around. It must be so for all daughters when there is a generation between the present and the past. The scene out there is perhaps what it's all about, adopted or not.

"Nana! Nana!" Karen calls, running to her across the grass.

One night, following one of those visits, Bob was restlessly turning the knobs on the television set after the late news when he happened on the David Susskind show. "Come here quickly!" he shouted.

The show was on adoption. A panel consisting of an adoptee, a natural mother, an adoptive mother, and a social worker from an adoption agency was engaged in the usual frenzied discussion that Susskind encourages.

I saw Florence Fisher for the first time. She is the Betty Friedan of the adoptee liberation movement. Short, blond, militantly aggressive on this subject, she was calling for the unsealing of birth records, the right of adoptees to know their origins.

The hostile adoptive mother and the intransigent social worker pecked at her, but she appeared unscathed by the ordeal—she even seemed energized by controversy. Her steely resolve had been forged in her twenty-year struggle to find out who she was; her consciousness was raised to the level of hubris.

She walked over taboos like holy men walk over burning coals.

I sat mesmerized by this fascinating coming-together of all the participants in the ancient drama of adoption. I felt for the uncomprehending adoptive mother who emerged as a tigress defending her cubs (much as my own would have done had she been there); but I identified with Florence, whose voice was like Cassandra's, telling all adoptive mothers that in the future some part of their children would have to leave them.

I wrote a note to her the next day asking for information about the adoptee organization she was in the process of forming. But it wasn't until a few months later that I heard from her—by phone. She had been swamped with hundreds of letters from the silent majority of the adopted who were daring to peek out into public for the first time. She was overwhelmed by the Pandora's box she had opened: the dead were rising, marching, writing, calling. She was finding herself the surrogate mother for emotional fledglings of all ages who were discovering that they could fly too.

Florence invited me to the next meeting of this organization which she called ALMA (Spanish for soul), the Adoptees' Liberty Movement Association. I dressed starkly that Saturday just as I had when I went to meet Bea. I told myself I was going as a writer, a recorder of events; with the lack of emotional responsibility that such a professional has, I would just drop in and observe.

The meeting at the Fifth Avenue Presbyterian Church had just begun when I arrived. I stood in the back for a few minutes. There were about eight rows of folding chairs filled with people of all ages, shapes, and sizes. Some were well-dressed, others rather plainly. There were more women than men.

Florence was seated at a table in the front. She was explaining that after going on her own personal search for her records, she had never intended to start an organization, but that somehow helping one person had led to another, and now there were letters in her mailbox every day asking for advice.

"Everyone has a right to know who they are before they die," Florence told the group assembled before her. "When I was a baby I didn't sign the agreement for my adoption, and I do not consider myself legally held by it now. In fact, I'm thinking of having mine annulled."

There was a slight stir in the room. As usual, Florence was soaring brazenly above everyone else, in realms that would take others a lifetime of guilt and ambivalence to reach. Perhaps it's easier to levitate when one's adoptive parents are dead.

She was saying: "They ask me, 'Why do you want to know?' I answer, 'Why wouldn't you?' Sealing our records is a violation of the Constitution. We have been indentured like slaves to our adoptive parents. We are told that the law is protecting the privacy of our natural parents. I say that my mother has the right to privacy from you, but not from *me*, her baby. She has no right to privacy at the expense of my anonymity."

There was a feeling of camaraderie as we listened to her daring declarations. Surely such impassioned rhetoric brought about the vote for women, civil rights for blacks, helped end the Vietnam War. Every movement needs such a fanatical force pushing it to the outer limits if it is to get off the ground. Someday I would recoil from her lack of psychological subtlety, but for now I could value her scream of rage as a means of forcing public attention.

There were natural mothers at that meeting too. The success of a group such as this meant a possible reunion with their grown children. There was even a natural father hoping to find a way to get adoption rights to his own daughter; a grandfather searching for the baby his son had secretly given up; and two adoptive aunts helping their nephew trace his mother.

Gradually people began to speak up from the floor, and from the fragments of their stories and questions, I learned that some of these adoptees already knew their original names but did not know how to proceed with them; others were still struggling to unearth theirs. The chance to meet together had mobilized them into action. They were to become the radical fringe of America's five million adoptees, and hopefully the trail they would blaze would be as a paved highway to those who followed.

An elderly man spoke of his search for *forty* years to find his mother—in a nunnery.

"Did she tell you who your father was?" someone asked.

"No," he replied wryly, "she just told me to think of her as my 'spiritual' mother."

A natural mother asked about the pending thirty-day surrender bill that would decrease the time the mother had to reverse her decision on giving up the baby. "Why doesn't society try to help mothers keep their children, instead of just shortening the period they have to decide?"

"It would make the adoption agencies go out of business," an adoptee called out.

"They're out of business already," someone retorted. "It's almost impossible to find white babies now."

"If the abortion bill is repealed, they'll be back in business," quipped another.

It was no secret that the adoption agencies now had waiting lists of three to five years for healthy, white babies, what with the advent of the Pill and the easing of abortion laws. In fact, many couples were turning to the "gray market" and paying lawyers up to twenty-five thousand dollars to arrange private adoptions for them. Our generation of surplus babies had been a real bargain.

There was a lot of bitter humor and unresolved pain in that room. But there was a lot of love too, as if in discovering each other we had found our true brothers and sisters. I felt my resistance vanish completely as I came to understand that, like me, each person was carrying their own secret as if it were an ugly scar that until now had to be kept concealed. We were all cripples in a way, wounded psychically by our dislocation and stigma. We were all beautiful freaks, enlarged by our survival. We met at this moment in this space, and it seemed unimportant what we did or who we were outside this room. All that mattered was what we revealed about our past adoptive lives and where we were in our searches.

After the meeting we stood about in awkward clusters, drinking punch, strangers sharing intimacies: "Did your adoptive mother tell you that, too?" "Did you feel that way with your adoptive father?" "Did you have that fear too?" "Did you also keep it a secret?"

There was a feeling of adventurism about the searches in process, but also an undercurrent of dread. We were still in uncharted waters.

I was one of the few who had already found their mother. Everyone was surprised that I had not gone on to search for my father. They wanted to know what my mother was like, how she had received me. They were startled when I told them I had not seen her for over ten years, that I had not met my half-brother.

"I'm going to keep on searching whether my mother wants to meet me or not," one of the women said. "I just want to see her face and hear my story."

"I don't know how I feel," another woman, herself the mother of a teenager, mused. "To be perfectly honest, I'm not sure I want to meet my natural mother if it means taking on new responsibility. What if she's incapacitated or on welfare? I see old women on park benches, shabby and alone, and I think, what if one of them is my mother and I have to take care of her?"

"I don't agree," an intense young man from an advertising firm broke in. "I want to know the truth at any cost." A veteran of A.A., gay lib, and psychoanalysis, he felt that an adoptee organization might be his last chance to put his emotional life together. He suspected that his ignorance of his past history was responsible for all his problems.

"I know I came from an orphanage near my home in Virginia, when I was three, but my adoptive parents told me nothing else. I never felt I belonged in that family. My father was cold and critical of everything I did."

His remarks were my first insight into the special difficulties that boys have in adoption when they cannot relate to their fathers and have overly domineering mothers. Docility in this situation seems to come easier to the female than the male: at least the price paid is less visible. And yet the majority of those searching were women. Perhaps women have more genetic concern for the children they will bring into the world. Or perhaps men have more aggressive rage toward the mothers who have abandoned them and handle their hostility by avoiding the problem. These differences have not been studied yet; one can only speculate now.

Later a group of us went to dinner at a small Italian restaurant on the West Side. It was so cozy there, such an exhilarating feeling being among our own, for truly we had more basic things in common with each other than we did with our most trusted friends. Seated at that long, narrow table I saw us as travelers at a way station, resting and taking courage before each began the next stage through the labyrinth alone.

At first I was disappointed to find I was seated between two natural mothers. I really wanted to go on talking with other adoptees about the experiences we had in common. But as I got into conversation with Susan and Margaret, I had the eerie sensation of hearing my story from the other end. Bea was the only natural mother I had been interested in until now, but here were two women of a younger generation who cared enough about the children they had given up to be working toward their eventual reunion.

Susan, on my left, was a Catholic who had signed her son away at birth, six years before, because she didn't want her ailing mother in Missouri to know. She said she was pressured into this action by the social worker who told her it was best for her child. But when she had pulled herself together a few months later, she changed her mind, and eventually tried unsuccessfully to get him back through the courts.

"A married couple is better than an unmarried mother," the judge had chastised her. To him, she was the proverbial fallen woman. She still remembers the hatred with which the adoptive mother looked at her across the judge's chambers. "And to think that woman is raising my child!" she said sadly.

Still unmarried, Susan has the dream that someday when her son is of age, the records will be unsealed and she can explain to him why she had to give him up. She has even kept track of the various addresses of the father, a married man, so that should her son want to find him, she will have the necessary information.

In a way, like Bea, Susan is still in hiding. Neither her mother nor her friends at the office know that she has given a child up for adoption. But on the other hand, she is keeping a place in her emotional life for her son to fit into should she ever see him again.

Margaret, on my right, was older: her son would be eighteen. She, too, had her child with a married man and could not keep him alone. She has no idea where he is. When she wrote her name and phone number on a cocktail napkin for me, she put his birthdate below it. "I always do this," she said. "Until the time I don't have to any more."

Talking with Susan and Margaret that night I began to

realize that, like the adopted, natural mothers have their own guilt and fantasies. They assuage their guilt for a while by imagining that the adoptive family will be wealthy and educated and give their baby all the things they could not. There is this paradigm of the perfect, almost royal set of adoptive parents somewhere, who will treasure the specialness of their child.

However, many of these natural mothers have their fantasies shattered when they hear the grim stories that some adult adoptees have to tell. They learn that babies such as theirs do not necessarily get adopted by families of higher social position, but just as often of lower status than their own. Many of the adoptees, especially those who had not gone through agencies, had ended up with poor, uneducated families where they had little cultural opportunity and even less understanding. Now that the mothers value themselves more, they begin to imagine that their children might have been better off with them after all.

Who knows?

Certainly the pain of the natural mother is of the same intensity as that of the adoptee—if not greater. But who can measure pain? What doctor can cure it? The symptoms can be treated, but who can hold anyone long enough, tightly enough, to make the agony go away?

Susan was saying: "I'd like to help set up a commune of unmarried mothers in which everyone shares the raising of the children. Then we could somehow manage to keep our kids while working."

Margaret was saying: "We should be subsidized like unmarried mothers in Finland are. They are encouraged to keep their babies there."

They were both saying that unmarried mothers should not have to give up their babies for life because they cannot take care of them in those early years.

That night at the restaurant I heard for the first time of

another active adoptee who had been grappling with all of
these problems for many years—Jean Paton, who has her
own organization, Orphan Voyage, in Cedaredge, Colo-
rado.

A former social worker and double adoptee, (her first
adoptive family broke up when the father died), her voice
is more controlled than Florence's, more literary,
although just as anguished. She believes that the adopted
are "social" orphans, prevented by the sealed records from
ever finding their moorings in the world. She has written
two books on the subject and was the first to suggest
regional Reunion Registries in which adoptees and natural parents can leave vital information about each other.
She also has been keeping her own Reunion File (as do
most adoptee groups now) and sends out a quarterly
newsletter in the form of a log which reports the latest
developments in the adoptee's legal and social struggle for
autonomy.

Jean's words to the adopted, and to the society which
has been repressing them, have been pouring out since
the fifties. Out there on the western slope of the Rockies
she has turned a little log cabin next to a burbling stream
into her Museum of Orphan Literature. I try to imagine
that museum there, high above the rest of the world, the
San Juan Mountains towering in the distance, the Grand
Mesa lying in the rear, and within, all those thousands of
volumes of poetry, prose, plays, and nonfiction that have
some connection with people like me. The Social
Orphan. I'm in Dickens, Shakespeare, George Eliot,
T. S. Eliot, Oscar Wilde, Plautus, Frances Hodgson
Burnett, Erasmus, Gilbert and Sullivan—and so on.

I think about Jean's word for the adopted a lot in the
next few months. *Orphan*. I never thought of myself as an
orphan before. I go to the dictionary: an orphan is a child
who has lost both parents through death . . . or less

commonly one parent / an orphan is a young animal who has been deserted or lost its mother / an orphan is a person or thing that is without protection, sponsorship / an orphan is bereft of parents.

Nowhere in the dictionary does it say that an orphan is someone who has been adopted.

We adopted are not bereft of parents. Do we not have those "psychological parents" who raised us? But now that I think about it honestly, the orphan wind has been blowing relentlessly through me all my years, although I've tried to masquerade about like other more insulated mortals.

Recently when I told my friend Ellie I was adopted, she said, "Oh, that explains the mystery about you. Now I understand."

What mystery? What did she understand? I didn't dare ask her then.

Is it that I never can stay with one group too long—no one community, no one country? I always have to move on.

Most women I know need what they call "security"— whatever that is. They burrow into their homes and social circles like moles and move contentedly about underground, blind to the temptations of the many moons swirling about in the constellations above them. I like to move in and out of communities, apartments, houses— love them, leave them, travel on. I am not the possessor but the possessed. I must escape.

Is it the orphan wind blowing through me?

I go for a leisurely bicycle ride through Central Park with Ellie one Sunday when the automobile lanes are closed to traffic. We are pedaling slowly side by side, past small clusters of guitar players, past a group doing folk dancing on the grass, past a horse-drawn hansom.

"Ellie," I say, "what mystery about me do you understand now?"

She knows what I mean. She's an old friend, and a writer, too, struggling as I have been to put together the strands of her life as mother, wife, and artist.

"Your plays and stories have always intrigued me," she said. "There is an obsessive quality in them—strange clues and reverberations—always the same mythic theme that puzzled me before, but that I understand now that I know you're adopted."

"Like what?" I ask, knowing what, but wanting to hear her say it.

"For instance, *The Many Lives of Chio and Goro*— the reincarnation play—where people keep missing the meetings they're destined to have. There's always the inability to return to what is past and irretrievably lost. And there's a touch of Ondine in some—you know, the little mermaid who lives on earth, but belongs in the sea."

We glide on one of the downhill stretches for a while, not saying anything.

"It interests me how people express the themes of their life through their work," she says. "I always felt there was something that had to be filled in in yours. Something you weren't revealing about yourself. Some secret you were keeping."

As she speaks I see the changeling that was me locked in the prison of herself, like an autistic child with a private world that cannot be communicated to others. I see her rocking back and forth inside it, dreaming her private dreams.

"I wonder if I would have been a different kind of writer if I hadn't been adopted," I muse. "Maybe I wouldn't have used fantasy and metaphor the way I have."

"It's fascinating to think how the form a person's art takes is compelled by the facts of his psychological life," she says.

She is silent for a while, pushing on ahead. I know she is thinking about her own journey from the Midwest to this point in her second marriage, her own experiments with style in poetry and prose to express what is unique in her as a woman.

"You're fortunate in a way," she says, slowing down. "Being adopted gives you your archetypal theme to hang everything on. The rest of us have to dig around in the fog trying to raise ours to consciousness. But for you the theme is crystal clear."

I hadn't thought of myself as necessarily fortunate before.

One morning just before dawn I bolt upright in bed, grope for a pencil and paper and begin writing frantically.

"What are you doing?" Bob mumbles, turning over.

"Searching for the real me."

"You'll never find her," he says wryly.

We both giggle like children. He is so right. He is a funny man, even in his sleep, in spite of all the serious subjects he has delved into. He's working on death-related concepts now, but he sees the absurdity of life and doesn't flee from it. He accepts it, even expresses it in his mocking bird cartoons which are his avocation and trademark. In one, the little bird says to the big one: "Now that you have completed forty years of scientific study on the nature and ramifications of death and dying, can you give us your conclusions?" And the professorial bird replies: "When you're dead, you're dead." But my favorite of his cartoons is the one where the little bird says, "All of a sudden I had this wonderful feeling: 'I am me'!" And the other answers: "You were wrong."

Now while I am scribbling on that paper it occurs to me that with all of my moving in and out of the various phases of my life, I have never moved away from him. And he, in true protean style, has always been ready to move with me. Something in the strength I have needed to call upon as an adoptee has given him strength too. We have, with the mysterious alchemy that exists between some people, been able to sustain each other.

As I correspond and rap with other adoptees, a new
me begins to emerge—the *me* who does not know her
father. Like Edward Dahlberg who carried his mother's
name through life, I might have cried out: "In what city
are my father's footprints? Does he walk, does he breathe
and is he suckled by the winds?. . . . Tell me, I must know
. . . or live and die unborn."

Until I find him, my journey is incomplete.

We have temporarily taken an apartment in New
York. My study window has a view of Central Park, the
same park Bea and I had overlooked at lunch so many
years before.

Why had I turned away from her before asking more
about my father?

One morning I sit at my desk and know I will contact
Bea again. I want to learn the rest of my story—my
father's side. I will call her and ask my father's name.

I pick up the phone.

I put it down.

I cannot make the call.

No one but the adopted will ever know what it is to

have a phone number like this in one's possession. One is afraid to dial. The number reaches across years, descends into the abyss, winds through the labyrinth.

Does the pain and longing never cease? I ask myself. I am so much stronger now, so much more self-assured. What I want from Bea will only take one more meeting. But I cannot pick up that telephone. I sit for hours staring at it and out the window at the park. Let sleeping dogs lie, I tell myself. Lot's wife turned into salt when she looked back. Keep going while you still can.

But I cannot keep going without my father's name. I write a note instead to her brother and his wife according to our old arrangement:

> I hope this note out of the past doesn't startle you. I am living in New York now and cannot help but wonder how Bea is now. I know her eyes were bad years ago, and I find myself hoping she has recovered completely and is in good health now.

> I would love to see Bea again or talk to her if she would like to. If she would rather keep the door to the past closed, I will understand. If she would like to meet again, I would be so happy. But please let me know in either case.

A few days later my telephone rings. It is Bea. I am startled, having expected to hear from her by mail. She, on her part, is nervous, apologetic about bothering me at this moment. Do I have time to talk? After all these years of broken connection, she asks if I have time to talk.

"I tried to call you yesterday but I hung up when another voice came on," she says.

"That must have been the answering service."

"I wanted to call immediately after Oran read me your letter. But I could not get the courage until today."

"How are you?"

"Oh, I'm all right. I was so moved that you asked about my eyes."

"How are they?"

"Not so good. I can't read much. I've got cataracts now."

"Are you getting an operation?"

"No, I'm tired of going to doctors."

"And how's your husband?"

"He died of a heart attack four years ago while visiting his sister in Florida."

"I'm sorry."

"Well, he was seventy-two. And not sick a day of it. He enjoyed his life."

She was living with her son now, my half-brother, in that same one-bedroom apartment we had driven past in Great Neck the night of the snowstorm.

"I wanted Howie to take the bedroom, but he insisted I have it. He sleeps on the day bed in the living room."

"And your mother?"

"She died the year before my husband. Five years ago, in her eighties. What a brilliant, beautiful woman she was. I looked nothing like her, but how I loved her."

I say nothing to this. She goes on about how she has been faring since her mother died. She has been ill for the past few years: immobilized by a series of ailments that keep her housebound. Indeed, she is practically a recluse. She has buzzing in the ear and dizzy spells, hardening of the arteries, allergies of the skin, cataracts in the eyes, and traces of the old glaucoma. A veritable casebook. My joy in talking to her is tempered by the thought that I might yet inherit some, if not all, of these symptoms. She is just sixty-three.

Shades of mortality hang over this conversation.

Bea says that her suffering from giving me up has brought her to this broken-down condition. But she is not complaining: rather she is apologizing for bothering me with the knowledge of her poor health. Her son, Howie, is wonderful to her, she says. He takes her out shopping on weekends: she leans on his arm to prevent herself from falling.

However, Bea makes a point of telling me that she does not want Howie to know about me right now. He is not married, and there is the implication that there is some insidious link between this knowledge and his future. She asks me never to phone her at night when he is home, only during the day when he is at work at an engineering firm.

"And please don't call for the next few weeks," she adds. "Howie will be home on vacation."

I have no intention of *ever* calling, I am so put off by her restrictions; but when I hang up I remember that what with the emotional turmoil of hearing her voice again, I forgot to ask my father's name.

I wait about a month to call. In the meantime, I think about Howie, this half-brother. I no longer care if I meet him or not. I am older, and my own biological children have relieved me of much of my former need to see blood relatives. I know he cannot be a brother to me at this late stage, nor I a sister to him. We have missed our timing together.

I think about the psychology of the relationship a mother has to the child who comes after the one she has secretly given away. That child is like the survivor of a dead sibling, but will not understand why the mother is so abnormally intense and clinging. At least one who grows up with knowledge of a dead sibling can try to integrate the fact and cope with it in various stages of life. But the second/first child, like my half-brother, is flying blind: he has been heralded as the first-born by a proud father and has never been told the truth about the hidden forces governing the relationship with his fearful mother. But does this overly protected second/first child sense that some terrible secret hangs over the family? Does this unnamable, unknowable force hold him pathologically to his mother?

When I do call Bea again, she tells me that my brother used to go with attractive girls, but not anymore.

"I don't understand," she says. "He is so good. He would make a wonderful husband."

Some years ago, it seems, he was going with a pretty girl from a wealthy family. It might have become serious. But when she took him home to meet her parents, it came out that his aunt—the very one who had arranged my adoption—belonged to their country club.

The next day the girl called my brother and told him she was forbidden to see him again. "I am sworn to secrecy," she had said. "Please don't ask why it has to be over."

Bea puzzles over this on the phone with me, as she must have alone so many times before. Did the aunt tell the girl's parents that Howie's mother was the *poor* branch of the family? Or did she tell them something else?

"Didn't Howie ask you what the girl could have heard?" I say.

"Oh yes, he did wonder about it."

"He must be suspicious. He must know that something is being kept from him."

She gets excited now. "No, he doesn't suspect anything. I swear to you he has no idea."

"He might have an idea and not be telling you." How can I explain to my natural mother about "middle knowledge"?

"He knows nothing," she insists. "And he must not know. He is not broad-minded like you. He has not traveled like you have."

"You said he served in Korea." I think of those G.I.'s I

saw in the dusty outposts of that forlorn country. I try to picture my brother among them. There is no face under the helmet.

"That's not what I mean. He is not international in his thinking. He walks out of the room if anyone says 'damn.'"

I cannot picture my brother at all now.

"Then this might help him grow!" I am getting impatient. My brother is slipping away from me, turning into a cardboard cutout. I cannot feel his life.

But Bea says she will not tell him. The secret must remain unspoken. She is adamant. As we say goodbye, she reminds me that there has never been a day when she hasn't thought of me.

I have not asked about my father.

I call her once every week or so. She is afraid to call me: it might be an inconvenient time, someone might be there. Sometimes we are relaxed and chatter about mundane things as people who are intimate do, but usually we talk about the past. That is the space we have in common. We keep bringing up the baby—me. I am still in the infants' home. Is it me or my double? That other self, the baby, is permanently infantilized. It cannot grow up. Like a grotesque, oversized mechanical doll it holds out its arms when it hears "Boopsy" or "Bubbaleh" from the young stranger who comes to visit once a week; at other times it walks down the hall toward its new mother and father saying "Mama!" "Daddy!" or whatever. But like a true toy, it never evolves beyond that stage. Just as death at an early age assures a person eternal youth, so too does adoption keep one eternally young, helpless, infantilized.

To pick up the receiver and dial Bea is like dialing a time machine, each digit the number of years going back, until I reach that golden era we shared together. Her voice is always on the other end, anxious, expectant, breathless; she is queen of the Realm of Limbo. But I am getting tired of this exercise in time, tired of the child waiting there with her. I want to be my living adult self for a change. I want to be me—wife, mother, writer.

She does not ask much about my children. She has never asked to see their pictures. Maybe she doesn't think she has a right—that they were relinquished with me by the agency: me, my children, and my children's children all signed away in one big package deal.

In one of these phonecalls my mother tells me about her two marriages: they were both unsatisfactory in their own way. The first husband she married because her mother wanted her to, and divorced for the same reason. He was tight with money and small-minded. The second she married even though her mother didn't want her to. He was a sport and loved the races; he always wore a pink jacket on Pink Flamingo Day at the track. But now I hear another little detail—he left her when she would not follow him in retirement to Florida.

"I couldn't desert my mother," she explains. "And besides there was nothing for me to do in Florida. The sun hurt my eyes."

It turns out that the second husband met someone else down there. Bea knew about this woman, but still she did not join him. He died there while living with that woman. There was never an official divorce: just an unofficial separation.

Bea admits this second husband was like my father in being a sport. She obviously has a weakness for the flamboyant. She describes my father's open sports car, how impressed she had been with it as a girl. I am thinking that, to her, that car must have been a symbol of movement away from the oppressive yoke of her mother: it must have been like a spaceship to the moon. For those few nights she spent with my father she must have thought it would propel her there too. The shock was when she was thrown off the vehicle to fall alone through space.

This talk of the sporty men in her life is an opening wedge and I squeeze through. "Is my father still alive?" I inquire cautiously.

"I don't know. I did hear from my older brother that he had married a schoolteacher with two children and then left her. But I haven't heard anything since then."

"I'd like to know his name."

Her voice gets tense. "Do not ask me," she says. "You once promised not to ask me."

"I don't remember that promise."

"But you did. And Bob promised me that first time we were together. Don't ask me, because it is the one thing I cannot tell you."

I do not ask again—for a while.

Names.

Asian people often choose names they hope will bring good fortune to the family or beauty to the bearer.

"Why did you name me Blanche?" I ask my mother in one phonecall. "Was it after someone you knew?"

"No, I was told it meant pure. . . . clean. I wanted to think of you that way. I thought it was a beautiful name."

Many adoptees take their original names when they learn them, discarding the other like a snake sheds its skin. I have no desire to take mine. Blanche is a fictional character in a fairy tale: "Once upon a time there was a baby born in a dark wood, and its name was Blanche, which means light."

During all of these calls Bea resists any suggestion that we meet. "I am too weak to come into the city," she says.

"I could drive out. It's only about a half-hour away, isn't it?"

"More like an hour."

"I could still do it easily. I have a car."

"No, the neighbors might see you," she says. "We've all lived here together so many years. We've grown old together. They'd wonder who you were."

"You could tell them I'm a niece visiting."

"Where would I suddenly get such a niece?"

At other times when I probe the possibility of my visiting, she might say: "My place is too humble for you to see. I had to get rid of the rugs and upholstered furniture because of my allergies." Or she would insist: "I look too terrible. I wouldn't want you to see me like this. My hair has been falling out lately. Howie says he'll go with me sometime for a wig."

"But don't you want to see *me?*" I ask her one day. It just slips out.

"Oh, I saw you on television, didn't I? You looked so beautiful. I was so proud of you."

She is referring to one of the talk shows I did for a book I had written with another journalist, *Children of Vietnam*. I had alerted her to the program, and then wondered how she would feel hearing me discuss those orphans and abandoned children on another part of the globe. But she has never mentioned the subject matter to me, just how well I looked. Here we are living down the lane from each other, and she settles for seeing me on her television screen. I am larger than life there, part of that fantasy world that can be turned on and off at will.

I am aware that she is watching me as I speak on that show. Before five hundred thousand people, or whatever the number is, I have the privilege of talking to my lost mother on daytime TV. "Hi, Mom, use Geritol," I should say. Instead I tell her how it was in Vietnam: how babies are separated from their mothers in the fighting—how children, living by their wits on the streets, are called *Bui Doi*, the dust of life—how whole families had been scattered like dust, and may never find each other again. The suffering of the Vietnamese people is beyond your imagination, I tell my mother publicly that day on this special hookup, just for us.

But my mother, like most of the American public, has tuned out on subjects like this a long time ago. She, too, is tired of hearing about Vietnam. And why shouldn't she be, when she learned about suffering so close to home.

"You look like I did when I was younger," is all she has to say.

One afternoon after I have hung up from Bea, my son brings his homework into my study. It is a blank family tree that he must fill out by the end of the week. Bob has just completed the paternal side for him: that is, he has put in what he knows along with a vague reference to a great-great-grandfather who was said to have been a wise man in his village, if not a rabbi. At the age of thirteen, when he was married, this precocious ancestor was given a coat with a three-foot-long hem to let out as he grew. His name was Hyamyakov, which translates into Jay in English, and which my son carries as his middle name, the same as his father. How can I compete with that bit of mythology?

"Now Mom, your tree," Ken says. My son does not like homework, but this is like a game.

I look at the graceful silhouette of that tree whose barren branches are waiting for my bitter fruit. But to be truly mine this tree would have to be artificial, like that vinyl Christmas pine of my childhood which hibernated in the closet all year under snowy tissue paper until its appointed moment to spread nondenominational holiday cheer on the living-room table.

Ken is waiting eagerly by my desk for a response.

"I am too busy now."

"Later?"

"I have to work tonight."

"Aw, Mom!"

I'm a spoilsport. But if necessary I would work every night all week to avoid my family tree. What tree, anyway? Does the adopted person go on the tree she was placed on biologically or on the tree onto which she was transplanted?

Who's to say?

It would be so easy to fill in my adoptive parents' names and just forget the whole thing. The children do not know I am adopted. I am keeping secrets from them just as secrets were kept from me. I tell myself it is because I don't want them blurting anything out to their only living grandparent—my adoptive mother. She is due for her ten-day visit soon and still ignorant of my preoccupation with the past. The children look forward to her arrival—the presents, excitement, fuss over them.

But do I really belong on her tree, which she can hardly fill in herself? Now that I think of it, I have never felt any connection to either of my adoptive parents' biological origins beyond affection for my immediate aunts, uncles, and cousins. And in truth, there is no connection. For although my mother and father gave me identity as a child—were the "psychological parents"—they could not connect me to my own historical or biological past. No adoptive parents can do that for a child not born of their blood. It makes them not less the parent, but only one part—albeit, the major part—of a child's identity.

"If you give historical perspective to psychoanalytic thought, the issue of parentage and origin becomes important," Bob once told me. But even that insight wasn't helping me with my arboretum now.

A few weeks before, I had clipped an amusing article from the newspaper about how Americans were searching for their ancestors in England, paying up to seventy dollars a century for professional genealogical guidance. Many of them were disillusioned to learn that the Victorians had cheated on their backgrounds, faked their lineages, and claimed coats of arms they had no right to. They had even disguised their illegitimate offspring so cleverly that now the experts can't tell where they belong.

If the experts can't tell, how can a family skeleton know which tree to swing from? I wondered if I wouldn't be better off repressing the whole thing.

For the next few days I fretted about genealogy in general and mine in particular, going to the library, consulting the good books. One Anthony R. Wagner, C.V.O., Richmond Herald, the College of Arms, London, and a Fellow of the American Society of Genealogists, put it this way in his King Penguin book published in 1946:

> To be aware that one is here, has continuity with the past, and is, as it were, a link between past and the future, gives one a sense of belonging, of being part of God's plan of history, however humble one's progenitors may have been. Even though an ancestor here or there in the family tree may have been licentious or a profligate, a horse thief or a scoundrel, a criminal or a convict, one can always be thankful that there were such exceptions in the family who in spite of their personal propensities or uncontrolled appetites, (and in some instances, the forces of circumstances which surrounded them) failed to break the continuity of the family, however much they may appear to be abnormal growths on its branches.

Was I the offshoot of an abnormal growth?
He continues:

> In contrast, the rest of the ancestral line
> stands worthy and reliable, and the descen-
> dants may take justifiable pride in the fact
> that they have conquered the tendencies
> which, for a brief space, got out of control,
> and have done their part to restore the family
> to wholeness.

Was I the fruit of the branch that got out of control?

I gave up on the genealogists.

Maybe I should be thinking on a larger scale, I told myself. If there's a Buddha tree, there must be a Christ tree and a tree of Abraham. As a Jew I did feel a sense of continuity with my heritage—did not one tribe of Israel turn me over to another? It was in that sense a family affair. And if I was in the Diaspora, so was everyone else.

I considered claiming the whole tree of Abraham. Or was that too cosmic for the purpose of my son's assign- ment? And wouldn't it take a tree at least three miles high to do it justice? My son would never forgive me for making him write so much.

And so by the end of the week, I had done nothing. My tree went back to school a blank, a barren twig. Ken's homework was only half-finished—the legitimate half. It was not mentioned again. The teacher didn't seem to care, and my son did not give it any further thought—or did he?

I mention the tree incident to Bea in our next phone-call.

"You should have put your adoptive parents' names," she says quickly.

"Do you mean that?"

"Yes, please don't tell anyone my name. Your children should never know about me. I don't want them to be ashamed of their background."

"My children will know the truth someday," I hear myself saying. "What has happened to me is their heritage too."

"Oh spare them the pain," she says.

I shift the subject to neutral ground, something about the baby squirrel my daughter found in the park and brought home. She is glad for the change of subject, moves with it. For in truth she does not want to end these occasional chats with me. I am no threat to her this way. The videophone is not yet available, so I do not see her with the various conditions she has described. Is it possible, I wonder, that all these symptoms are an excuse to retreat from life; that natural mothers punish themselves as severely as adopted people do? Is she her own Fury, one of those unpsychologically oriented handmaidens of justice who punished anyone who infringed on tribal law, regardless of the motive?

That's what it's all about, isn't it, sin and retribution? How else explain my mother's debilitated condition? Or is it just inadequacy that keeps her from fighting actively to regain her health so that she can move about independently, without leaning on her son's arm, so that she can see her daughter openly?

I wonder how many natural mothers have maimed psyches like mine has. "Hie thee to a nunnery, mother," I want to say. How happy she would be nestled in that pine and maple forest with Anshu-san, listening to the spring rain on the thatched roof, writing haiku, and burning incense each morning to the wooden statue of my father sitting smugly up there on the altar next to Kiyomori and the Buddha.

Mother, I want to say, why couldn't you have had the courage of Mary Wollstonecraft, Mary Shelley, Claire Clairmont, Eleanora Duse, Isadora Duncan, Rebecca West, Liv Ullman, Bernadette Devlin; to mention just a few—the list is longer than one realizes—the brave, clever, strong-minded, creative, talented, independent women of history who said NO to giving up the babies born of their passion.

I try to hold on to the absurdity of it all.

One day Bea tells me rather agitatedly that Oran's daughter is getting married. Do Bob and I want to come to the wedding?

"How can I come to the wedding when I can't even visit you?"

"I could say you're someone else—from California."

"And what about Howie? What would you tell him?"

"I'd think of something."

"It's impossible to disguise us." I try to imagine Bob being introduced as an insurance agent from Los Angeles.

"But I wouldn't want you and Bob to be hurt if you weren't invited."

She flounders about in her bourgeois trap of what to do with this daughter, who by nature should be a member of the wedding. I help her out of her misery.

"Bob and I will be away that weekend."

"Then you wouldn't be hurt if you weren't invited?"

"No, we wouldn't be hurt."

"Then I don't have to worry?"

"You don't have to worry."

"I probably won't go anyway. I look too terrible."

"You should go for Oran's sake."

"I'd have to get a wig. Maybe Howie can go with me."

There is a madness in our relationship. No one not adopted would believe it: it is too unnatural, this tabooed relationship between a mother and the daughter she has given away.

The time has come.

I am determined now to learn my father's name. What

am I doing in these phonecalls with Bea? They are going nowhere.

"I want to know who my father is," I say firmly one day.

"I cannot tell you."

"Look," I plead, "I'm not asking you to introduce me to Howie. He is your son and I have no claim on him. I can live without knowing my half-brother. But I have a right to know who my father is."

"It will make me ill just saying it. Do you want to make me ill?"

"I don't want to make you ill. But I want to know my father's name."

"I cannot tell you."

"Then I can never call you again. Goodbye, Bea."

I hang up.

The next morning the phone rings. It is Bea. She is breathless, choking. She can hardly speak.

"I . . . I want to tell you your father's name," she stammers, "since . . . it means so much to you."

"Yes?"

"It is . . . Bernard Mitvak."

"What?"

She repeats it.

"Spell it." I grab a pencil.

She spells it. I am writing while she speaks. It is such an unfamiliar, truncated name. I can see the immigration officials on Ellis Island impatiently struggling with the original and butchering it into this abridged version.

"Promise me you won't look him up," she says feebly. "And that you won't try to meet him."

I give some kind of evasive answer. The truth is that I don't know yet what I am going to do. I thank her and she seems relieved, as if some terrible burden has been lifted from her.

Now it is mine.

I look in the New York phonebook. There are no Mitvaks listed. Incredible in a city like this, where the whole West Side closes down on Yom Kippur. They must be the only Jewish clan not represented here.

I dial Rhode Island information. I am testing this new name in the world. I have to spell it for the operator who can't seem to hear it right.

Who could?

She finds seven Mitvak's, but none with my father's first name. I thank her and hang up.

Rhode Island must have absorbed all of that straggly group of immigrants who traveled north to that princely state to find their peddler's cart. The air must have been better there than New York's Lower East Side, living conditions less crowded.

What do I do with my father's name?

Is he dead or has he just moved away?

I feast my eyes on it, unpoetic as it is. I keep writing it over and over on a pad of paper.

I call Carol long distance to tell her the news. We've lost touch a little now that we live in separate cities.

"I'd forget it," she says wearily. "It doesn't matter anymore who he is." She has advanced arthritis and is as deeply involved in seeking relief as I am in my search.

It *is* all a bit anticlimactic after all these years. But by now I am strong enough to go on without my surrogate mother.

"Who is my father?" the Water Jar Boy
asked his mother.

"I don't know," she said.

He asked her again. "Who is my father?"
but she kept on crying and did not answer.

"Where is my father's home?" he asked.
She could not tell him.

"Tomorrow I am going to find my father."

"You cannot find your father," she said.
"I never go with any boy, so there is no place
where you can look for your father."

But the boy said, "I have a father, I know
where he is living, I am going to see him."

The mother did not want him to go, but
he wanted to go. So early next morning she
fixed a lunch for him, and he went off to the
southeast where they called the spring *waiyu
powidi*, horse mesa point. He was coming
close to that spring, he saw somebody
walking a little way from the spring. He went
up to him. It was a man.

He asked the boy, "Where are you going?"

"*I am going to see my father,*" *he said.*
"*Who is your father?*" *said the man.*
"*Well, my father is living in this spring.*"
"*You will never find your father.*"
"*Well, I want to go into the spring, he is living inside it.*"
"*Who is your father?*" *said the man again.*
"*Well, I think you are my father,*" *said the boy.*
"*How do you know I am your father?*" *said the man.*
"*Well, I know your are my father.*"
Then the man just looked at him to scare him. The boy kept saying, "*You are my father.*"
Pretty soon the man said, "*Yes, I am your father. I came out of that spring to meet you,*" *and he put his arm around the boy's neck. His father was very glad his boy had come, and he took him down inside the spring.*

—Pueblo Myth

An adoptee's past is like a mummy bound in layers of shroud, wrapped in years of secrets, mysteries, lies, deceptions, confabulations, mythology. When one has finished unraveling one layer from the corpse, one must sometimes rest for years before moving on to another section of the old fabric. The exertion is too great to permit moving forward at an uninterrupted pace.

Fourteen years had passed since I had touched the last layer of the wrappings and uncovered my mother. Now I was going to try again.

I sent a check to the office of vital statistics in Freeport asking for records. Two dollars for the birth certificate, two for the death. I did this to cover the whole life cycle, and in the process to find out if he was still alive.

The following week a letter with my check came back from the board of health stating that more money was needed—three dollars for each certificate since a search would be involved. I sent another check and waited. This time I got a mimeographed form letter with my returned check saying that they had located birth and death records which might possibly be the ones I was seeking, but that in order to be sure, would I please furnish the following information: father's mother's name; deceased's occupation; residence last known, including the street number.

If I knew all that I wouldn't have had to write them in the first place.

I replied that having grown up abroad I did not have that information, but to please send the certificates they had found anyway. I was willing to take a chance they were the right ones.

That was the end of the correspondence. I heard no further from the office.

However, in brooding over the second returned check and trying to decide whether to tear it up or file it for posterity, I noticed an inked notation at the top of it: *B. Mitvak, Bernard 1900 / D. Mitvak, Bernard 1960.*

Those must be the dates of his life, I thought. My father is dead. He's been dead all these years.

I called Bea immediately to tell her the news that Bernard Mitvak was dead. She wept as I spoke. I wept. We mourned together by phone for this man who was a stranger to us both.

Now that I was certain that Bernard Mitvak was deceased, I was in no hurry to call those other phone numbers in Rhode Island information. I decided to wait a few months until the summer when I would be nearby on Cape Cod. Inquiries about his life would seem more natural from there.

I resolved to go at this material like a detached biographer tracing the main currents of her subject's life. Perhaps he kept a diary where he put everything down, hoping someday his daughter might turn up and read it. What kind of man was this former bootlegger, this careless lover, this irresponsible father? What was the fire that burned in him? What put it out?

"The smiles of her youth shall be her mother's / The tears of her maturity shall be mine," Lord Byron had written of his illegitimate daughter, Allegra, after he was separated from her. I didn't ask that my father be a Byron, but I wanted to know what he was.

One night in late June, shortly after we have settled for the summer at the Cape, we are driving in blinding rain from my son's camp in Vermont where we have just deposited him complete with gear. The highway sign indicates the next exit is Freeport.

"Let's turn off," I hear myself saying. "I'll look in the phonebook for my father's relatives."

"Now?" Bob mutters incredulously. He is exhausted from driving through the storm and wants to get home to Wellfleet as quickly as possible.

"Now—please," I coax, afraid to let the moment pass for fear I will never have the courage again.

We drive down the main streets and park in front of a hotel. On the lower level we find the phone booths lined up along the walls like upturned coffins; I am grateful to see seats in them.

I turn the pages of the phonebook: M for Mitvak. There is that emasculated name again, with Burton, David, George, Paul, and William all claiming it. I rip the page out of the book. It is a terrible thing to do. I feel like Abbie Hoffman ripping off society: Steal This Page. I stuff it into my purse. I now own all the Mitvaks in the area, perhaps in the world. I am a vampire seeking the blood of a dead man. But it is *my* blood.

Bob has gotten into the spirit of the stopover by making a long-distance call in a corner booth. I decide to try one of my numbers. If I don't do it impulsively, this very moment, I may never do it. My heart is pounding. I don't know what I am going to say. Do people who are legitimate lead more dignified lives than this? I wonder. I hope so for their sakes.

It is like a game of roulette. I pick a number from the middle of the list at random. If I were a professional gambler I could invent a system for doing this: for choosing the Mitvak my father was close to—for finding his son, his brother.

I dial. The phone rings about ten times. Please God, don't let it answer.

It doesn't. I hang up with relief. A reprieve.

Now I jot down some notes to read from. I rehearse: "Excuse me, I'm from New York. I am looking for someone who knew Bernard Mitvak." "Why?" "I have reason to believe I am related to him."

Perfect—it neither acknowledges nor denies anything. A real screen. I am going to wing it from there.

I choose the name at the top of the list: I am going to go straight down systematically. I need order in my life.

The phone rings a few times. A teenager answers with a casual "Hullo."

"I'd like to speak with someone who knew Bernard Mitvak," I say in a low, dignified voice.

"Who?" Her voice is incredulous. I might have been asking for the Abominable Snowman.

"Could you ask your parents if they knew *a* Bernard Mitvak?" (Putting the article in front of the name is a midwesternism I am stuck with.)

"Sure, just a minute," she says. I hear her calling, "Mom, do we know Bernard Mitvak?"

I don't hear the response. "We've never heard of him," she announces, and hangs up.

I sit there trembling. This name, Bernard Mitvak, has seared holes in my mother's being all these years, tolled the death knell in her heart, and here in this small town where there are only about seven Mitvaks, for Christ's sake, no one in that house has heard of him.

I decide not to dwell on this. I quickly dial another Mitvak. No answer. Another. No answer. And so on down the list. No answer. It is past eight o'clock on a Sunday night, Small Town, U.S.A. Where do all the Mitvaks who don't know each other go on Sunday nights? Is it a conspiracy against me? Are they having a witch's coven in the local graveyard?

Still I am relieved. I wasn't quite ready to talk yet, to pour out my shame, my bastard status, so casually on the ride from Vermont to Cape Cod.

Bob comes out of his booth with the news that there are floods raging in the area near where we've just dropped Ken off. My free-floating anxiety, always available for any impending disaster, becomes fixed again. Here I am worrying about a dead man while my own living flesh and blood may be struggling for his life at this very moment in the swollen mountain waters of Vermont.

We call the camp.

"The children are not getting wet," the office girl informs us. "The floods haven't affected this region. Everyone's busy at Naming Night and cannot be disturbed."

We walk out into the Freeport streets. The elements are still raging but we need nourishment after our ordeals. We seek it in a shiny metal behemoth that sits on the corner like a creature out of science fiction. We enter its jaws half expecting it to rise up into space. It is, unbelievably, an ordinary diner.

The man behind the counter is a clown, wisecracking about dogs with or without, coffee white, black, or tan. I laugh at his jokes. He is corny, but crackling with life. Did my father ever stop here? Did he kid with him? Could he be my father not really dead? A clerical error on the check. Why hadn't I thought of that?

My father stands before me—prankster, fun-loving bootlegger emeritus, simple working-class man. I wouldn't mind at all. I'd settle for an alive man. I have pursued my father to this point, just as Orpheus pursued Eurydice, as Izanagi pursued Izanami, but I cannot go beyond here. I have not Orpheus' musical talent, Izanagi's wild abandon. I must accept that it is too late for my father and me in this life: we are separated until our next karma.

Will we recognize each other then?

Concentrate on the living, I tell myself. I wolf down my hot dog with, coffee without, and exit into the real world. I do not breathe easily again until we pass the Rhode Island limits.

Back in Wellfleet I study the page torn from the phonebook like a stock market report. I am resolved to call those numbers until one of them pays off with word of my father.

Again I start at the top of the list. From where I sit at my desk I can look out over the dunes and the sea. It is a familiar landscape, part of me; I am grateful to the Indians who loved it, preserved it, and passed it on to us unspoiled.

I hear the ringing of the number, rhythmic, like a drum with my message.

A young woman answers. She has a soft, kind voice. She tries to be helpful on hearing my request about Bernard Mitvak, "to whom I might be related."

"There was a Bernard Mitvak, an eye doctor, who is now dead," she says. "I married into the family after he died so I didn't know him. I think he had two daughters. If you want more details you should call his sister, Bernice.

She could tell you better than anyone about him. They used to double date."

"My father was an eye doctor," I rush out to tell Bob. "He could have cured Oedipus!" I feel giddy now and dial Bernice with great confidence.

A woman's voice answers the phone. It is aged, suspicious. Yes, she had a brother named Bernard, now dead, and he had two daughters, but why am I looking for him?

I aim for the bull's-eye. "I have reason to believe I am his daughter."

There is a stunned silence on the other end as if I have hit it. Then a recovery. "That is impossible," she says emphatically. "It must be the *other* Bernard Mitvak you are looking for."

"You mean there are *two?*" For a moment I feel a surge of hope that my father may be alive.

"There *were* two," she comes back quickly. "Both of them are dead now. But the one I think you're looking for died just seven months ago. It sounds like him. He lived with many women and who knows how many illegitimate children he probably had. Do you have any specific information on the Bernard you are looking for?"

"I only know one thing, that he was a bootlegger."

"That's the *other* Bernard all right," she says triumphantly. "He and his three brothers were all of them bootleggers. The one you're looking for was called "Boots." He was my first cousin and the Black Sheep of our family. I hope you don't mind my saying that."

I assured her I didn't.

"But I will say one thing," she continues. "He was a handsome man. An Adonis. He always had a beautiful woman on his arm."

"I'd like to see his picture."

"I might have one of him as a child, but I can't get at it now. Well, I'm sorry to give you such bad news about your father, but I can guarantee you it's not my brother you're looking for. My brother was at medical school during Prohibition, the only one of our generation in the family to go to college."

"Are any of Boots' brothers or sisters alive?"

"The brothers are all dead. Your father was the youngest. But there is a younger sister Alice, who has just had heart surgery and should not be disturbed. The older sister, Fanny, hated your father and probably won't talk to you."

"Is there anyone I can get more information from?"

"You could call Boots' best friend, Sammy Cohen. He had a store next to your father's dress shop and was as close to him as anyone. Sammy loves to talk and will tell you many stories. He's married to my sister."

She gave me his number. "It's too bad you just missed your father," she concludes, trying to be kind. "He was out of town on a business trip when he died."

Through all of this she seems torn between not wanting to acknowledge that she even knew the Black Sheep and wanting the glory of being the first to give out some information on him. She asks me nothing about myself, as if any woman Boots had spawned could be no better than the ones he consorted with.

I thank her and say I will call Sammy. Only a man can handle such business as Boots has left behind. It is not fit for a respectable woman.

I hang up. The sun is still shining brightly over the dunes as if nothing has happened. I know I would have liked the Black Sheep better than this proper cousin I have just talked to, but I cannot keep the tears back. I weep for myself, still the outsider, whom no one wants to take in.

I weep the tears of maturity which belong to my father.

I called Sammy the following night, after seeing O'Neill's *Moon for the Misbegotten* at the Provincetown Playhouse. It seemed a fitting title for the occasion. The moon was loitering on the horizon, as if waiting, as I dialed.

"Is Sammy Cohen there?" I asked the elderly woman who answered.

"Who?" She repeated his name suspiciously as if she had never heard of him. I was sure it was Bernice's sister and that they had been warned about my call. I shouted his name a few times into the receiver. The connection was bad on all levels.

Sammy's voice when it came on was thick with age and muffled by the accent which speaks of birth in other lands.

"Are you sure this man, not the *other* Bernard was your father?" he asked when I went into my routine again. Like Oran before him, he was proving he could not easily be duped.

"I heard he was a bootlegger," I replied. And that information, as infallible as my driver's license in the previous situation, dispelled Sammy's doubts and turned him on.

Bernice was right, he was garrulous. But this cousin by marriage, this confidant, was without doubt my father's loyal friend. He fell right into the spirit of things by referring to Boots as "your dad."

"Your dad liked life," said Sammy. "He didn't want to be tied down. You shouldn't judge him for being a bootlegger. His three older brothers were in it and called him in. He was only fifteen then, the baby. He got money too early and it spoiled him. You understand what I mean?"

I did.

"Your dad was not a drunkard or a gambler. He was no big deal, but I want you to be proud of him."

"I do not want to judge him," I said. "I just want to know his story."

"I admire you," said Sammy. "You show a human interest. I want you to know in your heart and soul you don't have to be ashamed of your dad or your background. Your dad was independent. He did what he wanted to do. He wanted to be top banana. You had a good father. A gentleman."

Sammy had all the warmth and openness of a Jewish uncle as he bumbled along. He obviously wanted to paint a little white on the Black Sheep he must have known his sister-in-law, Bernice, had tried to slaughter.

"Your dad was outgoing. He loved life. He was a good spender. He loved to entertain. He was happy-go-lucky. He had personal charm. He was an Adonis of a man. He idolized himself."

"Is that want you want to know?" he kept interrupting himself to inquire. "Ask me anything, anything, and I'll tell you."

"Just keep talking," I said, hoping that from the natural flow of his words a portrait would emerge more vivid than anything a methodical list of questions might produce. It would be an action painting, dripped and dribbled without the censorship of form.

"I will admit this," said Sammy. "Your father had the temper of a lion. When he had a tantrum, forget it. You had to get out of his way. If you understood him, it was all right. He would get over it in a few minutes and apologize. But few people would accept this. 'Cousin,' I would say, 'I understand but the others don't.'"

There was a pause, as if he was waiting for my father to give his usual response.

"Yes," I said, reminding him that I was still there.

"It's hard to talk on the phone," he said. "I'm semi-retired this summer. If you like I'll meet you halfway between the Cape and Freeport. How about Plymouth? I could meet you at Plymouth Rock."

We made an appointment for the following Monday at noon.

A novelist could have done no better than Sammy in choosing Plymouth Rock for our rendezvous. Here where

the traveler comes to seek the pilgrim father, I came to
find my bootlegging father, hoping to trap that perfidious
ghost which was probably even then busy gamboling
amorously among the famous and infamous ghosts of
history.

I must be strong, I told myself, as I drove off the
highway into the town looking for the ocean drive that
leads to Plymouth Rock. I must not become waiflike,
clinging to Sammy like a surrogate father, or weepy and
sentimental like those other women whose hearts my
father broke in the course of his promiscuous career.

Sammy Cohen was standing by the fencing around
the rock, scanning the cars going by. His thick mane of
white hair blowing in the ocean breeze around his sun-
tanned face belied his seventy-five years. He was six years
older than my father would have been. He grasped my
hands as I approached him. "I could see as you crossed
the street it was Boots' daughter," he exclaimed. "He
never told me about you, but there is no mistaking who
you are."

Arm in arm we walked the main street looking for a
seafood restaurant among the souvenir shops and quick-
order diners. The honky-tonk tone of this historic town
startled me. I had expected Plymouth to have the quiet
dignity of Mount Vernon instead of the carnival atmosphere of Coney Island. But I was getting used to surprises
by now.

Sammy had taken my arm as an uncle, but his stride
was that of a virile friend. Like my father, he was a man,
first and last. Perhaps that was what they appreciated in
each other. "I'm too old for lots of what I used to do," said
Sammy, "but I can still enjoy the fringe benefits."

Yet, Sammy, unlike my father, had stayed with one
wife for fifty years, and though he was complaining to me
now that she would not retire to Florida with him, he
wore the cloak of domestic respectability emblazoned

with sons and daughters and grandchildren. It was a garment my father never valued, although I was to learn he had once tried it on briefly for size.

As Sammy picked through the bones of his fish at the restaurant, he seemed to be sorting out the choice morsels of my father's life to present to me. Boots emerged as a cross between Jesse James and Don Juan, perhaps somewhat akin in spirit to those intrepid founding fathers who had forged their way through an unknown land whose wilderness had to be conquered and tamed.

The American-born son of Jewish immigrants from Russia, my father had had to chart his own survival course in hostile territory. It was scalp or be scalped. He got into bootlegging just after World War I through his eldest brother who had become chummy with an influential gambler who used his taxi service from the pier into town. While Minnie Marx's four boys—Groucho, Harpo, Chico, and Zeppo—were making it in vaudeville, Sophie Mitvak's four boys were making it in bootlegging.

There must have been a lot of orthodox boys making it in a lot of unorthodox ways in those days.

Sammy was an ideal narrator for he had always been an appreciative observer of the four brothers whose cousin he had become through marriage. He was always standing just outside the action, but close enough to give counsel in times of crisis—of which there seemed to be many. He was not unlike Nick Carraway commenting on Gatsby, and as he spoke of those thirteen zany years of the Prohibition era, I began to see Fitzgerald's words applying to my father too: "something gorgeous about him, some heightened sensitivity to the promises of life, a romantic readiness such as I have never found in any other person."

My father and his brothers, like so many other immigrants' sons, had seen the chance for a fast buck, but they, like Gatsby, were small fry, leaving it to the big-timers like Jack ("Legs") Diamond, Vincent ("Mad Dog") Coll, Frank ("The Enforcer") Nitte, George ("Bugs") Moran, and Charles ("King") Solomon, to amass the big fortunes and rub each other out. For the little fry, the risks weren't so great: the Volstead Act, which made it illegal to transport beverages containing more than one-half of one percent of alcohol, had no teeth. The penalty for a first offense was not over one thousand dollars or more than six months imprisonment, and less than one percent of bootleggers of any importance were ever apprehended or convicted. It must have been as much fun as cops and robbers, except they really weren't robbing anyone, just breaking an unpopular law that only the temperance people *(Ten Nights on a Barroom Floor)* held sacred. And the cops were always available for a free drink at the speakeasies.

I saw my father arranging for booze to be transported down Rum Row—the length of the eastern seaboard—in trucks filled with bales of hay to muffle the gurgling sound in the bottles; with boxes of nails to camouflage the sound of broken glass; with crates of bananas to disguise the rest of the contents. I saw those vehicles, unpainted, beaten up, so as not to arouse the suspicion of the Prohibition agents.

I also saw the old family wounds reopen as Sammy spoke. Once, when a cargo of liquor was going through Connecticut, it disappeared. My father was so angry that he put a gun to the head of the "good Bernard's" brother, threatening to blow it off if he didn't reveal its whereabouts. He found his cargo, but that branch of the family, to which Bernice belonged, never forgave him.

It also came out that the "good Bernard" had indeed been a distinguished eye doctor, but one day, at the age of fifty, he ended it all by putting a plastic bag over his head, leaving his wife and two daughters. Perhaps he had seen too much. This scholarly and sober Mitvak had been too sensitive to live, a maverick in the species.

The incidents of familial discord added up. When Prohibition ended in 1933, Boots took his younger sister's husband as a partner into the "rectifying" end of the liquor business, since as a former bootlegger he could not get a license of his own. This brother-in-law was to eventually steal the business from him.

"People took advantage of him," explained Sammy.

He was trying valiantly to defend an old friend and relative by marriage, someone whose errant behavior he had always taken for granted, but never analyzed. Now he was being called upon to indulge in an exercise in perception that most men are never asked to make: it is the role of the sociologists, the psychiatrists, the historians, the writers, not the Sammy Cohens. But Sammy, the tailor turned dry cleaner, tried to rise to the occasion, and the challenge seemed to excite him, to spur him on to taller tales and unbridled verbosity (much of it about himself) which was eventually curbed only by the waitress asking us to leave so that the restaurant could get ready for the dinner hour.

As colorful as they were, the stories Sammy told were for the most part out of sequence, and I despaired at times of ever finding my father in the clutter. I thought of Mailer confessing in *Marilyn* how he tried in vain to conjure up the movie queen he had never met with a whiff of her perfume, Chanel Number Five, while knowing that nothing can recapture the actual essence of a person once he or she is gone. I was faced with the same problem: how to sense that ineffable quality that makes you know whether you would have liked or abhorred the one you are trying to resurrect. In all of Sammy's flood of words, I could only catch glimpses of Boots in the whirling debris of his businesses and loves. Just when I thought I had caught him rising in full view to the surface, he would be submerged by some conflicting evidence and drift away from me. He was proving as elusive in death as he had been in life.

After his liquor business fiasco, my father set up a dress shop where, because of his charm, he attracted a large clientele. But when the fad of discount houses promised instant fortunes, such as bootlegging had once done, he overextended himself with a second shop and had to declare bankruptcy.

It was downhill all the way from there.

My father finally landed a job with a liquidating company which sent him up the East Coast and into Canada closing the affairs of others no more lucky than himself.

"But before your dad went broke, he went about in great style," said Sammy. "He always had white Cadillacs, and once when a parade was going down the street, I looked out of my shop to see him perched on top of a white horse with a beautiful blond call girl riding beside him. They were leading the parade."

Now came the only time Sammy seemed critical of his buddy. "'Cousin,' I said, 'not on the same street where you do business!'"

But my father obviously did not ride with the herd. I imagine, like Gatsby, "he knew women early" and became contemptuous of them, especially of young virgins because they were so ignorant.

My mother was one of those virgins.

Boots did try marriage once when he was in the liquor business: a wealthy widow with two children, who gave not only herself but her money. Perhaps he felt trapped. His temper became more violent and he began berating her in public for loose morals: sleeping with him before they were married. She left him because, as Sammy put it, "She didn't want to take his abuse." Then he was free to take up with women whose morals could not be questioned because they didn't have any. No more Madonnas, just Whores. He lived with the blond call girl for ten years and was the only one, according to Sammy, who didn't know how popular she was on the Grand Central midnight run into New York.

When he was in his fifties, my father dyed his hair and set up a household with a redhead in her twenties. "She thought he had money and fell hook, line, and sinker," explained Sammy. "He ravished women physically and they ravished him financially. Charge accounts all over town. When she found out it was a hollow thing, she left him. There were three small children, but I don't think they were his."

Sammy wasn't even sure whether or not Boots and the redhead were married. "I wasn't invited to the wedding," he admitted, "but then I wouldn't have gone because she wasn't Jewish. I didn't even know there were children until he brought them into the store one day to have their clothes cleaned and altered. He seemed very fond of them."

As Sammy talked, my father was now turning into a hustler in the Westerns, riding his horse out to adventure, and always leaving for other frontiers at the end of the episode. Still he stayed in one small community all his life, separating his business space from his private space (except for that moment on the white horse). He differed from other men in that he didn't want what they wanted: a wife, even one to be deceived, and a child to carry his name.

"In the autumn of his life your dad didn't make money," said Sammy. "There wasn't much to be had in the liquidating business."

"Was he broken or dejected during those last years?"

"No, he was always confident and as full of cheer as ever. He loved life. He always smiled."

Sammy had left the picture of my father in his car and so now we walked along the waterfront to retrieve it.

"When your father started traveling, he had a stamp made with his picture on it," Sammy was telling me. "He put it on all his mail."

Now at the car he pulled out a post card of the Royal Canadian Mounties postmarked Amherstburg, Ontario. "This is the last card I got from him before he died."

I saw the miniature features of my father on a miniature stamp beside his signature.

Like presidents, like generals, like endangered species, my father had his own private stamp. There it was, made to order in his own image.

I looked at this picture of my father, the Adonis, and as with my mother, there was no shock of recognition. I saw the round, smiling countenance of a man still trying to charm the world—a grinning guru, a rotund Lion's Club member. His neck was short and thick, making the head sit close to the broad shoulders. He looked beefy, overblown.

Sammy was waiting eagerly for some reaction.

"He looks heavier than I imagined," I said lamely.

"He'd gained some weight when this was taken," Sammy explained, almost apologetically. "But he lost it again." Sammy would always see Boots as the irresistible Don Juan; still he conceded, "He was a large man."

I looked more closely at the stamp made by the instant flash of a night-club camera. My father's sandy hair had come out black, and there was no way of knowing if the same distortion accounted for the pudginess of the face, the smallness of the eyes. His high cheekbones gave him a Tartar cast which along with his conservative suit, white shirt, and long necktie made him resemble not Gatsby so much as an affable Chinese restaurateur. But then night-club cameras are designed to take people in groups: families celebrating birthdays and anniversaries, lovers celebrating each other. For five or ten dollars they could get the instant illusion of togetherness. Such cameras are not meant to take the solitary reveler, and when they do, as with my father, they strip the mask, exposing what all the gaiety was supposed to hide: the aloneness that is always there.

The former beauty of the man, the wildness, was not in this stamp. And although Sammy had said I was the image of him, I was not there either. I wondered what could have prompted Adonis to send around this flawed representation of himself when the memories of people like Sammy were so much more flattering.

The message on the postcard lacked distinction too. Part print, part script, it read:

Hi Cousin Sammy,
Im in AMHERSTBURG, ONTARIO, CONDUCTING
A GOING OUT OF BUSINESS Sale, 5 weeks.
Will be here Until Oct 28, 1972.
If I don't get another Sale Will Come
Back To Freeport. With Kindest Personal
Regards to all.
Sincerely Cousin BOOTS   [The Stamp]

When Boots did not return after October 28, Sammy figured another sale had come up. The next thing he heard, my father had died of a heart attack in New Jersey or Pennsylvania—he couldn't remember which. And it didn't seem to matter.

Boots had not realized that he was on his last "Out of Business Sale," that he, himself, was being liquidated: going out of the business of life. His body gave up suddenly, without warning. I think that's the way he would have wanted it. Illness would not have suited him; he showed good taste in his hasty exit. He was a burden to no one. Like an old fox in the forest, he died hidden from the others. After that, the responsibility was no longer his. They could do what they liked with the shell: he was no longer in it. They could control the acquiescent body as they never had the rebellious spirit. They could drop it into the family plot where its very location among all the prosperous Mitvaks who had preceded him, Mama, Papa, brothers, would give it the myth of respectability, which only the dead carry off successfully. The passions of his life would be buried over with grass.

And the four dashing bootleggers, united at last, would try to make it again in the next world.

"Thanks Sammy," I said as I got into my car to head back to Wellfleet. "I appreciate what you've done."

He leaned over to me. "You can always call on Uncle Sammy if you want anything, more information, to talk some more. I think of you as the one treasure that Boots left on this earth."

"You're great, Sammy," I said. And I meant it.

"Your father was really a kind of outlaw," Bob said after listening to what I had heard from Sammy. He was stretched out languidly on the living-room couch and I thought I saw a spark of admiration cross his face. He saw the flash of the rebel in Boots' flamboyant make-up, his larger-than-life behavior, though he warned me not to romanticize or mythologize him.

I like that word *outlaw* for him. That's what he was— an outlaw from the constraints of society. It was so much better than saying he was impaired in his formative processes or labeling him a psychopath, which any psychiatrist might be tempted to do. And which he might have been.

I knew I could not judge that "Black Sheep." He may have grazed the negative identity of the twenties, the dark

side of innocence, and abandoned my mother, the White
Sheep, but his temperament was tethered within me. As
the Gray Sheep, I had learned to keep my volatile emotions controlled. I had been nursed by separation and
loss, weaned by adoption, shorn by the conservatism of
the Midwest, set free by education. I needed order and
continuity now as the Black Sheep had needed emotion
and freedom.

But the rebel in me unashamedly admired that outlaw,
that eccentric, that original, who was my father. By being
larger than life, he was in Anaïs Nin's terms, one of the
myth people, even though his life was ordinary, not symbolic, and had color rather than significance.

And—did they not say he was an Adonis? In that
sense, I was, after all, the daughter of a god, if only a
demigod. For the beautiful Adonis, who sprang from the
bark of a myrtle tree which his mother had been turned
into for lusting after her own father, had been adored by
Aphrodite, the goddess of love. When he was killed by a
wild boar, she quickly made a deal with Persephone, who
also loved him, to let him spend half a year with each of
them, one above ground, one below.

From my father's blood sprang the anemone; from his
seed, me—and as Bernice said—who knows how many
others. The gods do not quibble over such things.

I called Bea from the Cape the next day although I had
not spoken to her for a few months. She seemed breathless as a schoolgirl hearing news about her former love.
But she had the bitterness of Medea in her heart; and like
Medea, she had gotten her revenge. Because she had
withheld his name from me for so long, my father was
never to see this daughter whom he had produced as
capriciously as Zeus. Only the Greek dramatists would
have understood the sweetness of her revenge. In the

"autumn of his life" there would be no comfort for this man who had wronged her, no forgiveness. It was my mother's one victory in life.

"Sammy said I looked like him," I told her.

"The image," she said. "I couldn't believe it."

"But you said I was a younger version of you."

"I said so," she admitted, "but I saw him in your eyes."

She was shocked to hear that my father had been dead for only seven months, as shocked as when she had heard from me in the spring that he died thirteen years ago. But this time she didn't cry. We were both getting used to his being dead, and we laughed when I suggested that perhaps we were the only two women who had ever wept real tears for him.

She did not comment on my having looked up my father after she asked me not to. She only inquired nervously: "Did Sammy ask my name?"

"Yes, he asked."

"Did you tell him? I told you not to tell my name."

"Tell me just one thing," Sammy had said, a glint of slyness coming into his eyes—so transparent I could see his wife and Bernice behind it. "Who was your mother? I only want to know if she was Jewish, nothing more. You don't have to tell me her name."

"Yes, Sammy, she was Jewish."

He seemed relieved. His trust in me was confirmed. I was not the daughter of another one of those *shiksas*. By Jewish law, as child of a Jewish mother, I was a Jewess. Boots had not failed him after all.

"No, I didn't tell him your name."

She was satisfied. Now she asked me more details about Boots' life: she was hearing the possible sequel to her own.

"You mean he went into the dress business too? Oh, just think, we could have been in it together." And again she was lost in her fantasies of what might have been. "If only he had signed that birth certificate. How different it all might have turned out."

"But he didn't sign it," I reminded her. "It is as it is now. We have to go on from here."

But my mother wasn't going anywhere. She had given up long ago.

The ocean, in inverse ratio to the weather, begins to get warmer in late August on the Cape. Just when everything golden seems to be slipping away from us and the twilights suggest an autumn sadness, the sea begins playing with us, making us think that the summer, like the very tides, will go on forever.

It was on one of those extended days at the end of August that Fanny, Boots' older sister, called. Sammy had told her about our meeting, that he considered it her responsibility to get in touch with me.

"I waited a while before picking up this phone," she said sharply, as if angry with me for putting her in this situation. "I didn't know what to do. My husband told me to forget it, that I would be opening a can of worms."

"I'm glad you called," I told her, ignoring the implication I was a canned worm.

"What is it you want?" She was getting right down to business. No nonsense here.

"I just wanted to learn something about my father and get a few pictures of him. That's all."

"I wish you had gotten in touch with me directly, instead of going through others."

"I couldn't. I didn't know your married name."

"That's true, isn't it? Well, I may as well be honest from the start," she warned me. "I always hated Boots."

"Why?"

"He wasn't sweet like my other brothers. But I was ashamed of all of them—that they were bootleggers. I changed my last name in high school so that no one would know I was related to them. Then since I was married twice, no one knew what my maiden name had been. Just recently though, I mentioned the Mitvak name, and someone said, 'Oh, are you related to Boots?'"

"What was it about him you disliked so much?"

"Oh, I don't know. How can I describe him? He was the type if he went into a night club and didn't like the waiter's service, he would say, 'To hell with you!'"

Fanny thought that Boots might have been married legally to that young redhead. "She was a blob of flesh," she snorted. "No intelligence. But I don't believe the children were his. After his death another woman he had gone with earlier told me he had had his tubes tied long ago. And the redhead has had two more children in the years since their separation."

Then she put it bluntly: "Was your mother a Silverstein?"

I hesitated, remembering Bea's constant refrain: "Don't tell them my name." But Fanny already knew. "That's right," I said.

"I remember vaguely some talk about it," she said. "Maybe that explains why your father became the way he did. But he never spoke of it to anyone."

I told her now a little of my life, my travels, my search for who I was.

"You waited a long time," she said. "But you sound gutsy. I like that. All the Mitvaks had guts. That's one thing I'll say for them. Neither of my husbands had them, nor my daughter. But you've got them. You've got the Mitvak guts."

She told me that my father had died in Monroe, New Jersey on that last business trip. She'd sent a man from her firm down there for his things. "He said he never saw such a fleabag as the place Boots was staying."

"Did Boots leave anything that might be of interest to me?" I asked.

"He left nothing but some letters to the three children of that woman. He really liked kids. But there was no will, just an insurance policy covering his burial."

Fanny said she'd call me in a few weeks and arrange to meet me somewhere with family pictures.

She never did. She didn't have the guts. And then the summer was over.

The Mayan Indians have a saying that those who see, dream well. I had this dream:

> On the night we were to meet, my father gave a party for me. But he had invited so many guests, I could not find him in the crowd. After all, I didn't even know what he looked like. I wandered around in that maze of people, all of them drinking, laughing, having fun, but I never found my father.

I was taking notes on my thoughts, dreams, associations. I was pulsing my unconscious as the Indian shamans pulsed the blood. I wrote on odd scraps of paper while I was driving in the car, walking on the beach or city streets, lying in bed. They were to be put into bottles and floated out to sea to be waiting for me on the other shore when the voyage was finished. They were not pleas for help, rather more like the jottings of one who dabbles in magic, but does not have the gift of prophecy.

What did it all mean, these dead facts about a dead man?

Now that Fanny had told me just where my father died, something that even Sammy did not know, I wrote to the bureau of vital statistics in Rhode Island for his birth certificate and to New Jersey for the death certificate. I knew how much money to enclose by now.

The birth certificate arrived neatly typed, simple and concise. It stated that my grandfather, a peddler, age forty-three, born in Russia, had created along with his wife, age thirty-four, born in Russia, a baby named Bernard Mitvak, born in Freeport, Rhode Island. The rest was empty space, promise.

The death certificate, in contrast, was a long muddle of illegible scrawl written by a doctor who had never seen the subject alive—a stranger writing a report on a corpse.

Accuracy wasn't the issue here.

It stated that the deceased had been neither married nor divorced; that he died at the hotel where he was staying of "terminal congestion of viscera due to myocardial infarction"; that the approximate interval between onset and death was six hours; that an autopsy showed that death was not caused by accident, suicide, or homicide.

At the bottom was the name of the Rhode Island cemetery where my father was buried two days later and the signature of the doctor who wrote the report—the word *Love* in the first syllable of his last name.

I made a special folder for my father: his birth certificate, death certificate, and the post card with his personal stamp were laid to rest in my file.

6 ❦ REENTRY

We do not have to risk the adventure alone; for the heroes of all time have gone before us . . . the labyrinth is thoroughly known. We have only to follow the thread of the hero path. And where we had sought to find an abomination, we shall find a god; where we had thought to slay another, we shall slay ourselves; where we had thought to travel outward, we shall come to the center of our own existence; where we had thought to be alone, we shall be with all the world.

—Joseph Campbell

Go back to yourself. For nothing can begin from nothing, and it is from your past, and from what you are at this moment, that what you are going to be must spring.

—André Gide

Everything should have been resolved now that I had found my mother, my father, and my story. But this was not the end, for I was learning that there is no beginning and no end: one is and constantly becomes.

Campbell warns us that the journey is not really over until one has crossed the Return Threshold, and that this can prove the most difficult feat of all. I had to integrate my experience into my present life now—to connect the personal meaning with the larger one.

But how could I make a successful reentry when my adoptive mother did not even know I was away?

My adoptive mother, now in her mid-eighties, is weakening slowly from so many years of accumulated living. She has a housekeeper-companion living with her in a high-rise apartment building on a main street, supermarkets and cheap restaurant chains the only landscape. She and the other widows who have retreated there ride the automatic elevators daily to each other's apartments; up and down they go from one card game to another until they reach the inevitable last stop.

I admire this geriatric community that shrinks yearly,

231

but is continually refueled by an unflinching instinct for survival. Like straggler bees who keep faith with the hive even when most of its chambers are empty, they swarm with the sweet hum of life to which they are addicted.

On the telephone my adoptive mother is asking me, as she has for so many years, if I want the silver tea set, the silverware, the silver trays, the silver candlesticks. Her life still glistens with the silver illusion that her generation followed like the Grail. But I do not want them. Silver tarnishes: my generation goes for stainless steel. For us the Grail is not in the cup, but in the quest for it.

Yet, if I do not take the treasures she offers, I am refusing her the immortality she sought in adopting me. I must not deny her the pleasure of giving that which she has to give.

"Yes, Mother, I'll take anything you want me to have."

One day I get a phonecall from my mother's younger brother in Corinth. She has been rushed to the hospital: cancer of the colon. She does not know. It has not spread, but considering her age and general weakness, it could be fatal.

I call the room the night before the operation. She says not to come down now but to wait for a few days until she is strong enough to see me. She tells me to go on with my writing. She does not know that I am not writing for children this year, but of a child she once adopted. I am filled with guilt after the call and cannot sit at my desk. I turn to books on Zen and Taoism for comfort. It is said you can judge a Taoist priest by his laugh. I want to laugh at living and dying with the Taoists, but there is no laughter in me.

That night I have a dream that Bob and I take my mother out to dinner and she is vitally alive, fun, sympathetic—everything that I had wanted her to be and us to be to each other. She is reborn in my dream as the woman she might have been had she had a chance for the education she gave me. By bringing us together in this empathic way, I express the longing that all people have to touch a parent before it is too late.

The dream startles me because it is such a direct expression of Freud's theory of wish fulfillment.

My uncle calls the next afternoon, after the operation: it was not completed because peritonitis was discovered. My mother is in the intensive care unit and must remain in the hospital until she is strong enough for another operation. Her condition is grave—touch and go.

I fly down to the city of my youth and rent a car at the airport. I am Thomas Wolfe coming home again. It is all there, but smaller, shabbier than I remembered even though broad thoroughfares now rush people quickly out of the center of town into the suburbs, as if ashamed of that very area in which they once took pride. I have trouble knowing where to enter, where to exit.

I pass through the neighborhood where I once lived. The inhabitants are black now. Where were they when I was growing up in a white, Jewish world? I think with regret that I had no blacks as friends. Now they inhabit my former turf. Jehovah is replaced by the God of Zion. History moves on. A new minority will move into the middle class and collect the things they are supposed to covet and call it happiness.

Maybe.

I find my mother in the Jewish hospital where all Corinth Jews go to be born, to be mended, and to die. She is glad I have come. She has not spoken to anyone since that exploratory operation—has refused even a word to the doctor—but now she speaks. She asks for make-up;

she sits up. She is going to live again. Her daughter has arrived. She is resurrected. I hold her fragile hand which shakes like the quivering body of a wilted bird and know that she who raises the child is the mother. My childhood will fade with her, revive with her. As long as she lives, my image, fluctuating through various stages of development, is reflected in her eyes.

That night I stay in her apartment which is dedicated to me, the only daughter. Every wall is hung with my visage—there I am at three, at five, at twelve, graduating from high school, then college, getting married. I multiply: there are my children as babies, at three, at five. I am sleeping in a shrine to myself, thanks to this mother. I look at myself in her mirror. Traitor.

For the next few months I fly back and forth through the time machine to visit with her. She has three operations in all. Every time I get into the plane I lose all the courage, insight, and bravery I have managed to build up in the East. I shed them bit by bit as the plane flies over New Jersey, Pennsylvania, and into Kentucky where the airport is located a few miles from the Ohio River.

Do we never grow up?

My mother speeds through the intensive care unit after the last operation as if the other procedures were just a trial run for this one. She sits up immediately; she means to live. She is not going to get ripped off by Death, not when she still has her faculties left.

"Bring the children next time you visit," she says.

❧ ❧

In New York I am busy observing two cases in which adult adoptees are petitioning the courts to unseal their birth and adoption records. As things are now, a judge can unseal them only if he feels "good cause" has been shown.

Who can define "good cause"?

The law does not specify—health reasons, property rights, or possible inheritance seem to fall into that category.

Adoptees say the only good cause is the Constitutional right to have access to one's own record.

Only recently have such cases been tried, and the few that succeeded were not won on Constitutional grounds.

The attorney for both of these cases, Gertrud Mainzer, would like a verdict based on the un-Constitutionality of keeping these records closed to adoptees. The daughter of a prominent German-Jewish lawyer, she spent most of World War II in hiding in Holland, and then smuggled herself into an internment camp in time to accompany her two children to Bergen-Belsen, the concentration camp where Anne Frank died. Gertrud's presence had kept alive in her children the will to survive. Now she holds firm convictions that children and natural parents who have been separated for any reason, have a right to be reunited if they so wish. Her experience has given her a natural empathy for the plight of adult adoptees.

Gertrud asked Rollo May, whose books *The Meaning of Anxiety* and *Man's Search for Himself* she thought relevant, to give written testimony on the first case. Rollo did, stating that one's name, birth, and past before adoption are an integral part of one's personality, and that such knowledge is a necessary prerequisite for the development of the person who dares to ask questions.

Rollo, a restless searcher himself, was embarking on a book on mythology.

"People have lost their myths," he told me. "Modern man is in exile because of the lack of a mythology."

Myths helped Rollo understand the adoptee's need to probe. "Hamlet, like Oedipus, was looking for himself," he said. "Even Adam and Eve were searching for the

truth when they ate the forbidden fruit. They lost Eden,
like Oedipus lost his eyesight, but they gained knowledge
of themselves in the process."

Bob testified in person in the second case.

The woman petitioner was a forty-year-old accountant
who had learned of her situation only after her adoptive
parents had died. She had broken off her engagement for
fear of possible incest until she knew who she was, and
was asking for the agency's records as well as the court's.

It wasn't as far-fetched as it sounded—this fear of
incest. One didn't have to go back to Oedipus: as recently
as 1971 a case was reported in San Diego of a forty-one-
year-old woman being tried for unknowingly marrying the
twenty-three-year-old son she had put up for adoption as
a baby, and bearing his child. She got six months in the
county jail, and her son nine months on a county work
farm. Both were fined five hundred dollars.

But at least they got off better than Jocasta and Oedipus.

The case at which Bob testified—the Case of the
Sealed Record—dragged on for six tortuous days, the
atmosphere much like that of a prize fight: the agency and
its expert witnesses on one side of the ring; the adoptee
and her various experts on the other.

The agency was basing its defense on "confidentiality"
for that long-lost natural mother it had not been in touch
with for forty years. (As it turned out, the baby had been
abandoned, and the agency never even knew the
mother.)

Bob pointed out in his testimony that the principle of
confidentiality, like so many other principles, begins to
become absurd when it no longer serves its original purpose. And he also refuted the agency's psychiatric testimony that an adoptee's need to know is compensatory
behavior or an expression of disturbance.

"This quest is healthy and necessary," he said. "It is the way it is handled that distorts it. For identity is not any one thing but a configuration, and depends on one's sense of relationship over the generations to one's heritage— one's biological and historical roots as well as one's immediate life history. The one is insufficient without the other."

He spoke then of the need for fidelity and honesty between adoptive parents and their children. "Telling the child he or she is adopted is a step toward fidelity. It should be conveyed in an easy, natural way; gradually, much as one gives sex education."

When the lawyer asked if such openness might not threaten the institution of adoption, Bob replied that adoptive parents feel threatened now because the whole subject is built around the illusion that one can block out the heritage of the adopted person. But if parents are honest with the child they adopt, the child's identity will take firmer root, and their relationship will be improved. As it is now, he pointed out, continuing secrecy about information poisons the relationship, and builds an aura of guilt and conflict around the very natural, very healthy, and very inevitable curiosity of the child. He concluded with the admonition that society must change its attitudes to the adopted if the situation is really to be improved.

I listened to him proudly—we had come a long way from that evening twenty years before when I had told him so tensely that I was adopted. I used to say that if Freud had been adopted, everything would be different, for he would have understood that the Oedipus myth was really about an adoptee's search; now I decided that if Freud had married an adoptee, it would have been just as good.

Unfortunately, the adoptive mother brought in as a witness by the agency did not hear Bob's testimony. It probably would not have reached her anyway, for her mind was set in its own clichés. She spoke self-righteously of the necessity of sparing *all* adopted children, including the three of her own, from the truth of their origins: the implication being that all adopted come out of the gutter. She was doing them a favor by withholding their history.

Those adult adoptees who were present that day could only look at each other in outrage as she spoke smugly of the virtue of her cause versus ours. We wanted to cry out to her: "Don't you recognize us? We are your children, now grown. We are the babies you dreamed of, for whom you underwent humiliating home studies with social workers who pried into your private habits and your sex life. We are the fulfillment of your barren womb. Our cause is the same."

But she did not recognize us. She walked by in stony silence at the end of the session. We were the enemy. And we knew that she and the large adoptive parents' organization which she represented would fight us to the bitter end.

In both cases the adult adoptees were granted access to their court records, but on grounds of emotional need rather than Constitutional right. And each adoptee had to go through time-consuming and financially draining procedures, as well as a humiliating experience. Once again each was reduced to a child standing before Big Daddy, the judge, "Please Daddy, give me my name. Tell me who I am. Break the seal. Let me go free."

There was talk in adoptee circles of raising enough money for a federal case: a class action, in which we would demand our civil right. (I was once reprimanded in a letter by a social worker for saying civil *rights*, when, as she pointed out, it was only *one* right we were being denied.)

The more we spoke and corresponded about that possible future trial which, if won, could influence all the state legislatures on our behalf, the more our hopes soared, until it seemed the very power of our convictions would make us succeed. Our illusions were becoming like those of the anti–Vietnam War protesters who had thought their moral fervor would raise the consciousness of the Pentagon. Only when our meetings, like those rallies, ended, did we realize that nothing had changed: the records were still sealed.

Meanwhile, adoptees throughout the country were pursuing their illegal searches for who they were. Master criminals, they probed all possibilities: forging names, lying on telephones, impersonating relatives. All of this to get the names that were their birthright. I felt like a veteran as I listened to their stories of false leads, frustrations, sudden breakthroughs, and then the carefully plotted plans for contact that would preserve the mother's privacy.

However, now that reunions were becoming more common, many adoptees were facing, as I did, the problem of what to do with the relationship with natural parents once it has been initiated. Here I, too, was a neophyte. For the natural mother, the one taken by surprise, usually needs time to work out her guilts and ambivalences toward this returned child, and the adoptee needs time to work out those toward her, as well as toward the adoptive parents who may or may not know.

But how long should this period of adjustment go on? The natural mother is now given varying lengths of time, depending on her state's law, to change her mind after parting with the child: how many days should she and her adult/child be given to stay reunited or to part once again?

Of course, every case was different. In some instances, natural mothers have been overjoyed to hear from their grown children. I have heard of situations where adoptees have pulled up stakes and gone to live in the same cities as their newly found mothers, where each has filled an emptiness in the other's life.

But there were other mothers, like mine, who were still in hiding. Like the Japanese stragglers from World War II who hid out in the Pacific jungles for years after peace had been declared, these mothers were habituated to the dark interior world into which they had retreated. No armistice could lure them out.

I knew, after all these years during which I had seen Bea only twice, that in spite of our innumerable phone-calls she and I were just dangling on opposite ends of an exposed telephone wire—one wrong move and perhaps one of us would be seriously hurt.

I had not called her for many months during my adoptive mother's illness, and the thought kept occurring to me that it might be best to end these inconclusive calls altogether. The relationship wasn't going anywhere: there was no precedent for it. It was still taboo.

But how did one disconnect?

As if to answer my own question, I called Bea late one winter afternoon. A man's voice came over the wire.

"Hello," it said. It was warm and enthusiastic, as if it were welcoming contact with the outside world.

I was silent.

"Hello! Hello!"

For a moment I was tempted to say: "Hello, Howie, this is your sister." To blow everything.

Instead I put the receiver down, just like the heavy breather. It was all so tawdry. Again I was the dirty secret, the bastard, the polluter who would put a plague on my mother's house if I were discovered. The resentment I thought I didn't feel toward her now overwhelmed me.

Did she think, like Jocasta, that once she had put her baby out on the mountain she was truly rid of it? That it wouldn't return to fulfill the prophecy of her sin: reveal her as a fallen woman? Did all natural parents really think that signing the release form is the equivalent of making the baby magically disappear: now it's here, now it's gone?

How dare she!

How dare she what?

How dare she not be my strong, beautiful, fantasy mother!

How dare she put her son above me, protect him at my expense!

How dare she protect herself!

One part of me wanted to tiptoe away again, and forget her and all the sordid past. Another part wanted to confront her and meet my brother.

But what if she was right, that the knowledge of his mother's secret would overwhelm my brother? What if he felt betrayed and abandoned her? Would I then take care of her? Would I go every weekend to the supermarket with her, push her cart, support her arm so she did not fall? Would I be there every night to eat with her, pay her bills, bring in her mail and papers?

Am I worth the trade-off: her long-lost daughter for her familiar, homegrown son?

I know the risk is too great for her. He fits her needs. He is the size of her life, while I fit only on a television screen.

I know all this, and still I have the need to push the relationship with Bea to its ultimate conclusion, to test if the ties of blood are not thicker than the binds of convention.

I was calling, then, for what might be the last time.

I dial the number.

"How are you?" I hear her voice in response to mine. It is eager, as if she'd been waiting by the phone. "Tell me what you've been doing. Is everyone in good health?"

"I called last night."

"I thought that must have been you."

"But what did Howie think?"

"Oh, he said it was the wrong number. He didn't think anything of it."

"I thought something of it," I said. "I felt uncomfortable when he hung up, like I was doing something illicit."

"Don't feel that way," she reassured me. "He didn't hang up on you. He thought it was the wrong number."

"I know he didn't hang up on me deliberately," I persisted. "In fact, I hung up on him. And I didn't like hanging up on my brother."

There was a silence. We had reached the border that lay between us, arriving there quite deliberately on my part, but unsuspectingly on hers. She sensed danger rightly. I could feel her tightening up like a wild animal when it hears a new sound in the night.

"Is it natural to keep from Howie that he has a sister?" I asked.

"It is natural for me," she said simply.

"Look at it this way," I said. "If family members have been separated most of their lives by some kind of disaster, war or incarceration in a prison camp, wouldn't they want to be reunited later if they could?"

"That is different."

"How is it different?" I prodded. "Ours has been a kind of natural disaster. The people in our story are still related to each other."

"When something is locked inside you for a hundred years," she said, her voice breaking, "it isn't easy—"

"But one can grow over the years," I suggested.

"My mind can grow in any direction, but not in this— it is locked."

"Is it shame? Are you ashamed of me?"

"Oh, no, I've told you, I think you are a wonderful, talented, intelligent woman. Your brother has not developed the way you have. He is not worldly like you. He would not understand."

"Then you are saying, in other words, that this is so terrible he could not understand?"

"No, oh, I'm so mixed up. I can't think." There is a pause. "He would think it very peculiar that I hadn't told him before."

"Then you are saying it is because of him, the fear of him knowing and thinking of you as a fallen woman."

"No, he wouldn't think that. You must think I'm terrible, don't you?"

"I pity you," I said. "I think you are ashamed, or else you are a limited, frightened woman."

"You are right. . . . That's what I am . . . limited . . . frightened. . . ."

"What are you frightened of?"

"Everything."

My heart ached for her. I was beginning to realize that she could give no more than this. And I wasn't sure I wanted more. I didn't know what I wanted—except the truth of our relationship. I kept thinking of that strong, defiant young woman who had held on to me those first two years. It was that period that bound me to her now, that made me test like this before giving up.

"Do you remember what that analyst told you in Boston?" she asked, recovering herself a little. She was on the offensive now. "Why do you think she told you not to search?"

"Because she was a *stupid* woman," I replied hotly, losing control of the situation as well as of myself.

"How could she be stupid when she is such a learned, famous woman?"

"In any profession people have differing opinions," I replied, trying to regain my cool. "I suppose she thought she was protecting me, since the assumption is that natural mothers are all loose women." And I added, "Many psychiatrists, including Bob, would not agree with her."

"Yes, I suppose you're right," she said. She had liked Bob, respected him. I hadn't meant to bring him into this, but I needed all my weaponry for the assault on her closed fortifications.

"But the main thing is," I continued, "most people haven't thought about the problem of the adopted adult. Social workers forget about the baby once they've turned it over to some family. There's very little psychiatric literature on what happens to that child after it's grown. You and I are making the data now. We are writing a new page of the adoption story even while we talk."

"This should not be written at all," she said tensely. Her voice was desperate. "This is private. Not something for the public to know."

"It is not private to me. It is part of the story of my life."

"It will hurt your children. They should not know."

"They will know," I countered fiercely. "I will tell my children I am adopted and about everything that has happened between us. It is their history too."

"I don't agree," she said lamely.

"In the adoption story, written or unwritten," I persisted, "do you think the records should be open for adoptees to look up their natural parents? You should know better than that analyst in Cambridge or the adoption agencies which never check with the natural mothers. You are the expert, the specialist, not them."

"Yes, the records should be open," she said emphatically. "People should be able to know if they want to."

"And then what?" I continued. "What do natural mothers and their grown children do when they are reunited? Do they just meet and exchange experiences over tea, or do they go on and have a relationship?"

"They could do what we're doing."

"You think this is the ideal way?" I challenged. "You're having it both ways now. You're sitting in your bomb shelter with your secrets while I have to sneak around surreptitiously like this."

"The way I behave is natural."

"Do you think it's natural to be afraid to see your own daughter?"

"Well then I change my answer. People who are happy with their adoptive parents shouldn't look up their natural parents. Just those who were unhappy—like you."

"You're confusing happiness and unhappiness in the adopted child," I reprimanded her. "I wasn't unhappy in the way you mean. My adoptive parents were good, kind people, they did everything they could for me. I was happy with them in that sense. But all adoptees, whether they're on the same wavelength with their adoptive parents or not, suffer when they don't know the facts about their origins. They feel they cannot be complete human beings."

"The others don't want to know," she said. "You are different. You are special. You are more intelligent and sensitive and that's why you've done this."

"Then it's the duty of the more sensitive to clear the path for the others to follow," I replied. "To make their way less painful. Everyone should know their own story, and I believe that someday society will understand this and unseal the records."

"It sounds so simple when you say it," she conceded. "And my mind knows that what you say is true. But the human heart is more complicated. I don't understand why I must behave like this. But I must."

"Perhaps it means that natural mothers no longer have room in their lives for those children they were separated from."

"Oh, don't say that," she cried. "I thought only of you all these years. And that's why I am the way I am now. But perhaps other mothers have more common sense than I do. Don't forget I *could* not come to you when you first called—I had just had the eye operation. I was happy to hear from you, but I felt something strange—I can't put it into words. I was shocked—I couldn't stand the thought of your being hurt."

"Do you think people must be hurt in this kind of situation?"

"Every case is different, I suppose."

"Do you feel that what we're doing now is the right thing—these clandestine phonecalls?"

"If you have some kind of satisfaction out of it," she said.

"I could forego that kind of satisfaction," I said brutally.

"Oh, I didn't mean it the way it sounded," she picked up quickly. "What satisfaction could you get out of talking to someone as limited and uninteresting as me? I meant that just to hear from you that you are happy gives me such a wonderful feeling."

I wasn't placated. I brought out the big guns. "Why do you feel so safe keeping this from Howie now since he could find out about it someday?"

"You mean after I'm . . . gone?"

"Yes."

She was clearly flushed out. "How would he find out?" Pause. "Only from you." I was the enemy again.

"Or your brother and sister-in-law."

"They wouldn't tell. Only you would be the one." She stopped. "And you wouldn't." It was half declaration, half question.

"Why not?" I chased her down the field. "What difference would it make? You wouldn't care about a secret then."

"I would care."

"But one doesn't have feelings after one is gone." I wasn't as sure of this as I sounded.

"I don't know what I believe. There might be something afterwards."

"You mean we must carry this secret through eternity?"

"Oh, I don't know what there is after life. I just don't want him to ever know—ever."

I stopped. I had forced her into treacherous terrain. She might drop from sheer exhaustion. I let her withdraw back into her safe retreat. I knew I would never betray her in life or in death.

"Don't worry," I said, trying to sound jaunty. "I won't tell him."

Now she asked about the children. Even that subject seemed safer than the one we had left. How was Jumblie, our large silver poodle, and the squirrel? We went through the menagerie—the birds, the iguana, the gerbils. It didn't matter what we talked about, we both knew it was goodbye.

"I can't phone anymore," I said. "But I hope you'll be feeling better soon. Take care of yourself."

"I thank you so much for calling," she said rather shyly. And she added softly, "Please think of me now and then."

I put the receiver down gently. I felt relieved, sure of the integrity of my action. Just as one must have the courage to find one's natural parents, one must have the courage to say goodbye, if necessary. To let go.

I could see Bea now as a Japanese woman, the spirit of renunciation deep in her soul: there is an acceptance of what cannot be remedied or cured. ("We must suffer the insufferable; endure the unendurable.") Like Anshu-san, she had the formal sorrow of one who has given up worldly joy. She might speak to me on the telephone in private, but she had separated from me in this life as surely as if she had entered a nunnery and taken the vows.

And I was saying NO to this. No, I will not agree to your terms.

I could console myself that I saw the limitations of the situation with clarity. I was not as devastated that my mother could not acknowledge me openly as I had been after our two meetings years before. I could concede that we had reached a place in our relationship with no room to maneuver, that we must give each other up. Like T. S. Eliot I could accept that the dead tree gives no shelter, the dry stone no sound of water.

I could even agree with a friend who told me "Blood is nonsense. Don't make the mistake of overestimating it."

After all, I was the one who was always telling others that we do not belong to one another in this life by legality or blood, but rather by a bond of the heart, by mutual caring and compassion, by "elective affinities," by a spiritual tie that was formed somewhere out in the stars in a time we no longer remember.

Yes, I could console myself in innumerable ways, but it was just that: a consolation prize.

I felt a maternal surge of anxiety for adoptees who were just beginning their search. What if those much younger, less settled than myself, were turned away by the natural parents they so ardently sought? The mature part of me could forgive Bea's rejection, or what seemed like a rejection (is there a word for such turning away?), but it might destroy a more vulnerable person who came upon an ambivalent relationship without the necessary psychic underpinnings.

Could we veterans help the others understand that all adoptees have an unconscious fantasy when they are searching that they are following a path that leads to *home*; but that when they get to that destination there is no gingerbread house with Mommy and Daddy waiting inside with presents under the family tree. There never was. There was just a moment in a void when two physical bodies met like meteors colliding in the night. There was no meaning in their contact. The meaning is in the life that survives the crash: what the survivor makes of it.

The poet Muriel Rukeyser says it so well:

> . . . . I cannot fully
> have language with my mother, not as a
>   daughter
> and mother through all the mazes and
>   silences
> of all turnings. . . .

That night I discussed my phonecall to Bea with Bob—the frustration, the breaking off.

"It's a primal situation," he said. "People take stands and build their lives around them. If one party wants to alter that stand, the other might not be ready to make the shift."

"But shouldn't a natural mother be ready?" I asked. I understood so much, and yet a part of me, the waif, still could not comprehend.

"No."

"Why?"

Bob was thinking it all out for the first time too, although many of his concepts about how people react to holocaust and historical change seemed to fit the condition of the adopted.

"Because nature is not determinative," he said slowly. "What a mother feels for her child is a biological tie, but feelings around that tie are open to influence. In cases like this when separation is necessary, it is too painful to hold on. One continues with life and builds an alternative set of ties that replace the former one."

"Like getting married and having other children."

"Right. Then when the adopted child, now the adult, encounters the mother decades later, the biological tie is divested of some of nature's components. The memory of what happened when the child was born is there in the mother, but it hasn't grown or deepened. The meeting must open the original wounds. The mother awakens with great ambivalence. She fears she may reexperience the original pain in reestablishing the old bond."

"That's it," I said. "She can't bear to suffer again." And then I added, "But why does there have to be so much pain?"

In my mind that old refrain that had haunted me as a child continued its adult course—*the pity of it, the pity of it.*

A few days later Ken comes to me with another homework assignment. "Mom, I have to write a biography of
someone in the family. Dad isn't here so it has to be you."

"I don't give away my biography," I say lightly. "Try
your sister."

"Her! Come on, Mom. Please!"

"Oh, all right."

He runs and grabs a piece of paper and a pen from his
room. He pulls up a chair and settles down at the other
end of the desk. The pen doesn't work.

"Do you have a pen?"

I offer him a felt-tip marker. It is too thick. In despera-
tion he finds a pencil in the hall. It has to be sharpened.
Finally he is seated, ready to write.

"Where were you born?" he asks.

There it is again, that question that has plagued me all
my life on applications for schools, jobs, grants, licenses.
For the first time I am going to give the correct answer.

"Staten Island, New York."

My twelve year old looks up. Fuzzy on some things, he
can be sharp as a tack on matters like this.

"Staten Island! I thought you were born in Corinth!"

251

"No, my parents took me there at the age of two." I know the time has come dangerously close to telling my son the truth. Still I might manage to get away with this.

He writes conscientiously: *Staten Island*. Then he says, "What did you do your first two or three years?"

"You don't need that kind of detail," I object. In *his* first two years, he had lived in Tokyo, Kyoto, Hiroshima, and New Haven, but I'm not going to tell him where I spent mine.

"I do need it."

I look at him closely. No, this is not a deliberate trap—probably nothing more than the suggestion of some teacher taking an advanced degree in child psychology.

"It's on my questionnaire sheet."

"I'm writing a book on that," I say playfully. "Wait and read it. It's got all my secrets."

"I want to hear your secrets."

Until now the only interest Ken has ever had in my secrets was what I kept in the Secret Closet in my study where I hid presents during the year. Secrets between us had been fun and fanciful. When he was five, I had even written a book, *The Secret Seller*, about a little boy named Ken who was desperately in need of a secret to match those of his friends.

"You don't want to hear them," I tease, perched on the edge of my revelation.

"I do."

"Are you sure?"

Again I look at him closely. His round, beaming face so trusting, his bobbing head so energetic. I am tired of keeping secrets from him. Didn't I tell Bea just that? I am about to dispel them completely from my life.

"All right, I'll tell you," I say. "I spent the first few years of my life in a home for children. I was adopted from there by Nana."

His eyes grow wide with amazement. "You were an *orphan?*"

"Well, I don't know if I'd put it that way, but I was adopted."

"You mean Nana's not my real grandmother?"

"She is not by blood, but by personal ties."

"What happened to your real parents?"

"They . . . couldn't keep me."

"Have you seen them?" He is not even pretending to write. My story has become his.

"My father is dead. I saw my mother twice years ago. I talk to her on the phone though. Remember that time a few months ago when you came into my study and I let you say hello to someone you didn't know?"

"You mean that nice lady I talked to? I thought she was your friend."

"She is. But she is also my natural mother. I didn't tell you then because I've always wanted you and Karen to think of Nana as your real grandmother. It would hurt her to know you felt differently."

He turned away. "Oh, I knew something terrible was going to happen!"

As a young child he had had nightmares, expected the worst. Was it living in Hiroshima, marching with us in antiwar parades, learning about Anne Frank and six million Jews, that made him so fearful of impending disaster? Was it watching replays of his president, John F. Kennedy, shot on television, and then Bobby Kennedy, and Martin Luther King, Jr.? Only while watching sports was he truly relaxed, and then during the Olympics brought by satellite from Germany, he saw the armed Black September group scale the Israeli compound. Nothing was sacred; no place was safe. From the age of seven he was either brooding about being drafted to fight in Vietnam or being annihilated in a nuclear war. "I don't think I'll be able to live a full life," he'd say every once in a while. What was the world doing to my son's generation? He wasn't even in his teens yet. What was I doing now?

"What do you mean—something terrible?"

"Something is going from the box in the back of my brain saying that Nana is not my grandmother."

"She is your grandmother—but not by blood. By blood you are Russian on both sides."

"I'm a Russian? I have Russian blood!" This excites him. I know he is seeing a cosmonaut on TV as he speaks. He is, besides other things, a news freak.

"You're not really Russian—you're a Jew whose ancestors lived in a village in Russia."

"Can we tell Karen?"

"Not just yet. Karen's still not old enough. I want to wait—until Nana passes away. Karen might blurt it out somehow. Nana always wanted it to be a secret. She wanted people to think I was her real child."

"You were an *orphan!*" He savors the word.

Does he associate it with Little Orphan Annie, that tousel-haired moppet who still wanders about from one comic-strip home to another with her large shaggy dog, Sandy, always winning through no matter what the odds? Or with the James Whitcomb Riley poem: "Little Orphant Annie's come to our house to stay / An' wash the cups an' saucers up, an' brush the crumbs away . . ." He used to be afraid of the ending: "An' the Gobble-uns'll get you / Ef you / Don't / Watch / Out!"

I wonder what the word *orphan* really means to him.

"I didn't think of myself as an orphan when I was growing up," I say. "I had adoptive parents and that made me feel I belonged. It was much later that I learned why my natural parents couldn't keep me."

"Why?"

This is it. I face it straight on. "They were not married."

Again the eyes fairly pop out of the head. "You mean you were a *bastard?*"

We both burst into laughter, struck by the melodramatic absurdity of it all. Ken has always had a ready sense of humor.

"I wouldn't put it that way," I say, wondering which way I'm going to put it. "I was illegitimate."

We explode into laughter again. I'm grateful for that humor now.

There is a pause. "I always thought you'd tell me someday *I* was adopted," he confesses. "That I was an orphan."

"All children have the fantasy that their parents aren't really theirs and they're adopted."

"You sure I'm not?"

"I'm positive. One of us is enough."

We giggle this time. He rises to go.

"Wait a minute," I say, evolving from orphan into the old taskmaster. "We have to finish this. We've only covered the first few years of my life and you've all the rest to go."

He sits down again.

"Why don't you leave out what we've been talking about," I suggest, "and just start with elementary school? My life is pretty ordinary from then on."

But he doesn't want to go on. He needs time to dwell on this. "Just think, I have no grandmother."

"You still have Nana," I repeat. "She's still my mother. The one who raises you is the one you think of as your mother because you've shared everything with her."

I try to make it more concrete, something he can grasp.

"If we had adopted a baby—say a girl—I'd think of that child as my own, as your real sister. But we'd tell her she had other natural parents. And someday we'd help her find out what she could about them. But that child would still belong in our family."

What am I saying? I ask myself. I am making it all sound so uncomplicated.

Still Ken looks so vulnerable sitting there. I have given him something new in his life, but I have also taken something familiar away. I want to reach out and hold him like when he was a baby. He is struggling to grow, and suffering as only children can, without the defenses adults learn to use. I want to tell him that we develop by bits and pieces, patching and reworking, throwing away and adding new parts. We glue ourselves together like a collage that is always changing, and yet always the same, hoping that each stage of our creation will be strong enough to survive the strains of each addition, pure enough to reflect the beauty of our vision.

I know that each generation must create its own collage. I can give my son and daughter some of the pieces, but not the design. That they must come to by themselves.

As if Ken senses the limitations of my power, he breaks off our session abruptly to call a friend. I hear him heatedly discussing the trade-off value of a certain stamp. He does not show me the report that he takes to school.

Ken has a hard time keeping secrets—especially from his sister—and every once in a while when the subject would veer close to children and parents or Vietnam orphans, I could see him bursting with the need to let Karen know he knew something she didn't. I felt guilty toward her, for I didn't want her to resent me someday for telling Ken something so important before I had told her.

A few weeks later the situation resolved itself. We all went to a fair at F A O Schwarz to raise money for the Holt Adoption Agency, which, after years of bringing orphans out of Korea, had been licensed to arrange adoptions from Vietnam. In the past when I pointed out Amerasian toddlers on the street with their American adoptive mothers, Karen would say she wanted to adopt one. She was always after me to have another baby, somehow.

"I will take care of her," she would say.

"You have a squirrel," I would reply, reminding her of

the mischievous creature who had taken up residence in her bathroom.

"That's not the same. She (this baby was always a girl) can sleep in my room and walk to school with me."

Now F A O Schwarz was filled with these children of Karen's fantasy, as well as with clowns, tumblers, puppets, and magicians. Round and round the Amerasian children went with the rhythm of the music, with the swings, with the slides, with the joy of the moment. Karen watched them gravely, the way she regarded everything, even this joy which she saw as something deeper, something foreign—which it was. Round and round she would have liked to go too, but this was something more than ordinary play.

And then she forgot, as children do, and became a child herself, going round and round with them; my Karen and those children merging and becoming a laughing jumble of mirth, closed off from reality as F A O Schwarz, itself, was closed off from the public that day.

Watching those little Vietnamese and Korean boys and girls, some of them dressed in their native costumes as if they had stepped right out of the doll department on the first floor, I couldn't help but remember the emaciated orphans I had seen in the shelters and orphanages of their mother countries: some sitting lost in apathy if they had already given up, others holding out their arms to be held if they still clung to life. Ninety percent of the abandoned Vietnamese babies died before they reached one year; a large percentage did not live to the age of five. Many of those who survived suffered malnutrition so pernicious that it couldn't help but affect their development.

I knew that in spite of these dire statistics, many Vietnamese felt it a matter of national pride that these children should not be cut off from their heritage by adoption in other lands; but I felt that for many of the orphans—especially the mixed bloods—it was their only chance.

I struggled with this belief when the first controversial airlift of two thousand children came the following spring. I knew that the reason for their finally being allowed out was in part a political ploy to dramatize South Vietnam's desperate plight; I knew there was something grotesque about the very nation that had helped orphan these children now claiming to be their savior, while filling its own need for adoptable children; I knew America might have been aiding the millions of displaced and desperate children left behind as refugees with the money it cost to take these few out.

And yet there was still the human dimension. I also knew that many of the airlifted youngsters, especially the babies, would not have survived this long in their homeland had not American adoption groups been providing special shelters for them in Saigon over the past few years while waiting for their papers to be processed. Their destiny had been determined in a way then. And now at least they had a chance for nourishment and medical care, as well as some kind of parental love.

Still I wished that the conditions of the airlift could have been different—that the children could have been brought out under a foster plan rather than for adoption; that we could have helped care for them temporarily until the political crisis in their country was over, and then tried to sort out the real orphans from those who had some family members with whom they might be reunited.

As it was, the American style of adoption, which denies the past, was sealing their records for them even more irrevocably than it had sealed mine.

Watching the Korean and Vietnamese toddlers that day at F A O Schwarz, I wondered if their journey through the labyrinth would be like mine. Because they were a different race, at least it could not be kept a secret that they were adopted. But would they feel they had to be grateful to these well-meaning people to whom they were now clinging? Would they be able to belong, become part of our melting pot, or would they grow up feeling alienated and alone? Would some part of them resent these adoptive parents who had so unthinkingly buried their cultural identity under American names?

I remember that dinner party in New York for Madame Sawada a few weeks before. I had asked what became of the children she had raised.

"The Colonel's daughter, what is she doing?"

"The Colonel's daughter?" She had to think. There had been a few colonels' daughters. "The one I think you mean is a nurse."

"And Tōjō?"

"He is managing a night club."

Many of the children were married now and came to visit her with their own children. Some had become entertainers, some ordinary workmen, and a few were in jail for petty crimes. I knew from magazine reports that in general the mixed-blood children had trouble making their way in that closed society which stresses family ties. There was one notorious rape-murder by a half-black teenager just a few years before. "I hate my hair and skin!" he had screamed at police.

"He never had a chance," said Madame Sawada. Perhaps the mixed-blood children from her orphanage fared best. She put them through the high school she had built on her own grounds and often helped them get jobs. She even arranged the migration of some of them to coffee plantations in the Amazon until Brazil refused to give any more visas to such immigrants.

"What of the children who were adopted in America?"
I asked her. "Have any of them ever come back asking for
more information about their natural parents?"

"Three of them did. They wanted to know who their
mothers were."

"And what did you tell them?"

"I told them to leave their mothers alone. That even if
I knew where they were, I would not tell them. I
explained that their mothers probably had Japanese husbands and other children now, and that their appearance
on the scene could only disrupt their lives."

Round and round my thoughts had gone as we sat
there, two polite guests at a buffet dinner, balancing our
plates on our knees, far from that fairy ring.

"One of the boys had a father who was killed in
Korea," she said. "He was on his way to fight in Vietnam.
I heard recently that he was killed there."

He had died without knowing who he was.

I did not tell Madame Sawada how I felt on this
subject: that those former orphans of hers had a right to
whatever information she had. Who could say that they
would have destroyed their mothers' lives if they had
barged in on them, or even walked in softly, leaving their
shoes at the door.

Perhaps their mothers would have been relieved to see
them—perhaps not. That wasn't the issue. What mattered was that Amerasian, Eurasian, American, or Euro-
pean, one has the right to know one's origins.

I knew I would tell her—some day. I had to tell the
people of my own culture first.

That night of the F A O Schwarz fair, Karen was very
tired. As I was turning off her light, she said, "Am I
adopted?"

It came from nowhere. "No, why do you ask?"

"I always wonder. You're always talking about adoption."

Bob was in the doorway and we looked at each other. I heard myself saying: "You aren't, Karen, but I am."

She raised herself up on one elbow, startled. "Really?"

Bob said: "Yes, Mommy was adopted."

"Then Nana isn't your real mother?"

"She's my adopted mother. She raised me."

Karen was sitting all the way up now. "Did you know who your real mother was?"

Karen's nature is serious, reserved, but muffled within it is a wild sense of fantasy, along with an artist's intuitive need for concrete details. She is always asking me what I felt when I was her age, always aware of the response in the person with her.

"No, I didn't know."

"Didn't you wonder?"

"Yes."

"I would wonder."

"Well, when you're adopted you're not told who your real mother is, and you're not supposed to wonder."

"Then you shouldn't be told you're adopted!" she exclaimed.

"You mean you shouldn't know?"

"They shouldn't tell you until you're . . . fourteen." She said this rapidly, fiercely. She had the gift of seeing situations in their totality. Now she was feeling into the adopted person's skin.

"Why so late?" I asked.

She lay back on her pillow and considered before making her pronouncement. "Because you would wonder who your real mother was and feel sorry for her. You would wonder what she looked like."

"One wonders at fourteen too," I said.

"Did you meet her?"

"After I was grown up."

"Do you have a picture of her?"

"Somewhere in my files."

"Did you meet your father?"

"I spent last summer while you were in camp looking for him. But he died seven months before I could meet him."

"Why didn't you tell me you were adopted?"

"I wanted to wait until Nana was no longer alive."

"I think it's sad."

"What's sad?"

"That you found your father too late, and couldn't know either of them."

"In adoption you're not allowed to know. It must be kept a secret."

"I think you should be able to visit them when you're little."

"You do? Think how complicated that would be."

She thought about this. "You should be able to visit them—but not sleep over."

We all laughed at this. Karen was forever after me to sleep over at friends' houses, even on school nights. But her certainty about when one should know and what one should be allowed to do was already dissolving. She was being caught like the rest of us in the complications of the adoption web.

A little later in the evening she called me from the living room. She was lying there as I had left her in the dark, clutching her frayed pink security blanket which she had since birth, and the small brown Pooh bear that we had bought her in London when she was one.

"When you found your mother did you have to tell her who you were?"

"Yes, why do you ask?" I thought of Oran asking me for proof.

"Because otherwise someone else could be pretending to be you." Her grasp of the psychological dynamics at play here amazed me.

"Why would someone want to do that?"

"Someone mean—like you know, at Halloween people put razor blades in apples and candy to hurt children."

"Good night, Karen." I kissed her gently.

A few moments later she called me into her room again.

"Yes."

"You mentioned about an adopted baby who was not given to her real mother. And the real mother wanted her."

"That's right, Baby Lenore." I tell her again about the famous case that had been in the headlines for months. The New York court had ruled that the child, then two, should be returned to the natural mother who had been trying to get her back before the adoption papers were signed. But the adoptive parents, the DiMartinos, had fled the state and settled in Florida with her and their other adopted child, where they were out of New York's jurisdiction.

"That was mean," Karen said. "The real mother should have her. She belongs to the mother who gave birth to her."

I had always felt that when Baby Lenore grew up and learned how her real mother had changed her mind immediately on giving her over to the adoption agency, that she would never forgive her adoptive parents. But still I said, "The adoptive parents felt that she was theirs too. If we adopted a Vietnamese baby like you want us to, and she was my and Daddy's daughter, and your and Ken's sister, and a little later her mother came and wanted her back, we'd be very sad."

"That's hard."

Whose side am I on anyway? I thought, as I heard myself actually saying a word in defense on the Di-Martinos. I had been infuriated by their defiance of the court ruling, their lack of regard for the future of this child they supposedly loved, their callousness in not letting her grow up with her own mother. They could have taken another baby, I had declared at the time: true love is the ability to think into the needs of the other, even if it means giving up that person.

I still believed that, but again it came to me that the way the adoption triangle is set up now, everyone in it is victimized. The whole system had to be reclarified, modified, if any of the participants were to feel the inherent richness of its possibilities. Right now everyone at one time or another was dehumanized, limited, cheated, guilty.

I thought Karen was asleep when I heard her voice again.

"Do you still see your real mother?"

"I used to talk to her on the telephone. But not now."

"Why?"

"It's difficult. She has a son . . . my half-brother . . . and she won't tell him about me."

"You could say you were someone else."

"Then there'd be more secrets. I don't want any more secrets."

"But you were keeping secrets from me."

"I won't anymore. Now go to sleep, darling, it's late."

"Just one more thing."

"What?"

"Can I see pictures of Nana and Grandpa Harry when they were young?"

"Now?"

"Now."

I brought in a picture of my adoptive mother and Bob

managed to find one of his father, who had died shortly after Karen was born. We propped them both up on her night table and then contentedly she settled back on her pillow.

"It's late, honey," I said. "Please go to sleep right away."

But her eyes were closing even as I said it.

In the living room Bob and I discuss the significance of some of the things Karen has said. Asking for pictures of her adoptive grandmother and Bob's father—the only grandparents she knew enough about to identify with since the other two had died long before, was showing a need for origins. To reaffirm all her connections—"bio" and adoptive—she had to reconstruct a family line.

"Freud emphasized the sex instinct, but the need for origins is more basic," said Bob.

He'd been thinking a lot about Freudian theory these days as he was painstakingly breaking away from it to form his own system of thought based on symbolization, and on death and the continuity of life.

"When children ask where they come from, Freudians see it as sexual curiosity, but they are really asking for the origin of their lives, and the origin of life itself. They are expressing a need to be connected with those who have gone before and those who will come after."

"If everyone has this need, why are people threatened when adoptees ask this question?"

"Because adoptive parents feel that the continuity of their own family line is threatened when the child is looking elsewhere for biological roots."

That made sense. If you adopt children to give you what Bob calls "symbolic immortality," you don't want them abandoning your heritage. You feel that your chance to live on in them is jeopardized by their interest

in their original line. You join up with an adoptive parents' group to fight opening those records.

I thought of my friend, Janet, an adoptive mother,
whose son had been on drugs from the age of fourteen
and in and out of private schools. When I told her I was
working to get the records unsealed, she had lashed out at
me: "Is it fair that after raising a child for eighteen years,
we should give him a chance to go off with strangers?"
She still could not connect her child's pain with his
adoption.

How could I explain that the child/adult doesn't want
to go off; there's no place to go. He just wants to lay to rest
some ghosts—his own and his natural parents'.

❧ ❧

As Bea's birthday approached, I began thinking of her
again—wondering how she was, if she was suffering over
our last conversation. I was surprised to find myself wanting to wish her happy birthday. I thought I had resolved
our relationship by ending it, but are things ever resolved?

When the day arrived, I couldn't not call her.

The phone rang only twice before she picked it up. "I
knew you would call," she said.

She sounded weary and her voice kept breaking as if
she might burst into tears. But she also sounded bitter,
like a woman who has been thwarted for too long.

"I'm all right," she replied when I asked about her
health. She said she'd been brooding about what I had
said about looking Howie up after she was gone.

"I told you I wouldn't do it."

"But for a while you were threatening to. And I was
thinking that when you first contacted me, you said you
just wanted to meet with me once. And when we met you
said you didn't care about knowing anything about your
father."

I reminded her that I only said this when she told me she would never give me my father's name: that I hadn't wanted to hurt her then.

"Oh, I don't know what to do," she said. "Maybe I should have done what I wanted to do years ago."

"What's that?"

"Never mind."

Was she referring to suicide? This frightened me. I didn't want to hurt her anymore and I knew that my *not* calling had hurt her: that once I had opened that door between us, we were both trapped with less freedom than we thought we had.

"I wish you could do things on my terms," she said. "Call me even though I don't tell Howie. You must understand that I can never tell him. It is the one thing I am certain of."

I assured her I would phone from time to time. She seemed relieved, more cheerful. But it was still a sad call. There was to be no birthday dinner for her that night. Howie wasn't coming home until late.

"I don't celebrate anymore," she said. "It's a day like any other day."

"I'm sorry I can't be with you for just a toast," I said.

"I feel as if I'm always with you," she replied in a hushed voice, "because you are a part of me. Just knowing that your life has turned out well is enough for me. I feel I have no right to more."

Her words—so warm and sincere—threw into place so much of what I had been struggling with, what I could have told Janet. The natural mother does not want to snatch her child, now grown, back from the adoptive parents. She is content and grateful for what they have done for her baby. She is not the enemy. She only wants to know what happened to her child. She understands the adoptive parents are the *real* parents in the most meaningful way.

Every liberation movement has its backlash.

"Listen to this," I told Bob one night, reading him some of a newspaper article about a group of adoptees in Michigan, APAT (The Association For the Protection of the Adoptive Triangle), which was opposed to unsealing the records. The founder had looked up his own natural mother with what he claimed was success, but had decided it was too dangerous for others to embark on a similar quest: his followers should be satisfied with what information they could get short of the name of their original families. He was a self-declared savior of the "adoption institution," and perhaps not coincidentally, an adoptive parent.

"It's all very well and good for him to tell others not to look up their natural mothers when he couldn't resist doing it himself," I said impatiently.

I knew by now where the fallacy lay in his position. The records as they are kept by the agencies do not go beyond the day of adoption. Unless one looks her up, one is unable to know what happened to that young mother, invariably a teenager, how she developed as a person in

later life, and, in terms of genetics, what hereditary ill-
nesses she suffered, and might have passed on to her
child.

Ideally the adoption files had to be kept up to date,
either by the agencies or state registries. The development and medical history of both the child and the
natural mother had to be recorded, and this information
made available to both parties when the child reached
the age of majority.

Perhaps if the past were not sealed off so irrevocably,
adoptees would be satisfied with updated files and not feel
compelled to go further. I wasn't sure about myself.

"I wonder if I'd still have the need to see my mother's
face," I asked Bob. "Even now, why do some adoptees
have to search for their natural parents while others
don't?"

He verbalized so well the things I half knew and the
things I half didn't want to know. "Some of the adoptee's
need to search probably does have to do with relationships
with the adoptive parents," he said, putting down the book
he was trying to read. "But it also depends on how ques-
tioning the person is. I would say that if one is twice born,
one has to carve out a new self distinct from the one
society assigned you."

"Sometimes I think it would have been enough to
have been born *once!*" I declared melodramatically.

But I didn't mean it. I was beginning to understand
that being adopted brings its bonuses too. What had been
a shameful secret had evolved into a unique condition
that had led me into mythic realms, deepened me as an
artist, enriched me as a woman. It had, as Ellie said,
given me my archetypal theme.

It had allowed me to create myself.

"Everyone survives some kind of trauma in early life,"
Bob reminded me, lest I get too carried away with my
uniqueness. "In that sense everyone is a survivor. But an

adoptee does have a particular kind of separation," he
conceded. "It can be debilitating or it can give special
insight."

I remembered being shocked when a woman adoptee
blurted out to me: "I wish I had been an abortion!" And
when another said: "I feel the end of my life will be as sad
as the beginning. I am always waiting for the next disaster
to happen."

Both of them were stalemated in their searches.

But I was glad I wasn't an abortion. I loved this experience called life. I was grateful to the mother who had
given it to me, and to my adoptive one who must have
done a lot of things right for my life to have turned out
so well.

"It all comes down to the fact that we have to develop
a different sense of parenthood," Bob said, rising to take
Jumblie out and hoping by this ruse to end the conversation that never seemed to end.

"Being a parent has to be seen as something more
than the possessing or owning of a child," he added as
his canine child dragged him off to the elevator.

Adoptee organizations were springing up all over the
country.

Besides ALMA and Orphan Voyage there were:
AIM—Adoption Identity Movement (Detroit); Yester-
day's Children (Chicago); Adoptees in Search (Washing-
ton, D.C. and Ardsley, New York); Adoption Forum
(Philadelphia); Search (Denver); Link (Twin Cities,
Minnesota).

Every month there would be more. *Jean Paton's Log*
and personal letters of encouragement were helping them
keep in touch with each other.

I was no longer affiliated with ALMA, for although
Florence Fisher would always deserve credit for having
sparked the adoptee liberation movement, I felt there

were others who could follow through more effectively. I was glad to see new groups forming independently. It was healthier. And someday when the moment came for them to pull together, I was sure they would.

Even now Yesterday's Children was soliciting funds throughout the country for that civil rights case we'd all been dreaming about. The group had filed a suit in the federal district court in Illinois charging that the sealed-records doctrine violates adoptees' rights to equal protection, freedom of speech, due process, and freedom from involuntary servitude according to the First, Fourth, Fifth, Thirteenth, and Fourteenth Amendments to the Constitution. Its members were prepared to go all the way to the Supreme Court if necessary.

The attorney, Pat Murphy, was no neophyte in the struggle. He had made legal history when he won the *Stanley* case which established that in an adoption procedure the natural father, if known, must be notified.

"Of course, even if we win and the records are unsealed, our problems as adoptees won't be miraculously over," Margaret Lawrence, one of Yesterday's Children's founding members reminded me. "But at least a victory will be the spur to make the agencies restructure their procedures."

Someday, of course, the records will be unsealed—perhaps not too long from now if that case is won—and in the future people will look on today's strange attitudes toward adoptees as we look on many of the Victorian's irrational prejudices.

Already we are seeing a much less conventional generation than our own in action: one openly experimenting with communes, with extramarital sex, with bisexuality, with homosexuality, with open marriage, with common-law marriage, with single motherhood, with single fatherhood. No one can say yet what these experiments will lead to, whether this generation will have a lower divorce rate than ours, more or less achievement in love or life.

But the waves of liberation are washing over many fields, including the social services.

There are many hopeful signs.

About ten years ago, psychologist David Kirk's brilliant *Shared Fate* favored opening the records when the adoptee reached the age of majority. And now recent books like Alexina Mary McWhinnie's *Adopted Children; How They Grow*, and John Triselotis' *In Search of Origins: The Experience of Adopted People*, based on interviews with adopted adults in Scotland (where, as in Finland, the records are open to adoptees at the age of seventeen) also confirm the adoptees' need to know about their origins.

In this country psychiatrist Arthur Sirosky and social workers Annette Baran and Reuben Pannor have been interviewing natural mothers, adoptive parents, and adoptees before and after reunions in an attempt to explore the myths about the attitudes each group holds.

They have concluded that the birth mother does need to have further information about her relinquished child; that the aura of secrecy is often more of a burden than a protection to the adoptive parents; and that the adoptee's need to search cannot be labeled maladjusted or emotionally disturbed. They too are recommending the unsealing of birth records for adult adoptees and are urging adoption agencies to keep their records up to date for all the parties concerned.

They are also exploring the subject of "open adoption," as it's come to be called—an agreement by which the natural mother might meet the adoptive parents and retain the right to have contact with or knowledge of the child as it develops over the years. This arrangement, common in Polynesian and Asian cultures, was not unknown in this country prior to World War II when a couple might take in a pregnant unwed young woman, care for her through delivery, and then adopt her child. The natural mother had the satisfaction of knowing the character of the people who were raising her child, and the adoptive parents had the security of knowing their baby's heritage.

What if all these things came to pass: unsealed and updated records, agencies treating adoptees as clients instead of enemies, adopted children knowing that when they are grown they will have a chance to search out their origins freely?

I tried to imagine what those future adoptees growing up in such utopian circumstances would be like. Already I envied them.

Or would they have problems too?

I thought a lot about what kind of psychological worries the next generation of adoptees would have when the old problems—like the sealed records—were solved. Would the stigma of illegitimacy still plague them?

Erik Erikson has written of the "negative identity" that the illegitimate carry within them. This was a concept that spoke to me, for the adopted—whether born in wedlock or not—are always inwardly illegitimate. Our life struggle is to legitimize ourselves in our own eyes. It isn't enough to fool others. I knew some adoptees who acted on their "negative identity" by producing their own illegitimate offspring and putting them up for adoption: the self-fulfilling prophecy fulfilled.

Over the years I had been talking with Erik on the subject of adoption. Erik, himself, was what might be called a half-adoptee. He didn't know anything about his natural father except that he was a Dane who had abandoned his Danish-Jewish mother before he was born. At the age of three he had been adopted by his mother's husband, a German-Jewish pediatrician, Dr. Theodore Homburger, as his own son. It was not until

adolescence that he had learned the truth of that relationship.

It intrigued me that the father of the identity theory
had not known his own father—that he, too, had lived
with secrets within secrets.

Perhaps that's what had given him his heightened
psychological sensitivity.

Now it is summer and Erik has come to Wellfleet
for the annual psychohistory conference in Bob's study.
During one of the lunch breaks, while we are soaking up
the sun, I ask Erik what he thinks the identity of the
adoptee will be when society allows him not only to learn
about the natural parents, but also to meet them. It is,
in effect, a psychohistorical question.

Erik is cautious, even stretched out there on the beach
chair, seemingly relaxed and defenseless. His face, a
ruddy glow of tan and age under that shock of white hair,
turns away from me for a moment.

"You use the word 'natural,'" he observes. "It is loaded
because it implies the other parents are *un*natural. I have
always used the term 'biological' here."

"I use the word deliberately," I admit. I tell him all the
names that have been used for those forbidden mothers:
original, birth, biological, bio, physical, real, true, other,
blood, and even other lady or the other woman. I explain
that "natural" is used in old documents and I prefer it
because "biological" seems to deny the emotional experience of bearing a child and giving birth. Natural seems
right. There are nine months of a woman's life involved
here.

"But let's not get hung up on that," I say. "I am really
concerned with how you think unsealing the records
could affect the identity formation of an adopted child."

"You must remember that once conditions change,
everything will be different," he reminds me. "For a while

there will be a transition period. Some children and, indeed, some biological parents, will suffer, some won't. When customs change, the adopted will react differently from the way you did, and any prediction could only be relative to the changing society."

"But is there any reason it might not be a good idea to tell a growing child that she can know who her natural parents are at the age of eighteen?"

"It may be a good idea," he says simply. "But there should be some careful study as to when a child is ready to receive such information—and not when the adoptive parents (or society) feel they are ready to give it. And even then the child should be told that at the age of majority he can have the *choice* of looking up the natural parents. It should be a choice, not an *obligation*. And the important thing here is that the decision should not be made by the 'natural' or the adoptive parents for the young adult: the adoptee should make it for himself.

"But," and he pauses here, "may not the question of that choice overshadow his whole adolescence?"

That was, indeed, something to think about.

"Could it keep the child from forming a deep emotional involvement with the adoptive parents?" I ask.

"We know from the extended-family situation in other cultures that a child is capable of relating to a number of adults in his environment. And in our present period the rights of all the members of the family are more distributed than in Freud's more patriarchal day. However, how an adolescent in rebellion, say, will live with adoptive parents while nursing the decision as to whether or not at some future date to look for the 'real ones'—that is impossible to predict.

"But look here,"—it is an expression he uses when he wants to make a particular point—"if you want to have a new principle you must experiment. And some new kinds of interidentified groups must keep an eye on what is happening and discuss their findings. You can't wait for the next generation of psychiatrists to tell you what damage *was* done. Only time will tell how it will work out."

Erik was rising now from the lounge chair on which he had been reclining and heading off for the more austere atmosphere of Bob's study to continue the discussion there on Watergate, world holocaust, and other such related disasters with which it was hard to my little disaster area to compete.

I watched him make his way over the sand. "Only time will tell," I repeated to myself.

We adoptees had to continue to probe our own experience, achieve our liberation from within, so as to be ready for the *Great Unsealing Day* when it came.

There were no experts here.

My book was almost finished. It was the vehicle by which I would make that reentry across the Return Threshold, where, as Campbell points out, one can be either honored or reviled.

The atmosphere that awaited me was charged.

My natural mother had begun calling me—apologetic but frantic. She had started worrying about what I might be writing. Do not use my name, she kept repeating. Do not give Howie's university or profession. What she wanted to say was, *Do Not Write This Book*.

My adoptive mother was in a nursing home. The small apartment had been broken up and she occupied a space no larger than a narrow bed and dresser in half of a double room.

"These people are too old for me," she says when I come down to see her. But she tires easily. It is an effort for her to walk down the long corridor that leads to the dining room.

"The food is terrible here and there's so little of it," she complains.

I understand the sadness that lies behind Jewish humor. But this is not a joke to her.

"You and my brother wanted me here," she says.

I try to be calm. I know that old age brings out paranoia. "You wanted to come," I reply. "You were complaining about the private nursing fees, that the doctor would not make housecalls."

"Yes, I suppose you're right," she concedes.

I understand that this is not just a problem for adoptees. It is America's problem—what to do with parents when they grow too old to care for themselves.

"You'll make some friends here," I say, trying to reassure her.

"Never," she snaps in her most adamant tone.

"But why not? There must be some nice people here."

"I'm my mother's daughter," she says.

"What do you mean?"

"I don't mingle."

I still don't understand what she means. What is being one's "mother's daughter"? Is it a condition passed down through blood that regulates behavior at various stages of life so that now it is making her "not mingle" with strangers?

Can an adoptee ever say: "I'm my mother's daughter"?

Does she think of me as a daughter—in that sense?

I sit by her side as she naps. I worry that she may hear about my book.

In the corridor I see the elderly doctor who has been treating her over the years. Stern patriarch, he walks erectly, suffering no nonsense from hypochondriacs, respecting only those who come into range of the Grim Reaper himself. He respects my mother now: she has passed close enough. She has proven her mettle.

I have been speaking to this man about my mother's various conditions on the long-distance phone, but I do not know him any more than I do the others who were just names to me as a child.

Now he stops to chat as if some of my mother's valor

has rubbed off on me. Remembering that I am married to a psychiatrist, he tries to make contact by speaking of his son, a psychoanalyst, who is visiting from California. He has been up half the night answering the son's questions about the family background, dredging up his own father and grandfather, and those of his wife. Even his grandchildren are showing a lot of curiosity about their background, he tells me proudly.

"Why do you think they want to know?" I ask him.

"All children do."

We are making small talk.

"What of people like me?" I say.

He pauses, alert to the sudden change of course. "What do you mean?"

I am not sure what I meant or why I have so precipitously propelled myself onto this ledge over the abyss. But it is too late to turn back. I look into his shrewd old eyes which have seen so much and are now seeing me.

"The adopted," I reply. "You do know I'm adopted, don't you?"

He tries to continue as if nothing has happened. "Yes, I've always known that," he says casually.

He knows—*everyone* must have known.

"Well, what about the adopted," I persist. "Do they have a right to ask questions about their background too?"

"I never thought about that." He thinks. "Yes, I suppose they do, unless . . . unless there is something that is too terrible. . . ."

"What could be too terrible in one's past that one should not know if it is the truth?"

I watch him mulling this over. I can see whores, psychotics, suicides making their terrible way through his mind.

"I guess nothing," he says at last. "Nothing that is the truth could be too terrible if one is an adult."

And then he understands. "Have you looked up your family?"

"Yes."

He cannot hide his curiosity. "You found your parents?"

"Yes."

"What . . . who did you find?"

"I am writing a book about that now."

"Good for you!" He seems to mean it.

"But I feel guilty as if I don't have the right."

"Don't feel guilty. Everyone has the right to know everything about themselves," he says with conviction.

"I worry that my mother may not understand. That she'll see it simply as a defection."

"Don't worry, it is a good thing you are doing. And it is important that someone like you should write about things that most of us don't know."

"You don't think it's wrong."

"Certainly not. Good girl, I am proud of you!"

He is a convert.

I throw my arms around this stiff, formal, shy man and embrace him. He has given me sanction in the land of my childhood.

❧ ❧

I open the door of our New York apartment and drop my bag.

Two huge paws grip my shoulders. It is Jumblie.

Karen appears in the hall and calls out to Ken, "Mom's back!"

They both come running toward me.

I am about to reenter the world.

ABOUT THE AUTHOR

Betty Jean Lifton is a journalist, playwright, and author of many books for young readers. Much of her writing reflects her interest in the culture and politics of the Far East, where she and her husband, psychiatrist Robert Jay Lifton, lived for seven years. In *Return to Hiroshima*, she wrote about the survivors of the atomic holocaust; *Children of Vietnam* is about the lives of the children caught in the war.

The Liftons and their young son and daughter now live in New York City.